UNIFIED THEORY of BUSINESS STRATEGY

Rod Samimi PhD

SENTINEL 9
BUSINESS EDUCATION & ADVISORY

Published in Australia in 2020 by Sentinel 9 Pty Ltd

Website: www.sentinel9.com
Email: confidential@sentinel9.com

ISBN 9780648973409 (paperback)

NATIONAL LIBRARY OF AUSTRALIA

A catalogue record for this book is available from the National Library of Australia

Disclaimer

The author has made every effort to ensure the accuracy of the information within this book was correct at the time of publication. The author does not assume and hereby disclaims any liability to any party for any loss, damage or disruption caused by errors or omissions, whether such errors or omissions result from accident, negligence, or any other cause.

Contents

Acknowledgements

This book brings together the knowledge and experiences I have gathered from both the corporate environment and academic research.

I have been fortunate to be a student of several prominent academics, who generously shared their knowledge with me. I was privileged to study under Emeritus Professor Ian Harper, learning about finance and economics. I was also a student of Associate Professor Clive Edwards, who taught me about international business strategy. In addition, I gained great benefit by being associated with the University of Queensland's Business School and Durham University's Business School during my doctoral and postdoctoral time. I also worked in the industrial sector with several experienced senior executives who introduced me to various operational disciplines and taught me a quantitative way of thinking. As an executive, I gained practical knowledge and training through my work with Shell, Pacifica Group, and Clark Equipment. I am thankful for the opportunities presented to me by those companies within their international operations. I will be forever grateful to those academics and practitioners.

The production of this book would not have been possible without the support of Dr Judy Gregory and her patient assistance in the writing and editing process. I would also like to thank Wayne Liu and Peter Winkler, who did extensive work on the graphics and related YouTube videos, and Dr Victoria Gonzalez for her academic research, and Kirsty Ogden from Brisbane Self Publishing Service for her work on the design and production.

Introduction and background

Unified Theory of Business Strategy provides a conceptual framework and practical method for understanding the strategic process, particularly as it relates to business. It proposes a practical methodology for business strategy that is nested in relevant theoretical foundations.

This book is the culmination of over ten years of postdoctoral research by the author, both independently and within large organisations. It combines the author's experience as an executive, business strategist, consultant, business owner and academic researcher. This book applies a number of well-established concepts in the field of strategy. It straddles the academic and practical business realms, with a main focus on offering useful material relevant to business practitioners. It, therefore, does not attempt to add yet another layer of descriptive ideas on discussions about business strategy. Instead, it translates those discussions into a pragmatic, causal planning tool to present a continuum from conceptual theory into its practical application.

It is not our intent here to refute (or specifically support) any well-established or widely used schools of thought in business strategy, nor to add to esoteric volumes in the field. Instead, we aim to provide a synthesised framework that draws together specific aspects of existing theories and theoretical standpoints. Our intended contribution to the field is to identify complementary threads and offer further interpretation to translate abstract concepts into a day-to-day, practical application.

The business literature includes many theoretical standpoints, but these are often prohibitively cumbersome for business planners, particularly for those working in small- to medium-sized firms. In addition, many existing theories require a significant academic background before they can be understood – a background that many business planners may not have (or not need). We attempt to address these inconsistencies. Managers focused on, and pressured by, day-to-day business operations rarely have the time (or inclination) to examine detailed, abstract theory. On the other hand, many popular ideas about business strategy are not based on theoretical foundations, may lack credibility or may simply advance personal gain.

The framework developed in *Unified Theory of Business Strategy* brings together input and output mechanisms and their modus operandi that are relevant to broader business. The main body of the book refers to well-known concepts and does not assume prior knowledge. The material is presented without recurring academic referencing for ease of reading. Instead, supporting academic detail is included in the appendix and bibliography.

This book offers a solid theoretical foundation drawn from multiple disciplines, but also offers practical versions and planning tools. Readers with less theoretical interest can access the planning tool by itself (Chapter 3), knowing that the underlying theory is also available (Chapters 1 and 2).[1] Chapter 1 provides a conceptual framework of strategy. Chapter 2 interprets that conceptual framework into an applied commercial and economic version. Chapter 3 applies the framework to practical business planning. In this way, the chapters are designed to be read either individually or sequentially. Readers seeking only practical application may find everything they need in Chapter 3. Readers seeking the underlying theory will benefit from reading Chapters 1 and 2. Case studies and supporting material are provided at the end of the book.

- Chapter 1, *What is strategy?*, presents the underlying theory of strategy and offers a definition of strategic process with relevant variables at play. Drawing on specific variables and simple elements of game theory, Chapter 1 also introduces different modes of thinking. It concludes by proposing that the strategic process can be understood through two theoretical axioms and the interpretation link between them. The concepts developed in Chapter 1 apply to all types of strategy, not only to business strategy. Chapter 1 is most useful for readers seeking a theoretical foundation from which to understand how correlated strategic intent can translate into a causal process.
- Chapter 2, *Strategy in business: An applied framework*, applies the theory developed in Chapter 1 to a commercial business context. It introduces the concepts needed to develop and understand strategic business planning process. Chapter 2 defines wealth as the desired economic outcome of business, addresses the issue of risk, and introduces three building blocks of strategic planning (formulation, implementation and evaluation). These building blocks correspond with the material identified in Chapter 1. Chapter 2 is most useful for readers seeking to focus on the basis on which business strategy is developed.
- Chapter 3, *Applied business strategy*, describes specific steps involved in developing a practical, workable strategic business plan. It includes links to an external software tool, which can be used to develop a comprehensive business plan.

1. This is not a get-rich-quick book, nor is it a do-it-our-way book. Instead, it offers the business community a practical, usable method that helps with 'how not to lose money' before advising 'how to make money'.

Chapter 3 is most useful for readers who are ready to develop their own strategic business plans.

- Following Chapter 3, we offer two examples from the physical sciences to illustrate the links between practical science and business strategy, and three case studies (Toyota, Zara and Amazon) that relate the content of the three chapters to actual external examples.
- The appendix summarises key concepts, tools and theories referred to in the main body of the book. It includes three parts: theoretical concepts, business strategy tools, and theories of business strategy. It acts as a brief overview with reference material to support the concepts presented in the book.
- The bibliography provides detail of further reading to support the ideas presented in this book.

Throughout the book, QR codes are used to link readers to additional material, including:[2]

- Short YouTube clips covering key content
- Online access to diagrams that may be difficult to decipher on the page
- Access to read-only versions of strategic planning software.

Key concepts in Chapter 1

- Strategy process
- Strategic variables
- Strategic games
- Modes of thinking
- Strategic axioms

Key concepts in Chapter 2

- Desired outcomes in business
- Attributes of risk
- Building blocks of strategy (formulation, implementation, evaluation)
- Correspondence with key elements of Chapter 1

Key concepts in Chapter 3

- Formulation (external analysis, internal analysis, gap analysis)
- Implementation (general operations; processes, procedures and communication; capacity-building programs)
- Evaluation (financial plan and review)

2. All QR codes and URLs are current at the time of publication but their accuracy and availability cannot be guaranteed going forward.

The diagram below summarises the content of Chapters 1 to 3 and shows the links between the chapters.

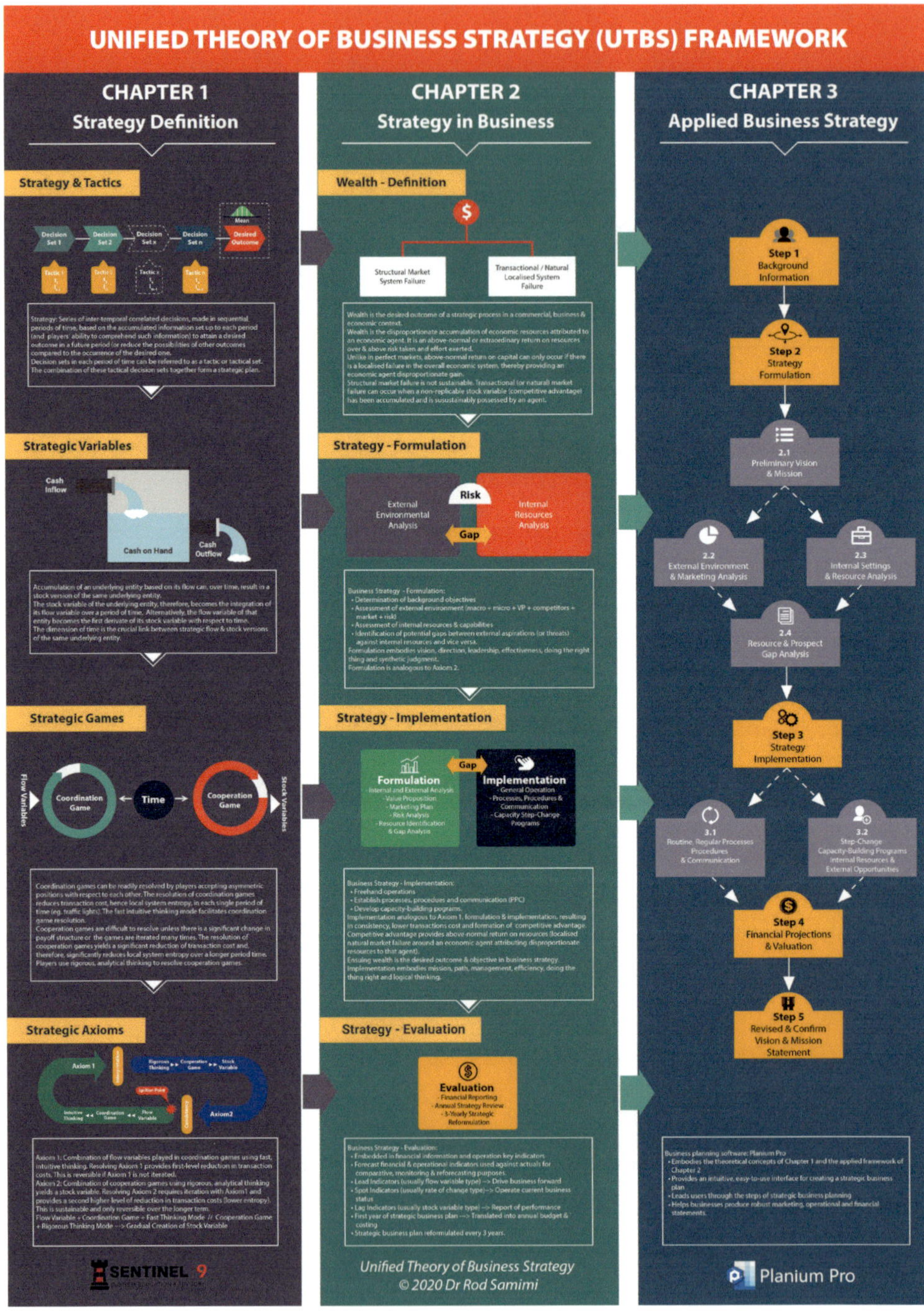

Figure 1: An overview of the links between this book's chapters (this figure is best viewed online; use the QR code for access)

Sentinel 9

Sentinel 9 is a conceptual framework that overarches the models developed in this book. It links nine interconnected bodies of knowledge to offer a synthesis that can be applied in many different contexts. The Sentinel 9 framework provides a holistic approach to understanding reality. Whilst this is not a book about the attributes of Sentinel 9, its framework has been used to configure the Unified Theory of Business Strategy (UTBS). Here, we apply Sentinel 9 to a microeconomic context by focusing on business strategy and competitive advantage. In a forthcoming book, we will also apply Sentinel 9 to a macroeconomic context.

Sentinel 9 draws on literature from the physical sciences, life sciences, social sciences and philosophy. Each discipline offers a slightly different perspective and provides a useful lens for examining reality. Sentinel 9 adapts key elements from these partially connected fields to develop a more complete theoretical standpoint. It attempts to create a more accurate set of paradigms to holistically interpret the reality (and its sub-components) around us.[3]

Some observers have suggested that universities should formally establish a cross-disciplinary faculty, tasked with examining similarities between disciplines and looking for relevant synergies in a way that is similar to the rationale of Sentinel 9. It is possible that artificial intelligence systems will assist with this process in the future.

Figure 2 illustrates the nine fields that contribute to the Sentinel 9 theoretical framework.

3. A full discussion of the Sentinel 9 framework is beyond the intended scope of this book.

Figure 2: The main interacting schools of thought included in the Sentinel 9 theoretical framework (this figure is best viewed online; use the QR code for access)

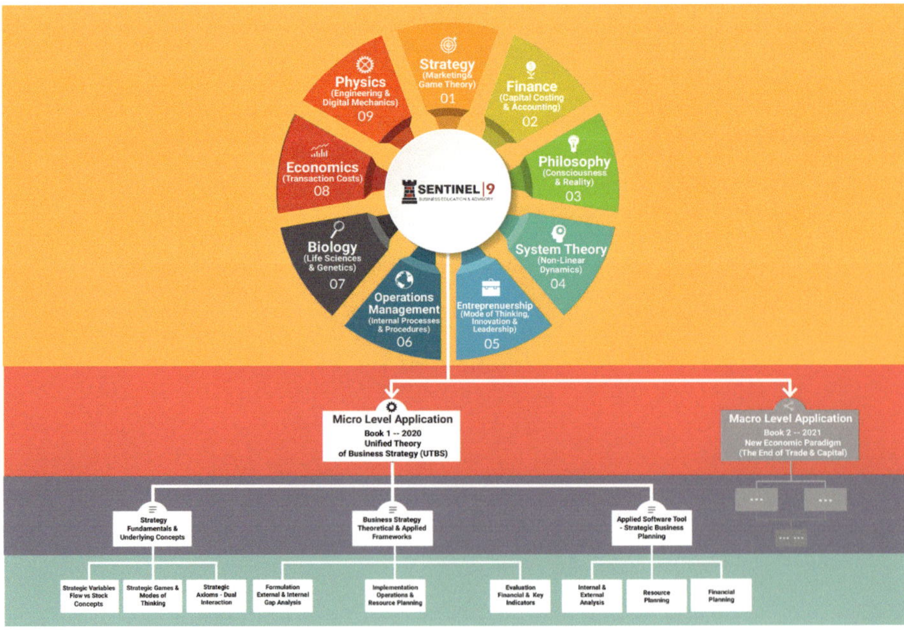

Figure 3: This book presents the Unified Theory of Business Strategy (UTBS) based on the application of the Sentinel 9 framework in a microeconomic context (this figure is best viewed online; use the QR code for access)

Use this QR code to access a short video about the Sentinel 9 conceptual framework

This book forms one of the linked elements between Sentinel 9's education material (particularly Unit 14) and the relevant YouTube channel and planning software, as described in Figure 4 below.

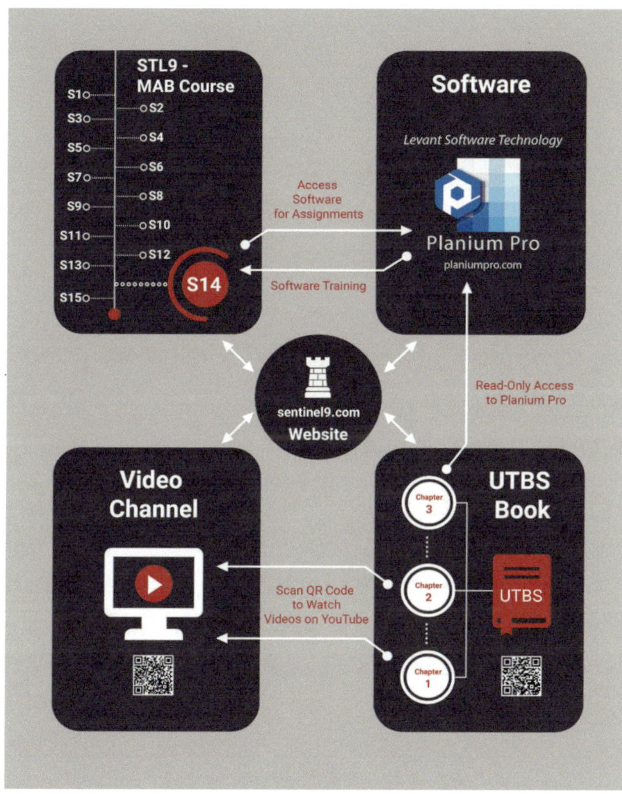

Figure 4: The interface between this book, Sentinel 9's framework, Planium Pro and the YouTube channel clips

Use this QR code to access a short video about the unifying theory and its application to macro-economics

Chapter 1

What is strategy?

Introduction

This chapter looks at the fundamental concepts that underpin strategy and provides a new perspective to propose that strategic processes can be configured within two interacting axioms in the Unified Theory of Business Strategy (UTBS).

Whilst the focus of this book is ultimately on business strategy, the strategic concepts discussed in this chapter apply to many fields, with relevance to politics, military and career development. The strategic concepts here also apply to everyday interactions and personal relationships.

In this chapter, we first make some general observations about strategy, including correlation, causality, outcomes, information sets and time-based decisions. We then look at specific components of strategy and introduce different types of variables, games within which these variables are engaged, and the ways players think when undertaking these games. We bring the components of strategy together in a theoretical framework with two interacting axioms.[4]

We provide the building blocks for a strategic process by:

- Defining strategy and the strategic process
- Introducing key variables present within the strategic process
- Using elements of games theory to explain how key variables are engaged
- Explaining different modes of thinking used by players in dealing with the games and variables

4. This chapter provides a broad discussion of the strategic process before applying it to business strategy. We assert that a shortcoming of many contributions to business strategy (including tertiary courses and general publications) is that they discuss business strategy without fully defining the underlying concepts in the field of strategy itself.

- Combining the concepts into two interacting axioms that explain how to develop a causal strategic process
- Connecting a link of interpretation between the axioms to close the loop for the framework.

In setting up a theoretical framework, we acknowledge that expounded theories may not be an absolute or unchallengeable reflection of reality. They offer a useful perspective and an improved way of interpreting that reality. Theories provide interrelated concepts, definitions and propositions that explain or predict events or situations. Most theories specify relationships between variables, offer a systematic way of understanding events or behaviours, and provide a simplified representation of how variables interact. Theories take a complex, real-world issue and simplify it down to its essentials in order to explain and make predictions. If done well, this enables decision-makers to understand the issue, problem or opportunity.

Strategy – general perspectives

Strategy is a word that gets used in a multitude of different contexts. In business, people talk about their 'business strategy', 'product development strategy', 'marketing strategy' and 'human resources strategy'. In their personal lives, people may talk about their 'fitness strategy', 'personal development strategy' or 'financial strategy'. People also talk about strategy as a type of intended action. People 'think strategically', 'invest strategically' and 'study strategically'. In government, the term 'strategy' is applied to concepts like 'economic strategy', 'employment strategy' or 'election strategy'. Here, the term 'strategy' is often vague, with some reference to broad thinking or boundary intentions. In this sense, strategy seems to convey an approach for a premeditated scheme.

One idea seems to link the various uses of the word 'strategy': it is often about forward planning – about putting in place a plan of action designed to attain a position in the future, with plans that are reasonably long-term and encompassing. This general use of the word 'strategy' makes it possible to identify some complexities with the term.

- Strategy involves making plans and taking action in the present, and implementing those plans over the medium- and long-term in order to achieve some future goal; it involves allocating resources now for some future higher-value outcome.
- Strategy involves an element of uncertainty and risk; whilst a well-developed and well-implemented strategy will internally (or endogenously) increase the likelihood of achieving the desired outcome, the outcome is not guaranteed due to potential external (or exogenous) influences.

- Strategy involves achieving an appropriate balance of breadth (scope), depth (scale), deterministic planning and indeterminate flexibility: if a strategy is too broad and vague, it is unlikely to be achievable; equally if a strategy is too closely defined and too narrowly fixed, it may become prohibitive to enhance opportunities as they arise. It will become increasingly susceptible to external influences.

There are three parts to developing strategy, which we will look at in more detail in the coming chapters:

- Defining the desired outcome
- Devising plans about the best way to achieve that outcome
- Implementing decisions in respect of those plans.

In the UTBS, we propose a definition of strategy as:

> **Strategy is a series of correlated decisions, made at sequential points in time, based on an available information set and players' ability to interpret that information, in order to attain a desired outcome at a future point in time.**

Within this definition:

- *Series of correlated decisions (or tactics)* – implies the interdependence between decisions and the accumulated residual impacts of previous decisions up to each point in the process
- *Sequential points in time* – implies the sequentiality of decisions (tactics) and the critical role of the time dimension
- *Available information set* – implies a state of play at each point of time with different accumulated values as the residual position up to that point of time
- *Players' ability to interpret* – brings in the human, cerebral element with their ability to analyse and/or synthesise a certain volume of information based on underlying complexity and players' level of knowledge
- *Attain a desired outcome at a future point in time* – implies that strategy is designed to maximise the likelihood of that desired outcome and reduce (or eliminate) the likelihood of other potential outcomes.

We will describe the above elements in more detail below.

A well-conceived and implemented strategic process, whilst maximising the likelihood of an optimal outcome (or reducing the likelihood of other, suboptimal outcomes), cannot on its own guarantee success. No matter how carefully a planner intrinsically defines and implements a strategy, there may still be extrinsic influences or events that change the outcomes of their correlated decisions. For example, imagine a person buys a new umbrella because the weather forecast suggests there will be heavy rain tomorrow. If the forecast was right and there is heavy rain, the umbrella will have a high value to its purchaser. But if the forecast was wrong, the umbrella's value is reduced. Whilst the price and functionality of the umbrella remain consistent, the strategic decision to purchase the umbrella may become suboptimal based on prevailing external elements.

Use this QR code to access a short video about strategy versus tactics

Correlation and causality

To define strategy as a series of correlated decisions is to recognise that each decision at a point in time is affected by the collective impact of other decisions at previous points.[5] Each decision that forms part of a strategy will influence the conditions for other forthcoming decisions. A change to one decision could have a residual ripple effect on future positions.

To better understand this, it is important to distinguish between correlation and causality. Correlation is the movement of parameters with respect to each other. Causality is when one parameter causes or resolves another or vice versa.

- Positive correlation exists when an increase in one parameter is linked to an increase in another parameter. For example, height and shoe size tend to be positively correlated: taller people will, on average, have larger shoe sizes than shorter people. Correlation can be measured mathematically through a correlation coefficient; when two parameters change exactly at the same rate in the same direction, they have a correlation coefficient of one.
- Negative correlation exists when an increase in one parameter is linked to a decrease in another parameter. For example, student performance on exams is typically negatively correlated with student absence from lectures. When two parameters change at exactly the same rate but in an opposite direction, they have a correlation coefficient of negative one.
- Uni-directional causality occurs when one activity or decision makes something else happen, and the outcome can only happen in one direction (A causes B, but B does not cause A). An example of unidirectional causality is retail spending

5. We discard a single-move, one-shot tactic that essentially does not constitute a longitudinal strategic process.

at Christmas. The approach of Christmas causes an increase in retail spending (A causes B). However, an increase in retail spending cannot cause Christmas (B cannot cause A) and it is spurious to examine retail sales figures in an attempt to predict the arrival of Christmas.

- Bi-directional causality occurs when causality can happen in both directions: (A causes B and B causes A). When a system has bi-directional causality, it is not able to explain its origin. The chicken and egg is a clear example here. A chicken causes an egg (A causes B) and an egg causes a chicken (B causes A). The system is unable to explain its own source or initial generation. The origin of such a system must be explained exogenously (from outside the system), because the system itself cannot (endogenously) explain its beginning.

It is important to note that causality and correlation are not always concurrent or co-existent (though they often can be). In particular, note that correlation does not imply causation. In the student performance example given above, to conclude that student absence causes exam failure would require more detailed testing and proof.

The correlation of decisions works both within and beyond a strategic process. This means that a decision made within one strategic step does not only have a direct effect on other decisions, but may also correlate with other parameters external to the context. Our framework here, in essence, describes how correlated variables in a broader definition of strategy can be configured to gradually induce causality and form a specific strategic process. Such a strategic process (towards an outcome) conveys the presence of causality between sequential decisions, generated from decisions that were previously only correlated.

In each step of the strategic process, at times a single decision is made at a corresponding point in time. At other times, a set of sub-decisions are grouped together to become an overarching tactical set at a point in time. In simple, short strategies, each tactic may involve just one decision. But in complex strategies or strategies that extend over a long timeframe, each point-in-time tactic may involve multiple sub-decisions.[6] For example, legislative change might be a set of tactics within a government's overall strategic goal to achieve a particular social change. The tactics of legislative change may each involve many decisions (drafting the legislation, engaging with stakeholders, seeking

6. Each tactic (which is made up of a decision set at a point in time) is, in itself, a microcosm of the strategic processes at play. Tactics combine to form a strategic process. But at the tactical level, each tactic (at a particular point in time) contains all the elements of the whole system at a microscopic level. This is similar to the concept of unfolding symmetry in fractal geometry, where each component incorporates all elements of the system, and vice versa. It also draws on the concept of holographic systems, where the same interactions apply between the part and the whole.

endorsement and so on). Together, these tactics will drive towards the strategic political outcome and, along sequential periods of time, form a strategic process.

Each decision (or tactical decision set) is based on the outcomes and learnings of previous decisions and will, in turn, influence future ones. In this way, the results of decision sets accumulate over time to influence the final outcome. For example, if a university student decides to miss a lecture one day because their time is better spent studying for an exam, the student has made a tactical decision based on the strategic goal of passing the exam. Each time the student decides to study by foregoing other activities, the combined results of those decisions accumulate towards achieving an eventual desired outcome.

Single decisions (or tactics) that are not correlated cannot form a strategic process. For example, a chess player who simply takes single moves without paying any attention to potential future positions is not engaging in a strategic process. For this player, each decision is isolated, made with no consideration of how these tactical decisions might work together. The player has a single-shot tactic (or a random walk), but these do not form into a causal strategic process. This player is unlikely to win. But a chess player who plans their moves based on a set of likely future moves (considering their opponent) is engaging in a strategic process. This player is putting together correlated decisions over time in an effort to achieve causality towards checkmating their opponent.

When implemented to sequentially correlate, tactics can progressively generate causal links. These causal links are essential for creating a directive strategic process longitudinally, gradually translating correlation into causality over time. In this manner, certain variables coming into the system can be transformed to cause other (desired) variables to emanate from that system.[7] The UTBS is a framework configured to systematically delineate this transition.

Sequential steps and available information

The correlated decisions that form a strategic process have an attached time dimension – that is, they need to occur in an ordered sequence and within a longitudinal timeframe.[8] Strategic processes can operate over a wide variety of timeframes – from hours or days, through to many years. The duration is not important, but a strategy cannot exist without a sequential time dimension leading towards a future position. Strategic planning is, therefore, intertemporal – it involves designing sequential decisions that consider

7. Whilst outside the scope of this book, correlation and causality are also apparent within probabilistic simulations for the military, economics and overall descriptions of reality frameworks.

8. The literature includes multiple definitions and interpretations of time. Passing or sequential time is the most common definition, but concepts such as block time and concurrent time are also used. In our framework, we employ the common definition of time as sequentially passing in one direction.

positions to date, the current situation and future outcomes. For example, if a student wants to graduate with a degree, they will participate in a series of events and activities over time (such as study, lectures and exams) designed to get them there. Each decision the student makes intertemporally moves their position towards graduation at a future point. Any strategy of reasonable complexity, therefore, involves multiple intertemporal decisions which, together at one point in time, can be grouped and applied as tactical sets that can yield accumulated causal results.[9]

Strategic decision processes do not embody access to full information and data along the way. Decisions are taken with respect to information sets that are limited, uncertain and, at times, superfluous. Strategic planning involves making the best possible decisions with the best available information, based on the player's ability to understand and interpret that information (that is, the player's knowledge and experience).

A good strategic planning process recognises that information is a work in progress: the search for information and the analysis or synthesis of information must continue throughout planning and implementation. This helps to refine and adjust planning throughout the life of a strategic process. In the real world, full access to information is unlikely (if not impossible). For this reason, decisions need to be analysed with respect to the source and accuracy of any information at hand. Strategic planning is often based on uncertainty and ambiguity caused either by a lack of information or a surfeit (excess) of information. Players attempt to best decipher information and interpret its value for their specific purposes (such as those engaged in stock market or derivative trading). They operate with bounded rationality (inability to be fully cognisant of all information) and make decisions involving logical analysis but also synthetic judgement (drawing on concepts that sit outside the deterministic information set). Ambiguity caused by a surfeit (excess) of information creates a particularly challenging scenario for strategic players, with acute application of the limitations of bounded rationality. Players need to be able to perceive and choose the relevant information in situations where there is such a surfeit or superfluous set. This implies that strategic planners should:

- Search actively for information
- Ensure the information they use is reliable and plausible
- Analyse and synthesise the available information to construct decisions.

It is possible that external events – things that are outside the planner's control and influence – can overwhelm the best strategic decisions. But over the length of a strategy, if a

9. Intertemporal decisions are made at different sequential points in time. The choices made at one point in time influence what is possible in the future (creating a causal relationship over time). In finance theory, for example, decisions regarding allocation of current consumption, or delaying that consumption by investing, are examples of this kind of intertemporal decision-making.

player keeps working with the strategy, they will be likely to attain better outcomes than others who do not engage in strategic thinking. The ability to deal with both endogenous and exogenous influences, combined with the ability to deal with either a lack or surfeit of information, are important aspects of the decision-maker's ability.

The desired outcome of strategy

The desired outcome of a strategic process should encompass the following characteristics:

- It must be realistic – that is, it needs to be possible and potentially achievable, both in terms of its quantum and the resources required
- It must be challenging and of value – that is, it needs to be something worthy of striving toward
- It needs buy-in from participants – the other players involved in achieving the strategy and implementing the correlated decision must believe the strategy is both valuable and realistic.

Decisions can then lead to a range of possible outcomes, which can be plotted in a normal (or another type of) distribution. From the statistical point of view, a well-defined strategy helps to reduce the variation of possible outcomes around the intended one, thereby reducing the standard deviation (the variation from the expected mean). Strategic thinking will reduce the range of possible outcomes, narrowing the spread of their distribution, increasing the likelihood of achieving the optimal outcome and reducing the possibility of suboptimal outcomes.

Figure 5 illustrates the strategic process towards a potential outcome. Each tactic (decision set) leads to the next tactic (decision set), and eventually leads to the distribution around the desired outcome (with an available information set at each point in time).

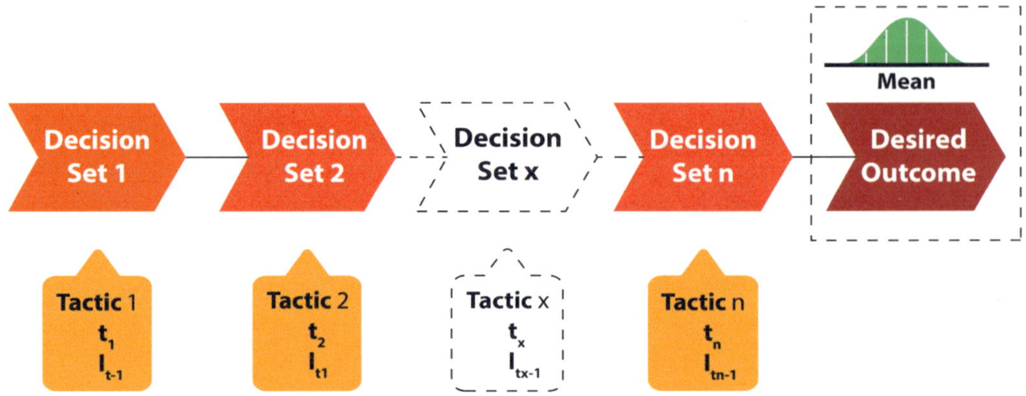

Figure 5: The strategic process involves a series of decision tactics at different points in time (t), based on the information (I) available to that point in time (I_{t-1}), which can contribute to achieving a desired outcome or reduce the possibility of other outcomes at a future point in time

Even the standpoint to avoid developing a strategy, in itself, becomes a strategic decision. It can be argued that not having a strategy, often described as a 'random walk' option, whilst a mediocre alternative, nevertheless remains a strategic decision. Instead of defining a desired outcome and making correlated decisions to help achieve it, a player adopting isolated moves could be simply engaging in the game randomly as it unfolds. The difference is that such a player makes decisions (randomly) without focusing on a causal process aimed at achieving a desired future goal. Over time, another player who makes conscious use of strategic decisions and combines those decisions into a process achieves better average outcomes than a player who engages in a random walk option.

The lottery makes an example here. Everyone knows that it is possible to win the lottery. Players who buy lottery tickets understand it is a gamble; they buy for the game, not because they fully expect to win each time. It is important to remember that the player's odds here do not improve each time they play. To stay with the lottery example: imagine that a person who purchases a lottery ticket has a one in 10 million chance of winning. If the person purchases two tickets in the same lottery, they double their chances. But next time they purchase a lottery ticket (for the next game), their chance of winning will once again be one in 10 million. Whether they won last time or not is irrelevant to their chances of winning in the future.

From a strategy perspective, a strategic decision to participate in the lottery gives very little likelihood of achieving the desired outcome: the chances of success are low, it is not effective to make sensible use of available information, and it is impossible to combine correlated decisions to improve the outcome. In a lottery, the outcome is both random and beyond the player's control. Applied, effective strategic planning is not like that. Of course, most people intuitively know that life is not like a lottery ticket. Most people make active, strategic decisions about their personal lives, their careers and their businesses. That is because most people want better-than-random odds of achieving their desired outcome.[10]

Another simple example from everyday life can illustrate this point. Imagine that a person drives to work each morning, with the desired outcome to get to work on time. They like to arrive at the same time every day. To achieve this, they make strategic decisions about the best time to travel and the best route to avoid traffic, minimise driving time and get to the destination. These decisions are correlated, based on the best available information each day. On a Monday, the person may leave earlier because the traffic is often heavier. If it is raining, they may choose a slightly different route. If schools are on holiday, they expect less traffic. This is an example of simple strategy being used every day. Each time the person makes the journey, they get better at making relevant strategic decisions because they have access to better, more complete information. The correlated decisions in this way gradually generate causality (that is, they help the person achieve their intended outcome). If, instead of actively planning the driving route each morning, the person simply drives to work whenever they are ready to leave, the variability in their arrival time will likely increase, and their ability to learn from driving experiences will decrease.

As mentioned before, at times, external adverse or unexpected (exogenous) influences may override a strategic player's internal (endogenous) plans. For example, a bus strike or inclement weather could completely overwhelm a player's intentions to arrive at work on time. In these circumstances, a strategic player has no advantage over players who pursue a random walk. Indeed, in these circumstances, the strategic player is worse off because they allocated resources to planning without achieving a superior outcome. Over time, however, the player who consistently attempts to arrive at their destination based on planning will, on average, be better off though a superior outcome is not valid for each and every occasion. These correlated decisions, therefore, become causal, progressively moving the player in the desired direction. That is the value of a strategic process: it increases the likelihood of achieving desirable outcomes within the overall system or reality framework.

Strategic variables

The previous section broadly defined strategy and the characteristics of a strategic process. In the following sections, we introduce a number of elements that are used to construct the framework of the UTBS and explain the actual workings of a strategic process. These elements sit within strategic contexts and are present when players make decisions. The first components we discuss are strategic variables.

10. The UTBS, discussed in this book, examines how do that in a business context.

A variable is a broadly measurable quality or entity that can change. Price is a variable. So are inflation, profit and temperature. Within strategy, variables are the factors that can be worked with and used in decision-making to help achieve desired outcomes. Some variables are things that can be controlled or influenced (like the number of hours worked, or the way resources are used), whilst other variables will be fully or partially beyond internal control but still relevant to the strategy (like the economic conditions of the time, or customers' interest in the product).

As a simple example, again consider that a person needs get to work on time, using public transport. The variables include the time they leave home to get to the bus (which is under their control), the bus timetable (which they do not control, but can discover), and today's traffic conditions (which they do not control and may not know). The person will adjust the variable under their control (the time they leave home) in response to what they know about the two variables that are not fully under their control in order to achieve the strategic outcome of getting to work on time.

Different disciplines are interested in different types of variables. In quantitative disciplines, for example, variables are classified as:

- Independent variables (also called explanatory variables) – the factors that researchers might manipulate in an experiment (the inputs to the process)
- Control variables (also called exploratory variables) – the elements researchers might hold at specific levels during the process
- Dependent variables (also called response variables) – the factors researchers are interested in measuring (the outcome of the process).

For example, in a study to examine whether students achieve better results if they have access to online video resources, the variables might be:

- Independent variables – the online resources available to students (the input)
- Control variables – the unit of study taken by the students
- Dependent variables – the results achieved by students (the output).

We refer to a subset of independent and dependent variables in the UTBS, drawing on common terms used in sciences: flow variables and stock variables.

- Flow variables are set in our framework as a subset of independent (explanatory) variables – they are the input to a strategic process.
- Stock variables are set in our framework as a subset of dependent (response) variables – they are the outcomes of strategic process.

Use this QR code to access a short video about strategic variables (flow and stock)

Flow variables

In broader strategic thinking, flow variables will be entities that may be measured or understood over time (such as how quickly a person is able to travel). In business examples, these are also any variable quality or quantity that can be measured over time – such as income, expenditure, depreciation, cash flow and profit. All these are understood per unit of time. A distinct attribute of flow variables is that their amount or quantity can be readily changed (increased, decreased or discontinued). In the UTBS, we see flow variables as those both measured over time and repeated over time.

Because flow variables are linked to time, they can be relatively quickly reviewed and adjusted. In the water tank example below, the inflow of water can be changed by disconnecting the entry tap, and the outflow can be stopped by closing off the drain. In the product production example below, it is possible to change the income flow variable by adjusting the sale of products or reducing expenditure.

Stock variables

Stock variables are relevant variables (quality or quantity) that are measured as an accumulation at a point in time (not per unit of time). For example, items in a balance sheet such as accumulated cash, assets and borrowings at a point in time are stock variables.[11]

Stock variables are the outcome of strategy, measured at a particular point in time. Under the UTBS, we extend the economic definition to see stock variables as a fixed-point outcome of repeated application of strategic flow variables over time. Concepts such as wealth, brand recognition, intellectual property and organisational innovation are examples of stock variables. We will look at these examples in more detail in the following chapter.

Stock variables are slow to change, difficult to adapt and cumbersome to discontinue. Because stock variables are an outcome of accumulation, they cannot usually be reviewed and adjusted directly. Stock variables change as a result of changes to underlying flow variables. They, therefore, have a time-based inertia in accumulation, which also implies

11. In a business context, flow variables are usually reported in a profit and loss (P & L) statement. Stock variables are described in the balance sheet.

that their effect will continue for some time after their accumulation or reduction dissipates. Stock variables are subject to diseconomies of time compression based on the law of diminishing returns. They exhibit inertia in their accumulation even if the underlying flow variables are progressively or rapidly increased.

Knowledge is a good example of a stock variable that results from accumulation based on analysis and synthesis of information. Whilst it is possible to change the rate at which information is accessed, knowledge is something that will grow slowly. There are clear limits to the rate at which it can be accumulated. A person who studies a course over a year will accumulate more knowledge of the same material than a person who attends an equivalent one-week intensive course covering the same material, even if both individuals begin with the same knowledge base and the same level of intellectual capability.[12] Trying to increasingly accelerate the formation of stock variables induces time-based inertia: less and less can be progressively accumulated, despite the faster movement of flow variables (referred to above as diseconomies of time compression).[13]

Relationship between flow and stock variables

Flow variables and stock variables are closely related.

- Each flow variable, through its repeated application, culminates in the presence of a stock variable.
- Growth or reduction in the amount of stock variables is an outcome of the repeated application of flow variables.
- A stock variable cannot be formed or changed in the absence of the underlying flow variable that created it over time.

A water tank is often used as a simple illustration of the relationship between flow variables and stock variables. The tank is designed to hold water that comes through a tap. The amount of water per unit of time flowing into the tank is a flow variable. The water only enters the tank during the time the tap is fully or partially open. In addition to its water inlet, the tank has an outlet: a drain. Every time the drain point is opened, water will flow out. It flows out at a set rate per unit of time, depending on the size of the drain. Just like the water flowing into the tank, the water exiting the tank is a flow variable.

Both the inlet tap and outlet drain can be readily adjusted by the owner (player). What the owner decides will influence how much water accumulates. If the tap is open, water

12. Intensive executive MBA courses clearly show this divergence when compared with the same MBA material covered over longer periods.

13. A similar effect is shown with the viscosity of fluids as described in the physical example later in this book.

will flow in. If the incoming flow of water through the tap is greater than the amount exiting through the drain, the water in the tank will increase. Conversely, if the reverse applies and there is more water draining out than is flowing in through the tap, the amount of water in the tank will reduce. If the drain is open to the same degree as the tap, the outflow is the same rate as the inflow; no water will accumulate and the existing levels will not change. *Flow variables may, therefore, be in operation without ever accumulating or changing anything.*

There is a mathematical relationship between flow variables and stock variables, which can be described through differential equations.[14] Stock variables are an integration of flow variables over a period of time. Conversely, flow variables can be seen as the first derivative (differentiation) of a stock variable with respect to time. Figure 6 illustrates the water tank's flow and stock variables, and provides their cash equivalents.

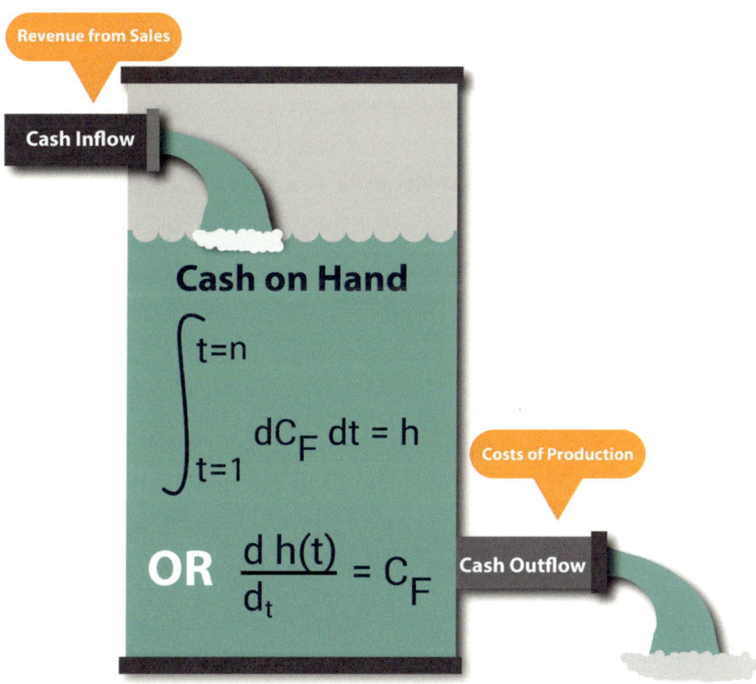

Figure 6: Flow variables enter and exit at each point of time whilst stock variables accumulate over time (in mathematical terms, a stock variable is an integration of a differential rate of flow variables over a period of time; alternatively, a flow variable is the first differentiation of a stock variable with respect to time)

14. Differential equations describe the relationships between physical variables that change over time. Whilst beyond the scope of this book, it is worth noting the importance of differential equations to describe fundamental relationships and, through their numerical solutions, yield underlying mathematical equations that can be used to predict outcomes in science, economics and engineering.

In this example, the water itself does not change – it is always made up of the same water molecule. It is how we interpret the water that changes its definition. When the water moves into or out of the tank, it is described in terms of flow. When the water accumulates in the tank, it is described in terms of stock. *The dichotomy is that the flow variable describes the process (and the way it changes over time), whilst the stock variable describes the outcome at a point in time.*

The same principle applies in business, most clearly with the sale of a product. Selling a product creates a flow of money into a business (income: a flow variable). The costs involved in making that product flow out of the business (costs: a flow variable). If expenses are less than the income from sales (as outlined in the P & L), money will accumulate inside the business (profit). This accumulated cash is a stock variable (as outlined in the balance sheet).

Flow variables and stock variables also operate in many different parts of life.

- Information is a flow variable. Individuals can search for and collect information. Knowledge (the ability to analyse and synthesise information) accumulates over time. It is an outcome of the continual application of information over a period of time. This makes knowledge a stock variable, linked to the flow variable of information.
- Operational efficiency is a flow variable. Businesses can refine their work processes to improve their efficiency and lower their transaction costs. Repeated efforts with operational efficiency could lead to the stock variable of competitive advantage.
- Advertising and promotion are flow variables. They are the tactical decisions a business makes to communicate with potential customers. Repeated advertising and promotion, backed by the attributes of consistent products and services, can create the stock variable of brand.[15]

Figure 7 illustrates some common links between flow variables and stock variables.

15. Mathematical integration and differentiation principles apply in all these examples.

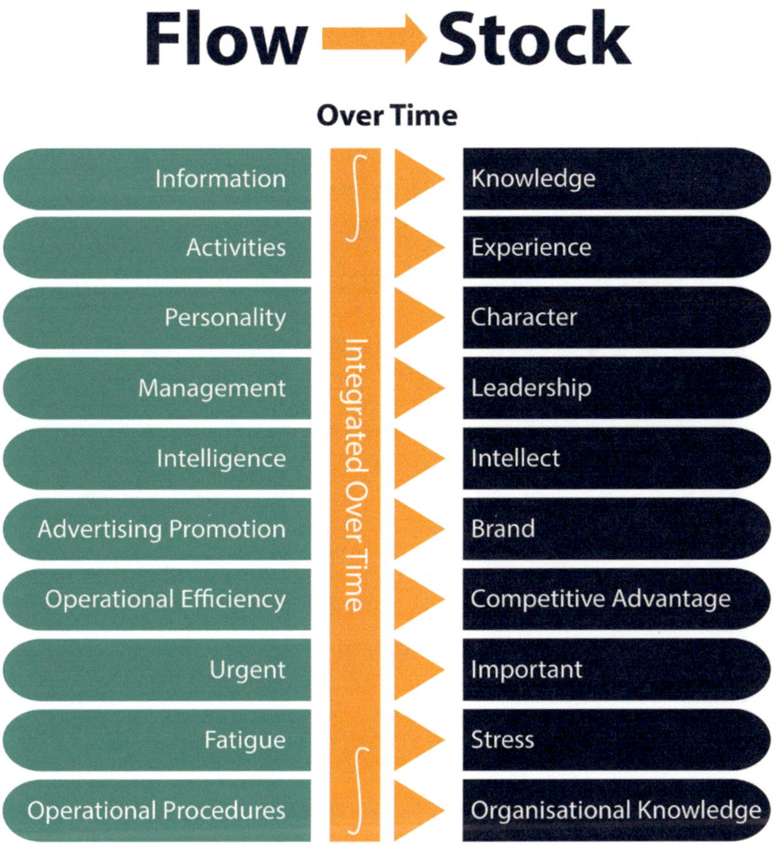

Figure 7: Everyday examples of variables: an integration of flow variables over time leads to a corresponding stock variable (alternatively, the first derivative of a stock variable gives a flow variable)

Strategic games

In the previous sections, we described strategy and strategic processes. We then introduced strategic variables as the first elements towards configuring our framework. In this section, we introduce the next elements of the framework by explaining how those variables become engaged in the process. We do this by briefly looking through the lens of games theory.[16] We employ the characteristics of two distinct types of games: coordination games and cooperation games.[17] These games tend to be associated with certain types of variables.

16. More detailed discussion of games theory is included in the appendix.

17. In his 1993 book *Foundations of Corporate Success*, John Kay includes an exquisite description and explanation of these games, including the conditions for mutually beneficial cooperation in various business structures such as joint ventures.

- Coordination games enable players to resolve simple issues using fast, intuitive thinking by pre-agreeing to asymmetric but mutually beneficial positions. These games primarily act on flow variables.
- Cooperation games achieve strategic outcomes with complex thinking, based on repetition and iteration. These create stock variables.

Use this QR code to access a short video about strategic games (thinking modes and transaction costs)

Coordination games

In a coordination game, players resolve the game by intuitively adopting relative asymmetric positions. In most cases, players use predetermined rules to achieve optimal or higher-value outcomes. This type of outcome, in essence, reduces or lowers the transaction cost of their undertaking.[18]

We see coordination games around us every day.

- Road rules provide a predetermined agreement about which side of the road to drive on to avoid head-on collisions. In addition, stop signs and traffic lights assist in the asymmetric flow of traffic without the prohibitive costs of collisions. These agreed asymmetric positions between drivers allow them to get to their destinations without the need to constantly circumvent incoming traffic (the road rules lower transaction costs by readily resolving the coordination games).
- Losing the connection during a telephone conversation provides another example of a coordination game. If two people agree in advance who will make the call (and who will wait to be called) if they become disconnected, they can reconnect quickly. Without a pre-agreed asymmetric position, they may both try to reconnect or both wait. The asymmetric positioning readily resolves the coordination game in this example, at low transaction costs compared with the indeterminate position.
- Queuing at the supermarket is an interesting example of a coordination game. Even without a formal contract to bind them, players organise themselves in a way that optimises their time and lowers their transaction costs. A strong or aggressive person could push their way through the queue, but that rarely happens.

18. Transaction costs are the implicit costs born by players over and above the direct cost. For example, if a person eats in a low-quality restaurant, the direct cost of the food may be low, but the overall transaction cost may be high (from the risk of food poisoning). Transaction costs are explained in more detail in the appendix.

Each player takes an asymmetric position in relation to the others, choosing the shortest queue and waiting for their turn. Players do this quickly and efficiently without a written contract, using predetermined rules that guide how to wait in line with confidence it will eventually be their turn. The overall transaction cost is reduced by asymmetric positioning in a queue and intuitively comprehended by participants with free will.

- An organisational hierarchy is also a formalised version of a coordination game. Through the rules of an organisational hierarchy, it is clear who can make decisions and who has limits to their authority. In this example, the asymmetric position resolves the coordination game (lowering organisational transaction costs) with formal contracts in place.

Coordination games are associated with rapid, intuitive decisions. These games, thereby, allow players to resolve situations through intuitive thinking because they can rapidly draw on their experience in regards to predetermined positions. The efficient resolution of coordination games helps reduce transaction costs (as described in economics) and reduce disorganisation or entropy (as described in the physical sciences).[19] Coordination games must be repeatedly resolved in order to maintain the lower level of transaction costs (and reduced entropy). As soon as the coordination games cease, transaction costs and entropy will both increase. *This means that the outcome of coordination games is straightforward and expeditious, but not enduring.* In contrast, the *cooperation games* discussed in the following section, *whilst not as straightforward and expeditious, have the potential to further decrease transaction costs (and entropy) significantly and tend to become more enduring.*[20]

Cooperation games

Cooperation games tend to be complex and difficult to resolve. In many cases, they may remain unresolved. They involve complex decision-making and it is often possible for a cooperation game to have an outcome that benefits one player at the expense of others.

The prisoner's dilemma is an example of a cooperation game. Under the prisoner's dilemma, two prisoners are kept in solitary confinement with no way of communicating. Prosecutors offer each prisoner one of three options.

- If both prisoners remain silent, they will each serve one year in prison.
- If both prisoners betray each other, they will each serve two years in prison.

19. Entropy, as an element of the second law of thermodynamics in physics, is the tendency of a system to reduce its organised useful state and move into gradual disorganisation over time. It is briefly explained in the appendix.

20. These cooperation games, in turn, require iteration of the underlying coordination games for their eventual resolution.

- If one prisoner betrays the other, the prisoner who talks will be set free whilst the other prisoner will serve three years in prison.

In this dilemma, the best outcome for an individual (betray the other person) conflicts with the best outcome for the group (both stay silent). The prisoner's dilemma creates a paradox for players where they cannot produce an optimal outcome if they act in their personal self-interest. Unlike coordination games, which are readily resolved by asymmetric positioning and predetermined rules, cooperation games require careful thought and rigorous thinking. But successful resolution of the cooperation game will create a long-term, significant reduction in transaction costs (and entropy). The outcome is more enduring than the outcome of coordination games – though the outcome is still not permanent. For the prisoner's dilemma, trust is a potential outcome. Trust cannot be built rapidly, but is an iterative outcome and reasonably enduring once established.

Cooperation games tend to be resolved in one of two ways: either through a massive change in the payoff structure, or through iteration and repetition.

- A massive change in payoff structure for the players may not always be feasible. An example is the realm of gangsters or bribery (cooperate or face dire consequences). Whilst this may achieve a resolution, this type of high bribery incentivisation or extreme threat payoff structure is not pragmatically replicable.
- Iteration and repetition of the cooperation game can achieve resolution. With each iteration, the players will have access to better information and be more able to make optimal decisions.

Rigorous analysis and iteration of decisions can produce stock variables measurable at a point in time (like trust or wealth). Trust is, in essence, the ability of a player to accurately predict the response of a player who is not present. It is established over an extended period (such as in a personal or business partnership) by consistent signalling, over and over.[21] Such consistent, iterative signalling can occur through the application of fast coordination games (discussed in the previous section) leading to the systematic resolution of cooperation games. Cooperation games cannot be avoided, because they are the only way to achieve valuable, longer-term stock variables.[22]

Figure 8 summarises the relationship between coordination games and cooperation games, showing how intuitive thinking combined with flow variables can resolve

21. A trusting relationship in a marriage or business partnership is built because each partner can predict the behaviour of the other, even when the other is not present. Trust comes about as an iteration of previous, consistent signals during their time together. For consumers, brand name exhibits the same characteristics.

22. In the case of the prisoner's dilemma, for example, successive iterations of the game could create trust, demonstrated through the ability of each player to predict the behaviour of the other even when they are not together. The highly valued stock variable of trust becomes the outcome of their resolved cooperation games.

coordination games and, over time, create consistent signals to resolve cooperation games and accumulate stock variables. This outcome results in a significant, enduring reduction of transaction costs (and lower entropy). We will employ a combination of coordination games working on flow variables together with cooperation games producing stock variables in our framework in the next section.

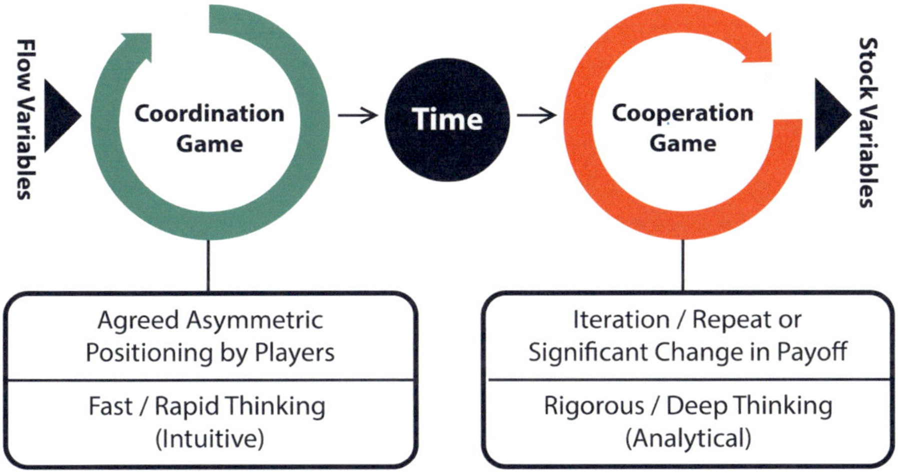

Figure 8: Links between strategic variables and games (the input of flow variables in coordination games, over time creates stock variables as the output of cooperation games)

Modes of thinking

In the previous sections, we provided a general perspective of strategy and introduced variables and games as building components of our framework for a strategic process. In this section, we discuss the final component of this theoretical framework and bring in a human element by considering two main modes of thinking applied by players.

Researchers have identified two different modes of thinking – a fast, intuitive mode and a slow, analytical mode.[23]

- Fast, intuitive thinking relates mainly to subconscious and habitual understandings that enable us to make rapid decisions. This mode of thinking can be deployed over a long, continuous period.
- In contrast, slow, analytical thinking involves conscious, rigorous processes that cannot be extended for long periods of time.

23. In his book, Kahneman (2013) incorporates a comprehensive treatment of these thinking modes. We employ a slightly simplified variation of his detailed exposition.

These modes of thinking correspond with the games and variables introduced in the previous section. Coordination games are usually resolved through fast, intuitive thinking. Cooperation games are resolved through slow, rigorous, analytical thinking. Some activities that initially may require slow, analytical thinking can, over time, become fast and intuitive. Literature also links these modes of thinking to the left and right brain, with left-brain thinking being more analytical and right-brain thinking being more intuitive. The frontal lobe is understood to be an interacting mechanism between the two.

For example, a learner driver needs to apply a great deal of conscious thinking and the task is difficult and exhausting at first. Once the skill of driving is learned and the activity becomes routine, the fast, intuitive mode of thinking takes over. An experienced driver can engage in conversation whilst driving and can drive for many hours – that would be difficult for a learner driver exercising continuous, rigorous attention.

Individuals' typical interactions in conversation make another useful example. Most of the time when people listen to others, they listen with an intent to reply. They typically use fast thinking to formulate a quick response, based on what they know, rather than examining to learn new concepts. There is another mode of thinking available, unique to humans – that is, the ability to think deeply with effort to learn before making a response. This type of thinking is conscious, detailed and rigorous, and can usually only be sustained for a relatively short time. An individual using this type of thinking to listen to a conversation is listening empathically to understand rather than simply to reply. Students' attendance at university lectures is an example of listening with intent to comprehend. The lecture cannot continue for longer than around three hours or students' attention will be dissipated.

Some players are able to pitch their thinking and understand which mode is most suitable for the situations they encounter. These players have more comprehensive, accurate paradigms of their environments and apply their synthetic judgement to the scenarios they face, successfully adopting either intuitive thinking or rigorous thinking as the situation requires. Synthetic judgement, thereby, is the ability to adopt the best mode of thinking; it is a trait that can be learned. All successful companies will include at least one player in their senior leadership team who is capable of this type of synthetic judgement. This ability is built through experience, based on a long period of successfully resolving cooperation games. These players are able to choose the most appropriate mode of thinking for the situations they face, whether in a coordinating or cooperative scenario. Individuals with this ability for synthetic judgement become superior players (game resolvers). These are the individuals who are likely to become successful entrepreneurs. Their success is just as much based on their ability to adopt the best and most relevant mode of thinking as on their natural intelligence or technical ability.

Unified Theory of Business Strategy (UTBS) – axioms

In the previous sections we described attributes of processes, strategic variables, games and modes of thinking. In this section, we bring those elements together to create an overarching theoretical framework. We will configure two interacting axioms (each containing corresponding variables, games and thinking modes) that together form the UTBS. Through these two axioms (and the interpretation link between them), we show how the components of strategy combine into a causal strategic process to yield stock variable outputs from flow variable inputs.

Axiom 1

Axiom 1 combines three components – flow variables as inputs, coordination games as engaging mechanisms, with fast intuitive thinking as the cerebral mode – to yield a position where transaction costs and entropy are reduced. This can only work in an iterative way. This axiom applies to the tactical decision level at each point of time along the strategic process. The successful resolution of this axiom will endure only for a short period of time.

Axiom 1 describes most of the decisions people make every day. In business, this axiom describes an organisation's everyday actions, including management, correct operational path, operational efficiency, ethical practice, and clear processes and procedures. The flow variables and coordination games create consistency: a solid foundation on which to build. In general, players can expect around 70 per cent of everyday activities to involve coordination games.

Axiom 2

Axiom 2 combines three different components – cooperation games, with rigorous thinking as the engaging mechanisms, to yield stock variables. Successful resolution of cooperation games and inducement of stock variables achieves a step-change with above-average outcomes, a greater reduction in transaction costs and entropy, and more enduring results. Axiom 2 requires rigorous thinking and careful analysis in interpreting outputs from the recurring implementation of Axiom 1 (towards the resolution of cooperation games and the creation of stock variables).

Axiom 2 receives the outcomes of coordination games emanating from Axiom 1 along a longitudinal strategic framework. The signals from Axiom 1 are interpreted together into more complex cooperation games that can only be solved through rigorous, analytical thinking. The potential outcome is stock variables that can reduce transaction costs significantly. Axiom 2 cannot be readily configured and implemented. It relies on the slow, progressive, iterative build-up of the outcomes and rigorous thinking achieved through interpreting the results of single-time-period, Axiom 1 signals.

In general, it makes sense to expect around 15 per cent of everyday activities to involve cooperation games.[24] The stock variables that result from Axiom 2 may include knowledge, leadership, vision, competitive advantage and the formation of new business capabilities.

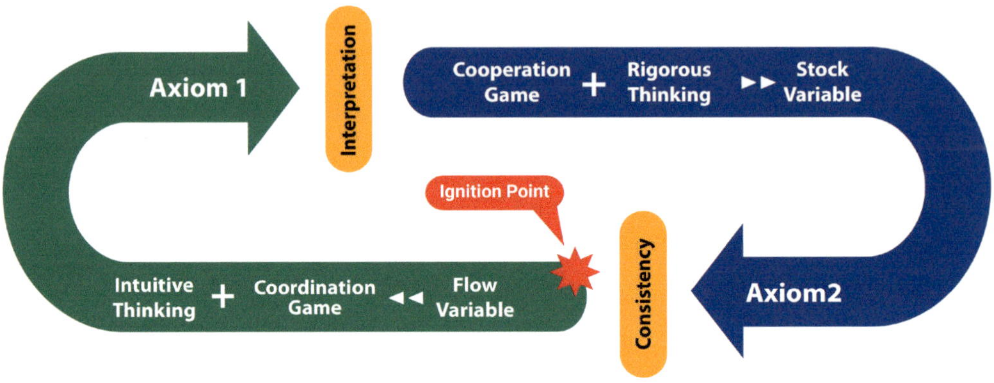

Figure 9: Axiom 1 and Axiom 2 and their elements interact via an interpretation link

Interactions between the axioms

Interactions between Axiom 1 and Axiom 2 form the causal loop of our framework. Axiom 1 at each point in time creates the tactical decision sets of the strategic process. Axiom 2, by interpreting the results of Axiom 1 signals, yields the desired outcome in the form of a stock variable at a point in time. This interpretation requiring rigorous thinking acts as the link between the two axioms to configure a closed-loop framework.

Figure 10 provides a full representation of the framework, superimposing Axiom 1 and Axiom 2 onto the generalised strategic process presented in Figure 5.

Axiom 2 yields the desired outcome of strategy, with Axiom 1 as the leading prerequisite for its formation. Axiom 2 cannot operate in isolation. It depends on, and builds upon, the outcomes of Axiom 1 and can only function through the regular interpretation of Axiom 1 signals using rigorous, analytical thinking.

24. This links to the discussion of capacity building in Chapter 2, where we note that businesses should not put more than 15 per cent of their effort into building capacity (Axiom 2 – formulation) or more than 70 per cent into processes and procedures (Axiom 1 – implementation). The rest should be an indeterminate degree of freedom in the overall system.

- Axiom 1 is a necessary but not sufficient condition for achieving the desired outcome of a strategic process at each point in time.
- Axiom 2 brings in sufficiency (creating the full conditions) to yield high-value, desired outcomes that are lasting stock variables.
- The link between necessary (Axiom 1) and sufficient (Axiom 2) conditions is the interpretation step between these two axioms.

Axioms 1 and 2 interact, and it is their interaction that induces causality (from simple correlation) within a strategic process. Axioms 1 and 2 must both be in play to create a strategic process, whereby certain inputs are dealt with over time, creating certain outputs that can be measured at a point in time. In this way, the flow variable input becomes a stock variable output (representing the strategic intent). Together, these axioms and the interpretation step create the foundation for the UTBS.

Figure 11 illustrates the theoretical framework (Axiom 1, Axiom 2 and interpretation).

Use this QR code to access a short video about the strategic axioms

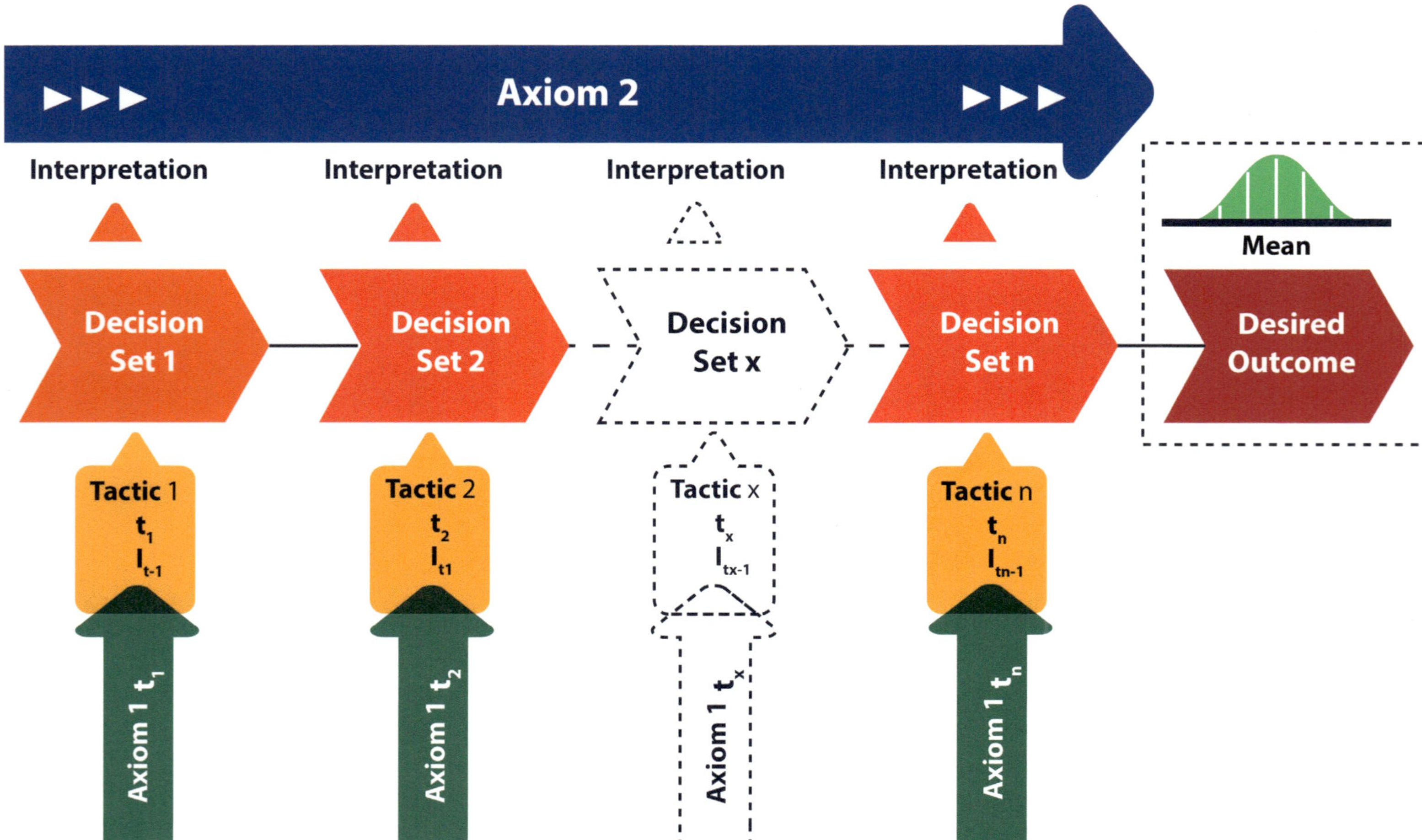

Figure 10: A more complete representation of the strategic process (from Figure 5): the tactical decisions of Axiom 1 and ongoing interpretation of the signals facilitate the workings of Axiom 2

Figure 11: Axiom 1 and Axiom 2 combined in the theoretical framework of the UTBS, with stock variables resulting from input flow variables

Chapter 2

Strategy in business: An applied framework

Introduction

This chapter applies the framework developed in Chapter 1 to a commercial business context. It introduces the concepts needed to strategically guide a business towards superior or optimal outcomes.

In Chapter 1, we identified variables, games and modes of thinking, which we then placed within two interacting axioms that essentially transform strategy from a correlated set of decisions into a causal strategic process. Chapter 1 included a general definition of strategy:

> **Strategy is a series of correlated decisions, made at sequential points in time, based on an available information set and players' ability to interpret that information, in order to attain a desired outcome at a future point in time.**

Chapter 1 identified four important components of strategy:[25]

- Strategic variables, which we categorised as either (input, explanatory, independent) flow variables or (output, response, dependent) stock variables
- Strategic games, which we identified through the taxonomy of coordination (rapid, iterative) games and cooperation (slower, analytical) games. Coordination games work with flow variables to reduce transaction costs (entropy) slightly, but to sustain this reduction the games need to be iterated over time. Cooperation games, on the other hand, produce stock variables and induce longer-term reduction in transaction costs (entropy) which can be measured at a point in time
- Broadly, two modes of thinking apply to these games. We identified fast, intuitive thinking to expeditiously adopt asymmetric positioning resulting in the

25. These points provide a brief summary of Chapter 1 for readers who are accessing this chapter as stand-alone material.

resolution of coordination games. We also identified rigorous, in-depth thinking to interpret the iterative conditions required to resolve cooperation games

- Strategic axioms – we defined two strategic axioms that together form our theoretical framework. These two axioms are interdependent and interact to progressively transform flow (input) variables across to stock (output) variables:
  - Axiom 1 combines strategic flow variables with coordination games and intuitive thinking to yield outcomes where transaction costs are reduced in an iterative way (Axiom 1 describes most routine business activities and operates at the tactical level)
  - Axiom 2 combines rigorous thinking and careful analysis (with respect to signals received from Axiom 1) to resolve cooperation games and yield stock variables which can lead to superior strategic outcomes (Axiom 2 describes activities that achieve a step-change and significant gain, and operates longitudinally along tactical steps).

In this chapter, we apply this theoretical framework to the commercial business environment in the following ways:

- Describing the desired outcome for commercial business – which we identify in a capitalist system as *wealth*
- Addressing risk as a critical element to understanding the risk-adjusted return on resources (capital) towards wealth
- Introducing the three building blocks of strategic planning – formulation, implementation and evaluation – by describing components within each and linking them back to Chapter 1 (Axioms 1 and 2 and the interpretation link)
- Demonstrating how these building blocks combine to create competitive advantage and wealth.

Commercial strategic outcome: Wealth

The capitalist system is not perfect, but it is currently the primary functioning system readily available to business. It is an economic system based on private ownership, law of contract and trade. Consumers maximise their utility and firms operate for profit maximisation. Various schools of thought, including maximisation of shareholder gains, agency theory, and transaction cost economics are used to justify the existence of economic value-added entities within the capitalist system.[26]

When businesses engage in commercial activity within the capitalist system, their goal is to attain returns on their investment through creating a profit. This is to attract resources

26. Some of these schools of thought are briefly described in the appendix.

through the sale of goods and services – higher than that spent on input resources (capital and human) employed to create those goods or services. The goal of a business operating within a capitalist system is, therefore, to achieve higher economic returns on stakeholders' investment.

Most businesses make a *normal* return – that is, they create a basic profit in return for their investment, commensurate with the risk associated with their venture. A reasonable return on investment is enough to enable the business to continue. Methodologies that attempt to measure the underlying profit of an entity include accounting profit, economic value added (EVA) and cash flow return on investment (CFROI).[27]

A non-business example can illustrate what a normal return might look like. Imagine that a person decides to study and become a doctor, but that person's friends all take full-time jobs straight out of school without going on to further study. During medical studies, the person will sacrifice many opportunities to earn money. They will invest a lot of time, effort and fees in studying and will encounter risks associated with their choice, including the risk of potential failure. When they finally graduate from medical school and enter the workforce, the individual will have the potential to earn a high income – probably much higher than their friends who started working without completing further study. Whilst the doctor will live a comfortable life and may appear to have a high income, the overall risk-adjusted return on investment is likely to be normal. When we factor in the delayed income stream, the effort of study, the time invested in study and the underlying risk of uncertainty, the doctor's return on investment is *normal*. There is nothing out of the ordinary about the doctor's income when we consider the investment made and the risk and time taken to achieve it.

In contrast to the above example and in rare circumstances, however, an economic agent may create a return that is abnormal – that is, a return that is disproportionately high for the resources allocated and the risks taken. An abnormally risk-adjusted high return is a desired strategic outcome: it is the creation of *wealth*.

In the Unified Theory of Business Strategy (UTBS), we define wealth in this way:

> **Wealth is the abnormal (or extraordinary) return on resources accumulated around an economic agent, over and above efforts exerted and risks taken by that agent.**

An abnormal or extraordinary return on investment is a return that is beyond risk-adjusted, normalised expectations. Whilst both abnormal and extraordinary returns create a higher-than-normal return on resources, a subtle distinction needs to be made

27. EVA and CRFOI are briefly described in the appendix.

between the two within our framework. Extraordinary returns are typically one-off, discontinuous gains (or losses), which may result from a decision to divest certain assets or to gain from an unexpected, fortuitous opportunity. Abnormal returns, on the other hand, involve a continual, superior return that is the result of some underlying capability or competitive advantage.

Wealth is typically measured by metrics such as share price, market value of assets, financial resources, market capitalisation or enterprise value. All these can only be understood in relation to the risk taken, but wealth is still essentially the main strategic commercial outcome desired by economic agents within the capitalist system.

Use this QR code to access a short video about wealth

Risk in creating wealth

Before we discuss the conditions needed to attain abnormal returns and create wealth, we need to look briefly at the concept of risk as relevant and at play in commercial contexts.

Risk is the possibility of other outcomes prevailing – outcomes that are different from the optimally desired one. This suboptimal position can transpire due to certain influences that can render outcomes incongruent with the targeted one. Using quantitative disciplines, two types of risk are prevalent in business: systematic risk and non-systematic risk.

Systematic (non-diversifiable) risk is the type of risk that is beyond the business's control (such as a natural disaster or an economic downturn). It may not be feasible to mitigate against systematic risk and, because of this, an allocation for risk must be built into the required return on capital. Mechanisms used to cater for systematic risk include the Capital Asset Pricing Model (CAPM), which takes into account risk-adjusted return on shareholder equity. When a business operates in a generally risky environment, it requires a higher return on investment. For example, when a bank lends money in a high-risk jurisdiction, it demands a higher return through interest payments than when it lends money in a jurisdiction that is low risk (that is, sovereign risk and return). This means that systematic risk has a direct influence on what can be considered a normal return on investment.

Non-systematic (diversifiable) risk is the type of risk that businesses can feasibly mitigate against by diversification. It does not necessarily become embedded into returns. Non-systematic risks can be specific to a particular industry or organisation, such as labour problems, quality issues or errors in leadership judgement. Two questions are particularly relevant to assessing non-systematic risk for businesses: What is known about the situation? What can be predicted in relation to the results of actions?

Mechanisms used to measure non-systematic risk and its possible overlap with systematic risk include models such as VUCA.[28] The combination of elements in the VUCA model can help businesses distinguish their position along the spectrum between systematic and non-systematic risk. Figure 12 shows key elements of the VUCA model.

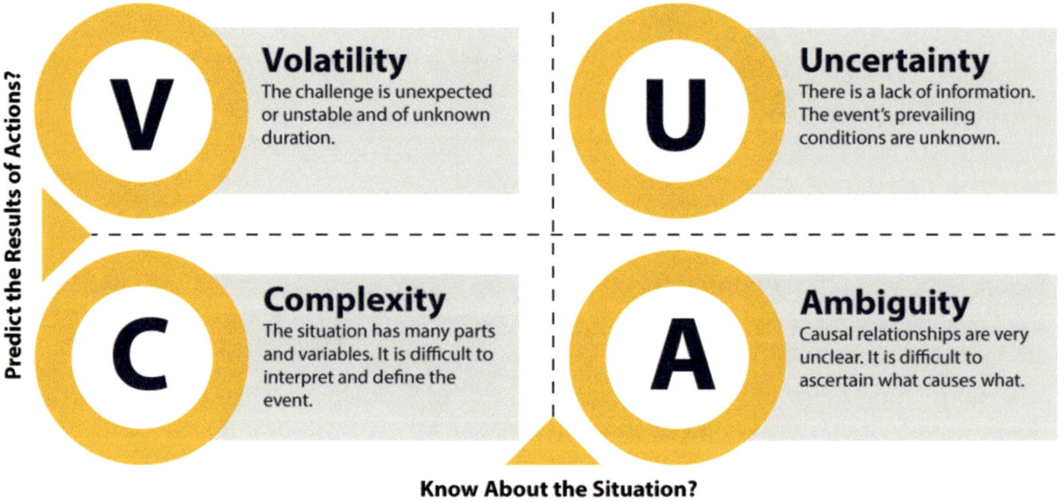

Figure 12: The elements of VUCA are useful in determining the systematic and non-systematic nature of overall underlying risk

Risk, being the likelihood of an outcome not turning out as expected or planned, is not necessarily negative or linked only to underperformance. Risk can also be linked to a trend of unexpected overperformance.

- Downside risk is the most familiar form of risk: the likelihood that the actual outcome will be less favourable than the desired outcome.
- Upside risk is less understood, but can be equally problematic: the likelihood that the actual outcome will be repeatedly more favourable than the desired outcome, indicating an uncontrolled underlying trend with characteristics of risk (that is, not achieving the expected, targeted outcome).

28. VUCA was developed by the US military to measure volatility, uncertainty, complexity and ambiguity.

Both downside risk and upside risk can create problems within a dynamic system. The market rewards control and predictable outcomes – that is, it rewards businesses that operate within a predictable performance–control band. If a business continually overshoots its predictions (upside risk), the business is clearly not operating within the control band as expected and a likely outcome will be a drop in its long-term valuation by the market.[29]

Downside and upside risk both tend to oscillate (as illustrated in Figure 13). It is rarely possible to readily transition from overshooting directly back to the confines of the control band. What typically occurs is that a dynamic system, for example, will overshoot and then undershoot, gradually oscillating to a steady-state position within the intended control band (in the absence of any further shocks). This is a fundamental factor of non-linear system dynamics, attributable to many different contexts including business activities.

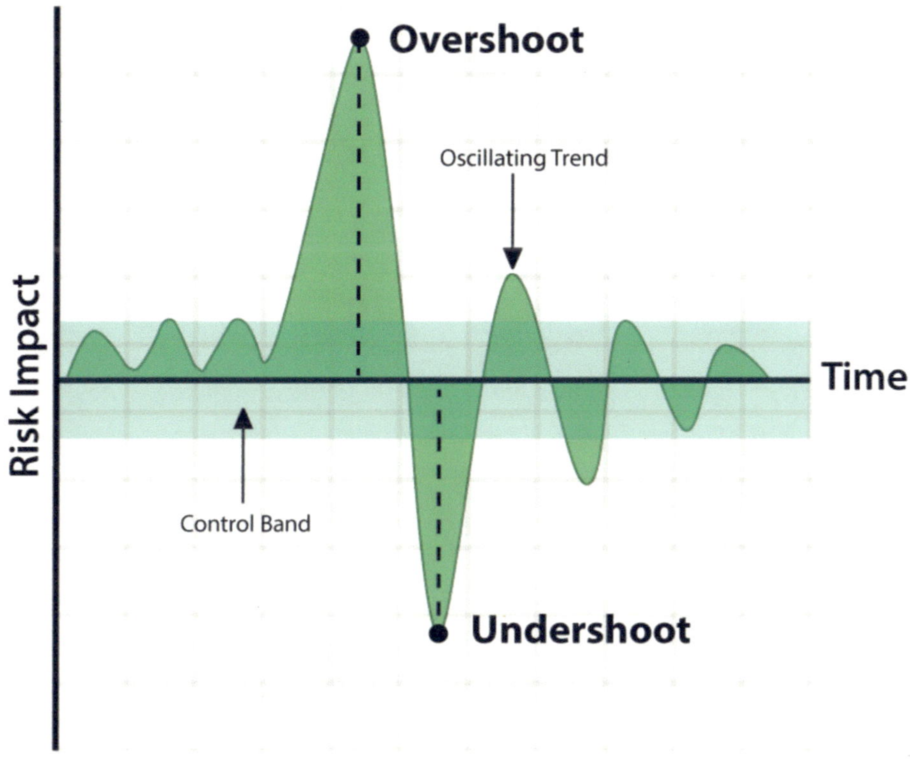

Figure 13: The implications of risk tend to oscillate towards steady state, and not adjust linearly (this is a common feature of non-linear system dynamics)

29. Alternatively, the valuation may be adjusted to cater for expectations of repeated higher outcomes. In the long run, no premium can be attached to continually overshooting.

Two dimensions are commonly used to consider both upside and downside risk: likelihood and potential impact. As shown in Figure 14, risk can be assessed on a matrix according to likelihood and potential impact.

- Risk considered as low likelihood and low potential impact can potentially be monitored without action.
- Risk that is low likelihood and high potential impact is often addressed with formal mechanisms such as insurance contracts (where available).
- Most risk-mitigating internal activities concentrate on risks considered to be high likelihood and high potential impact.
- As noted, prior to embarking on any mitigating mechanisms, a distinction between the systematic or non-systematic nature of risk ought to be made (using, for example, the VUCA method discussed). This remains, irrespective of the combined likelihood impact dimensions. Mitigation mechanisms would then only apply to non-systematic, diversifiable risk elements.

Likelihood	Negligible	Minor	Moderate	Major	Extreme
Certain	Medium	High	High	Very High	Very High
Likely	Medium	Medium	High	High	Very High
Possible	Low	Medium	Medium	High	High
Unlikely	Very Low	Low	Medium	Medium	High
Rare	Very Low	Very Low	Low	Medium	Medium

Potential Impact

Figure 14: The severity of risk is a combination of its likelihood and potential impact, which can be depicted as a matrix

Use this QR code to access a short video about risk

Attaining wealth in the capitalist system

Having touched on the elements and characteristics of risk, we turn our attention back to the conditions for potentially attaining the desired strategic outcome in a capitalist system, which we referred to as *wealth*.

Capitalism is structured to encourage economic agents to contribute to the economy by gathering some resources (earning a wage or selling a product or service) and distributing some resources (spending the funds earned by consuming or investing). Capitalism is successful (and the economy grows) when consumers spend and corporations invest (or distribute) earnings. If economic agents hold on to their money, capital flow becomes constrained and economic downturn is the likely result. *This means that capitalism does not (and can not) readily support the broad-based accumulation of wealth for all agents.*

Indeed, capitalism encourages the rapid movement of money between agents. This concept is known as the velocity of money, and it describes the way that a capitalist system spurs agents to spend money as quickly as possible so they can contribute to (and increase) the overall economic output. In advanced economies, the velocity of money is so fast that many people spend their money before they earn it, using mechanisms such as consumer loans or credit cards.

Capitalism also encourages a multiplier effect, where agents are encouraged to buy and sell different goods, turning resources over and over to stimulate the economy. This multiplier effect enhances the application of capital across the system, facilitating more economic output. It further accentuates economic growth if it happens faster and faster (with increased velocity of money).

The gross domestic product (GDP) is a measure of the output value of all the goods and services produced in a particular economy within a specific timeframe. It is directly and positively correlated with these multiplier effects and velocity phenomena. Divided by the number of players, as a per capita measure, GDP is also an indirect indicator of the purchasing power of the individual agents within an economy.

Within markets, economic agents may choose to consume goods within the current timeframe or, if they have surplus, decide to reduce current consumption and invest (save) with the aim of higher consumption capacity at a future period. Economic agents' decisions about consumption now versus future consumption (by saving) are referred to as the Golden Rule, which also forms some of the fundamentals of finance theory. The reward for an economic agent who delays consumption by investing to produce a higher capacity of consumption at a future period is called the time value of money, or cost of capital (e.g., interest rates).

There is a constant, rapid movement of money in a system that is operating normally (as shown in Figure 15). But generating the strategic outcome of real wealth requires an economic agent to accumulate a disproportionate level of capital and retain it ready to be used at some chosen time in the future. This means that wealth – the desired outcome of business strategy – is an exception to the normal functioning of the capitalist system.

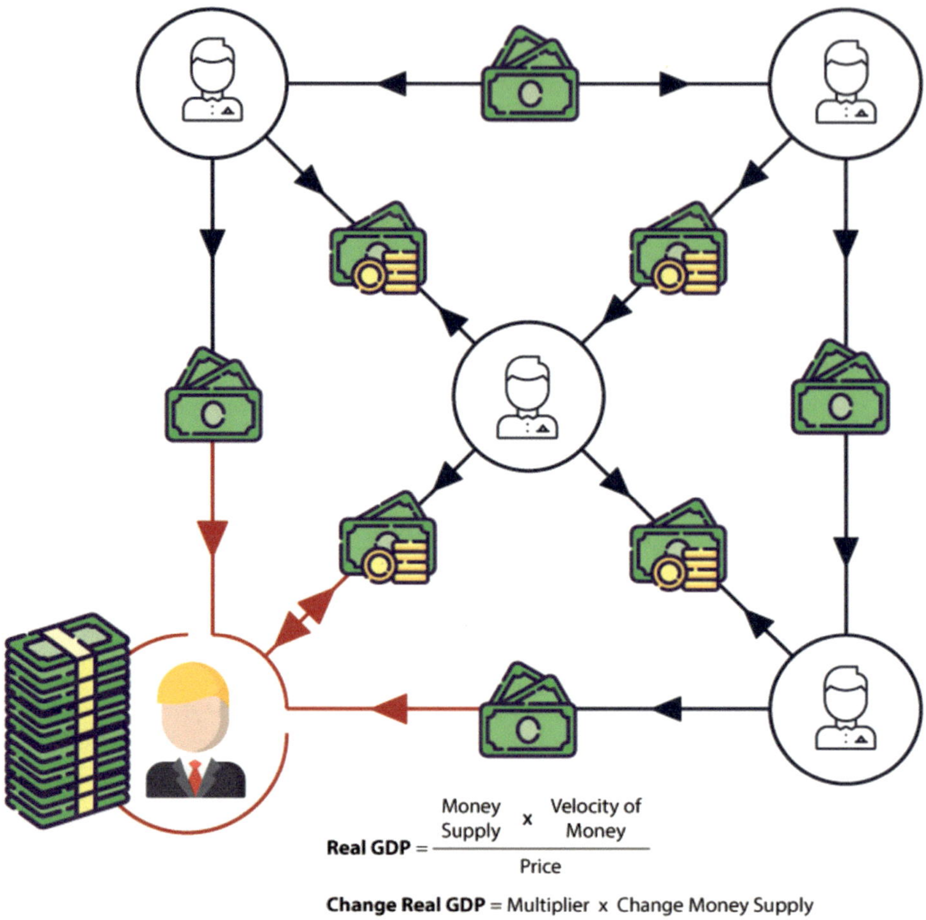

Figure 15: Within the economic system, most agents receive and move funds on quickly and accumulate little surplus; economic output (as measured by GDP) is positively enhanced by how fast money shifts between agents (velocity of money) and how many times it is exchanged (multiplier); only very few agents are able to systematically accumulate capital

Different types of market structure are described in the economic literature.[30] For example, perfect markets offer uniform goods and services, widespread knowledge, and many sellers and buyers. The price mechanism operates in an efficient way, with information widely spread and accessible to all agents. In a perfect market, it is highly unlikely that an economic agent can obtain above-normal returns on their resources. In contrast

30. Brief descriptions of market structure are included in the appendix.

to this, other types of more common market structures, such as monopoly, oligopoly or monopolistic competition, may provide conditions where specific economic agents are able to extract above-normal profit from their activities.

In most cases, the return on resources still remains at a normal risk-adjusted level. However, within these imperfect market structures, some economic agents are able to consume as much as they wish through current consumption, and also additionally allocate a significant amount of capital (as investment) for future gains and consumption. These agents must have access to some strategic asset or position whereby they can create a localised situation around themselves within the overall market. They are able to accumulate a disproportionate net amount of capital. Wealth, therefore, can be described as a micro disruption or a localised system failure in the capitalist system. The economic agent who becomes wealthy does not perform like other economic agents in the system and accumulates significantly more than they could spend or consume. As we will explain in the following sections, these agents may possess strategic assets that could be the result of a one-off structural failure (not replicable), or can be induced replicably through a process. We codify the latter in this section by applying the UTBS.

Wealth, being the desired strategic outcome in business, requires certain localised system conditions to be present around an economic agent for them to accumulate disproportionate net capital. This can broadly be achieved in two ways: either through a structural system failure or through a natural system failure. Both of these failures are localised around a particular economic agent and would not be broad-based across the market.

A structural system failure happens when some economic agents have privileged access to assets restricted only to themselves. Structural system failures are not replicable. Many are incompatible with legal compliance. Examples of structural system failure include having access to insider information, or using a political connection to create a favourable outcome. Other examples include an excessively high market share, pricing power or access to long-term mineral deposits through a special connection. Structural system failures may create wealth, but it is not the type of wealth that can be systematically attained, planned and replicated. In many cases, if a structural system failure is discovered, regulation will be gradually introduced within the system to disband or prevent it.[31] Even in cases where a structural system failure cannot be regulated against, the situation is rare, not replicable and may not be sustainable. Structural system failure provides, at best, a one-shot opportunity for wealth, often with compliance issues.

A natural market failure (also called a transactional failure), on the other hand, occurs when an economic agent possesses a particular type of advantage that gathers a great

31. Examples include formalised anti-trust or anti-collusion regulations in many industrial countries.

deal of resources – something that other economic agents struggle to readily replicate. These advantages are not readily tradeable (or transactable) through acquisition within the overall market system. Reasons for natural system failures might include specialised knowledge, intellectual property, extensive experience, refined work processes and other competitive advantage. These are outcomes of a successful strategic process that can be systematically obtained.

The capitalist system struggles to trade in this type of underlying entity. Intellectual property is an example of this. The value of intellectual property is that its owner knows something that others do not. Putting a value on it is difficult, because the buyer does not know its details. If the details were divulged by the seller, then the details are known and their underlying value is dissipated. The market attempts to use imperfect mechanisms such as non-disclosure (or confidentiality) agreements to alleviate this problem, so that such stock variables can be traded. This is because stock variables (such as competitive advantage, brand or innovation leadership) enable economic agents to charge a premium and generate higher profits. Knowledge, innovative capability, intellectual property and brand reputation all create such value. The economic agent possessing these makes an abnormal return on investment. This type of advantage takes time to accumulate and (as noted in Chapter 1) cannot be rushed. In addition, the position is not readily replicable by other players.[32]

This type of inability of the capitalist system's trade mechanisms (to deal with induced stock variables) is at the heart of the localised natural system failure that occurs around the agent that possesses such developed capabilities. The localised failure means the outward multiplier effect and the velocity of outward capital slow down around that agent. Conversely, it accelerates the inbound multiplier effect and money velocity. This economic agent (or a node in the overall system) can potentially magnify the inflow of capital and also constrict the outflow of capital, gathering it and accumulating it around themselves. The agent becomes wealthy (Figure 16).

The desired outcome of strategic business planning – wealth – can be induced over time by a natural system failure due to the formation and existence of a stock-type variable in the economic system. Wealth is firmly linked with stock variables (through the input of flow variables into strategic processes). *The application of the theoretical framework*

32. It is not possible to simply accumulate wealth through business-as-usual practices, as defined in Axiom 1 (Chapter 1). Axiom 1's iteration creates the preconditions for the mechanisms of Axiom 2 to operate. The formation of stock variables and localised events of a natural system failure then result in disproportionate resources accumulating around the economic agent. These resources come out of Axiom 2, by iterating Axiom 1 (as described in Chapter 1). Flow variable inputs become stock variable outputs through interactions of these two axioms.

discussed in the remainder of this chapter describes the building blocks needed to achieve wealth, linked to the axioms developed in Chapter 1.

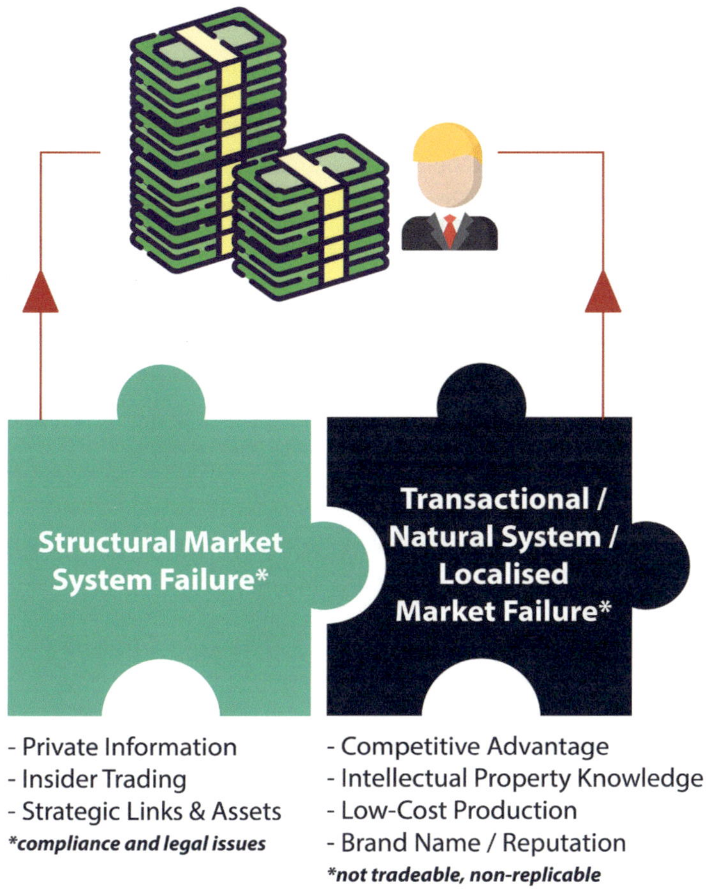

Figure 16: Two ways to achieve wealth: structural system failure (not replicable) or natural system failure (replicable and intended)

Use this QR code to access a short video about the underlying concepts of business strategy

The building blocks of strategic business planning

In the previous section, we described the desired outcome of business strategy and explained attributes of risk and preconditions for the formation of wealth. In this section, we look at how Axiom 1 and Axiom 2 (introduced in Chapter 1) can work together in business strategy to induce the outcome of wealth. Any firm that seeks to accumulate wealth and minimise risk needs a clear strategic plan that guides both the consistent iteration of Axiom 1 and the workings of Axiom 2.

A sound business strategy involves three building blocks:

1. Formulation – the analysis needed to understand what the business is seeking to achieve. This stage involves rigorous analysis of the business's external market and internal resources. The formulation stage of business strategy development essentially constructs cooperation-type activities and is analogous to Axiom 2
2. Implementation – the details necessary to guide consistent progress towards the desired outcome. This stage involves iterative processes, procedures and communication, applied over factor inputs (flow variables) to reduce costs, improve efficiency and provide the basis for a successful outcome of the formulation step. Implementation, therefore, is analogous with Axiom 1
3. Evaluation – regular monitoring that allows for self-correction and improvement. This stage provides an interface between formulation and implementation analogous to the interpretation step in Chapter 1.

The three building blocks of business planning should be implemented sequentially in a closed loop, with each stage clearly discrete from, but interdependent with, the one that follows.

- If formulation is not followed by rigorous implementation, it becomes little more than pontification or wishful thinking (that is, an effective vision from leaders without efficient mission from managers).
- If implementation is conducted without careful formulation, it may take the business in the wrong direction (faster than otherwise, even if done efficiently) and could result in failure (that is, efficient management mission or action with misguided leadership vision).
- If regular evaluation is not conducted after a set period between formulation and implementation, the business cannot assess whether it is making progress towards achieving its desired outcomes (that is, no interface between leadership vision and management mission).

In most businesses, formulation is undertaken at the senior leadership levels, by functions with most experience. Implementation corresponds more to the operational level of organisational management ranks. Together, the three building blocks of business strategy – formulation, implementation and evaluation – form a closed loop that allows the business to progress towards a desired outcome whilst continually realigning or self-correcting to maintain the correct direction. Figure 17 illustrates the three building blocks of strategic business planning.

Figure 17: The main building blocks of strategic business planning; formulation and implementation interact through evaluation

The building blocks work similarly to the autopilot function on an aircraft – with a desired destination set at the outset (formulation), a consistent set of activities designed to keep the aircraft on the correct path (implementation), and regular monitoring of coordinates (evaluation) that may lead to adjustment and correction. This type of negative feedback loop is an integral part of system dynamics applicable to business situations, commonly called a self-correcting server system.

Formulation

In this section we look at the first building block of business strategy development: formulation. The formulation stage involves three steps: 1) analysing the external environment, 2) identifying internal resources and 3) comparative gap analysis. We refer to these three steps as external, internal and gap analysis. These develop a concrete understanding of the direction the business will take. Formulation essentially culminates in the development of corporate vision.

Formulation must consider both the business's external environment and internal resources. Most of the external evaluation is embedded into a marketing plan (also discussed in Chapter 3). By comparing and juxtaposing the external and internal aspects and considering relevant risks, businesses can identify the resources required to reach and exploit external opportunities or, conversely, to extend available internal resources across to new uncontested market segments.[33] External and internal analysis together form a critical part of the formulation stage, which is built on the rigorous thinking outlined in Axiom 2 (in Chapter 1).

External analysis

The first stage of the formulation block involves analysing the external environment in which the business operates. External analysis needs to be conducted at the correct level and scale – considering both the macro level and the more focused, micro level.

- The macroeconomic environment is analysed to primarily identify systematic risk, using tools such as PESTEL (discussed in more detail in Chapter 3 and in the appendix).
- The microeconomic environment is analysed to primarily identify non-systematic risk, using tools such as Five Forces (discussed in more detail in Chapter 3 and in the appendix).

Microeconomic analysis broadly embodies two components – industry analysis and market analysis. It is important for a business to understand both its industry and its market, and to recognise whether they overlap within its operating value system. The business should consider what type of market it resides in – in relation to its industry position and where, in turn, its value-added chain operates. For example, a business in the automotive manufacturing industry that supplies vehicle components to original equipment manufacturers (OEMs) is likely to be interested in issues of engineering, technical performance and industrial B2B marketing.[34] In this situation, the business's industry sector and its market segments overlap. They are both in engineering (automotive) areas. On the other hand, if a business in the automotive manufacturing industry sells vehicles to the retail consumer market, it is likely to be interested in retail issues and consumer B2C marketing.[35] This relative position will have a considerable impact on the strategic formulation steps in external analysis. We distinguish and clarify this industry–market definition within our framework for business strategy.

- An industry is a place where a business undertakes its value-added activities. Examples of industries include manufacturing, professional services and

33. This, in turn, forms the basis for configuring the second stage of business strategy – implementation.
34. B2B = business to business.
35. B2C = business to consumer.

transport. Industry sectors can be broken down into further subsectors.[36] For example, automotive manufacturing is a subsector of the manufacturing industry; legal services is a subsector of the professional service industry; road freight is a subsector of transport.

- A market is a place where potential buyers of a business's goods and services may be located. Markets can be within or overlap an industry (such as the market for vehicle components being located within the same automotive manufacturing industry) or can overlap across multiple industries (for example, the market for legal services could come from any industry). Markets can also be completely separate from the industry relevant to the business. For example, a business operating in the freight industry could service the retail market or the fuel distribution market. Markets can be broken down into segments and subsegments.[37]

A firm's industry and market may be the same, may overlap, or may be entirely separate (Figure 18).

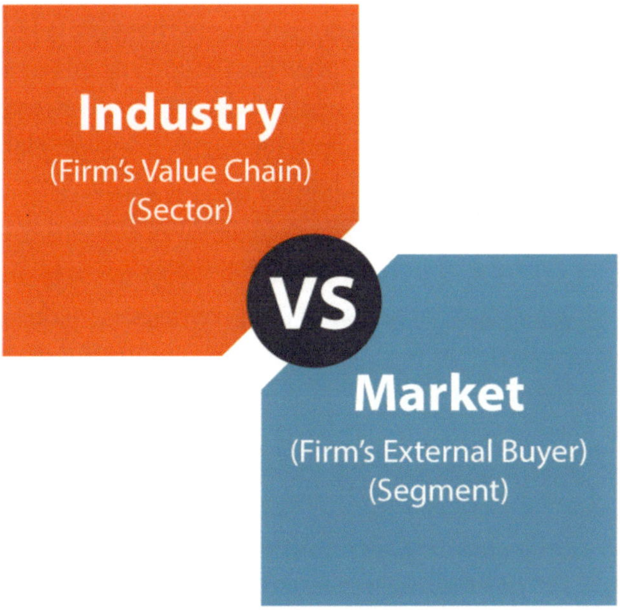

Figure 18: Industry and market may be the same, may overlap, or may be entirely separate parts of the overall value system of a firm

Once the analysis produces both a macro and micro picture of the industry and market within the external environment, the market may need to be analysed and segmented.

36. The terms 'sector' and 'subsector' are more appropriate for discussions about industries.
37. The terms 'segment' and 'subsegment' are more appropriate for discussions about markets.

Market segmentation

Markets can be divided into discrete segments, which can be useful in helping to understand who is purchasing the product (or services) and how to adjust the relevant variables in a way that best suits them. Clear understanding of market segments enables businesses to fine-tune their decisions about product package and service bundle, position, price, promotion, distribution and sales tactics.

Prerequisites for market segmentation are the economic concepts of price elasticity and information value of a signal. If one or both of these conditions are present, there is justification for market segmentation, where businesses use different pricing and positioning to improve potential economic gains.

- Price elasticity is the degree to which the demand for a product changes as its price changes. When price elasticity is high, demand for that product is highly sensitive to price changes, because sales can fall markedly when price increases. When price elasticity is low, demand for the product will change little when the price changes. For instance, discretionary items that cost a large portion of the consumer's income are often highly price elastic (such as cars or furniture). In contrast, essential items that require a small portion of the consumer's income (such as basic food items), are examples of products with low price elasticity. If there are different price elasticities across the market (for the offered products and services), there is then a valid case for dividing the overall market into discrete segments.
- Information signals indicate the perceived value of a product or service (rather than the actual price) to a particular market participant. Value signals like brand name and sales location can indicate whether a product is designed for, or desired by, a particular market segment. For example, a wealthy consumer may pay a high price for a jacket with a recognised brand name from a high fashion retailer. A jacket that closely resembles the expensive one may be available in a local weekend market for a fraction of that price. The price signal is, however, not of value to the wealthy consumer, who makes the purchase on brand, the location of the store and the prestige image created by displaying the label. In many cases, this type of information signalling is not feasible or available to consumers. If there are clear barriers to information signals across the market (or the signals are of no value) then there is also a case for segmentation of the overall market.

Figure 19 illustrates the two main prerequisites for market segmentation – price elasticity and information value signals.

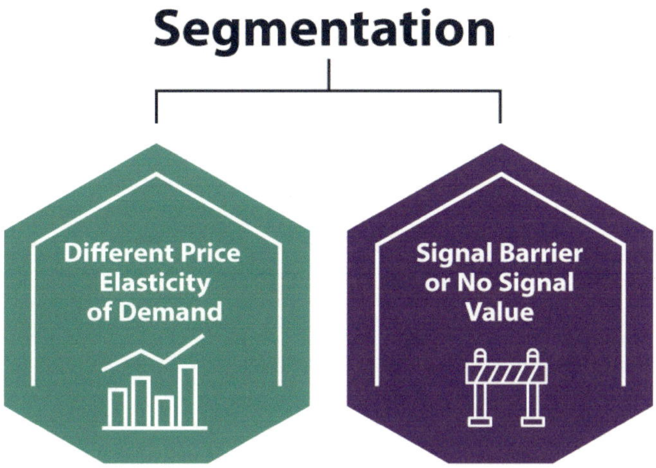

Figure 19: The two main prerequisites in economics that justify segmentation in marketing

Markets are typically segmented according to characteristics such as geography (location), psychographics (beliefs and interests), demographics (income) and buyer behaviour. When defining market segments, it is important to use the same criterion in order to create a logical segmentation. For example, if geographical location is used as the primary market segment, then it should be used consistently to create the segments relevant across the business (see Chapter 3). In complex markets, where these segmented elements may differ significantly across the segment, it may be useful to further divide the market into subsegments (also discussed in Chapter 3).

Once segments are defined, each will require appropriate elements such as product package and service bundle, pricing and positioning, advertising and promotion, distribution channels, sales tactics and after-sale incentives, and so on (these elements are discussed in detail in Chapter 3). Based on the segmentation (and on criteria such as profitability and margin), the business can decide which segments to target (contest). Not all identified segments may, therefore, be always contested.

Other steps in external analysis

External analysis also involves other steps to assess the competitive position, external risk, unique selling proposition (USP) and/or value proposition (VP). Together, these form a macro-level, micro-level and segmented view of the external attributes of the business. These steps are discussed in more detail in Chapter 3.

Once the external environment is understood as a complete picture, the next step in formulation involves a review of internal aspects of the business.

Use this QR code to access a short video about background corporate information in business strategy

Internal analysis

As a continuing part of formulation and after examining the external environment, businesses then need to analyse their internal capabilities and resources.

Several tools are available to support this work, including SWOT analysis (examining strengths, weaknesses, opportunities and threats), best conducted using a balanced scorecard approach (which considers four different perspectives of the business – financial, customer, internal processes, and learning and growth).[38] Another useful tool is the PROFIT model, which can be used to identify various classes of internal assets (such as physical, financial and organisational assets).

An understanding of internal resources enables management to construct a view of what can, and cannot, be achieved. The internal analysis of weaknesses and strengths can be compared with the picture that emerged from external analysis. For example, suppose a great market opportunity is identified through the segmentation and industry analysis, but is not contestable by the business due to insufficient sales capacity or financial constraints that prohibit the products in that contestable market. This type of mismatch can be identified through gap analysis to later become part of the implementation block.[39]

Care should be taken to also identify resources and assets that may not be readily apparent but may add considerable capacity to the business. Readily discernible assets generally take a physical form (such as manufacturing capability, transport fleet, personnel numbers or cash balance). However, other assets are less readily detectable, even though they may be equally valuable. For example, intangible assets such as organisational knowledge, innovation capability, access to licences and regulatory advantage should all be considered. This means that internal analysis is not simply an accounting exercise (focused on the balance sheet) as many valuable assets are not catered for in typical accounting measures. As we note in Chapter 3, accounting formats are suitable

38. These tools are also discussed in Chapter 3 and in the appendix.

39. The resource-based view of strategy, discussed in the appendix, is based on the premise that the firm's internal resources are the key determinant in formulating a strategy. The opposite approach is taken by the attractive or external market view of a strategy, which proposes that available external opportunities should be used to determine strategy. Our approach, here, attempts to bring these two schools of thought under one interconnected framework.

as reporting (evaluation) lag indicators, but are not suitable as lead indicators, which are generally relevant during formulation.

Comparative gap analysis

A comparative gap analysis is a useful way of understanding the relationship between the opportunities and challenges facing the business and the capabilities (or resources) at its disposal. Any mismatches pinpoint areas where the business should look to build internal capacity or, conversely, extend existing resources to broaden its external scope. This type of comparison is best spread across different aspects of the business, based on the balanced scorecard approach. It is particularly helpful when it identifies a latent market opportunity – that is, a gap in the market that the business can easily step into if it has the prerequisite capabilities. For example, activewear companies identified a latent market opportunity when they started to offer fashionable sportwear, which had not previously been available. This can be an application of Say's law: that supply can generate demand.[40] Chapter 3 also describes a comparative gap matrix.

The outcomes of comparative gap analysis (between external opportunities and internal resources) feed into the implementation stage of strategic planning as part of capacity -building programs. These are finite-period activities designed to develop required resources or extend existing resources into external markets. Capacity-building programs are the essential backbone of creating competitive advantage. Moreover, if these programs are firmly based on the comparative gap analysis, they will embody the correct and most relevant type of capacity for the business to build. This correct correspondence avoids building costly and irrelevant (white elephant) resources that, in the long run, do not generate even normal profits. This incongruent interface remains a common error in many corporations.

External analysis, internal analysis and gap analysis together form the formulation step of business planning (an Axiom 2–style entity). Formulation, therefore, identifies what overall macro and micro environments may be prevailing, what competitors are doing, what risk types may be confronted, which parts of the market to contest, and what capacity needs to be configured within the business. It, therefore, establishes the prerequisites for the second building block and stage of business strategy development – implementation (an Axiom 1–style entity).

40. In economics, Say's law states that production of one product creates demand for another product by providing something of value. That is, production is the source of demand. Because each person can only make purchases equivalent in value to the income they produce for themselves, the more each person produces, the more they are likely to purchase. Supply-side economics is primarily based on the same premise.

In practice, therefore, the strategy development process follows the reverse order to our description of strategic axioms in Chapter 1. Strategic outcomes are determined and formulation is configured first (Axiom 2–style entity), leading to implementation (Axiom 1–style entity). However, in Chapter 1 it was more intuitive, from a theoretical standpoint, to describe the process from Axiom 1 to Axiom 2 within our framework construct. In pragmatic business strategy, however, the configuration of formulation (Axiom 2) drives implementation (Axiom 1) which, in turn, caters towards formulation in the evaluation link (interpretation in Chapter 1).

Use this QR code to access a short video about the formulation building block of business strategy

Vision and lead indicators

The culmination of the steps in the formulation stage is the strategic vision, which embodies the firm's external and internal environment, where it is heading and what resources are available. Vision formed in this manner tends to be more accurate, pragmatic and plausible than vision declared too early in the planning process.

Many businesses try to define a vision first, and then formulate a strategic plan intended to realise that vision. However, strategic business vision is not something that can be simply conjured up. A clear and accurate vision is more than a vague slogan. It is a concrete guiding principle that is supported by analysis and developed through rigorous thinking. Through the formulation stage described in this section, vision is progressively constructed and shaped. A well-founded or grounded vision created through careful analysis at the end of the formulation stage will provide the bridge into implementation.

Lead indicators are primarily used within the formulation stage. They help the business to reduce uncertainty by providing an indication of the forthcoming potential conditions. For example, in order to forecast the price of housing, relevant lead indicators may include the number of building approvals, the amount of new land released and the volume of development applications submitted. They look into the future. To the extent possible, care should be taken not to look at backward-reporting indicators or spot indicators when creating a future vision. Whilst those indicators are useful (primarily in implementation and evaluation), lead indicators are the most appropriate indicators for formulation. Lead indicators look to the future and are suitable in formulation and creating a vision used to drive the business forward.

Implementation

In the previous section, we addressed the first building block of strategic business planning – formulation. We identified its three key steps – external analysis, internal analysis and gap analysis – and described the features of each step. We now move on to consider the implementation phase, which also involves three parts: general operations; routine processes, procedures and communication (PPCs); and capacity-building programs (which, being one-off step-change items, also have a similar format to ongoing PPCs). The implementation stage is analogous to Axiom 1, and involves establishing the required resources and correct routine activities to support the cooperative resolution of the configured formulation (Axiom 2).

Implementation involves developing PPC, then refining them through regular review and iteration to help move the business towards its strategic goals. These are likely to focus on improving efficiency, lowering (transaction) costs and responding to the external environment as needed. In this way, implementation deals with operational efficiency (the flow variables of Axiom 1) and progressively transforms it into competitive advantage (the stock variables of Axiom 2). Tools such as TQM, 5S and Kanban are useful to support the implementation of strategic planning. These tools and other organisational attributes such as corporate governance address factor input and their iteration.[41] Continuous application of these aspects ensures operational efficiency (a flow variable) over time, that in turn can gradually induce competitive advantage (a stock variable). Therefore, the relationship between operational efficiency and competitive advantage can be described using mathematical notation:

$$\int_{t=1}^{n} (\textit{operational efficiency})\, dt = \textit{competitive advantage}$$

or

$$\frac{d\,(\textit{competitive advantage})}{dt} = \textit{operational efficiency}$$

Based on this approach, a mathematical integral of operational efficiency will yield competitive advantage; equally, operational efficiency is the first derivative of competitive advantage with respect to time. The steps discussed next collectively represent the making of this mathematical relationship in business strategy, showing how to create operational efficiency to then, over time, render competitive advantage.

41. TQM is a continual process of detecting, reducing and eliminating errors; 5S is a workplace organisation methodology; Kanban is a scheduling system for just-in-time manufacturing. These concepts are briefly described in the appendix.

General (freehand) operations

The first part of the implementation block is the general operations that should be left relatively flexible by the business. Broadly, approximately 30 per cent of the business's activities should be left in this manner to provide some degrees of freedom. This leaves space for operational tasks that cannot be readily accommodated (or are not suitable) within a formalised procedural framework.

The degrees of freedom provide open choices that keep flexibility and vigour to take advantage of opportunities and explore options for innovation. In this area, management has the ability to conduct business in a way that directly responds to the internal and external requirements of the business and the opportunities presented. These may not be determined in advance. Having flexibility in some parts of the operation within a semi-structured framework keeps the organisation nimble. It helps to ensure the business is not over-structured and, therefore, not in danger of suffocation from 'doing business internally with itself'. This flexibility can remain in various parts of the business – from marketing to operations – leaving room for creativity and ad hoc innovation. If few (or no) activities are left unstructured, the adverse ramification may smother the business due to overly constraining processes and procedures.

Processes, procedures and communication (PPC)

The second step in implementation is characterised by processes, procedures and regular communication (PPCs). PPCs are a critical aspect of implementation. They address many of the risk issues facing a business, bring control and consistency to business operations, and create a steady state. PPCs encompass the repeated, iterative, correlated activities that gradually achieve the business's goals and lower transaction costs. By reducing transaction costs (for both the business and its customers) through that improved consistency of approach, PPCs achieve the desired strategic outcomes identified in formulation.[42]

Through this application, PPCs can be used to develop things like operational efficiency, corporate governance and knowledge, which, in turn, will help to create competitive advantage. PPCs should only apply to approximately 70 per cent of the business's operational activities. They are relevant for generic activities including financial and operational management. A subset of PPCs can also be applied directly towards the resources required to build stock variables (identified through gap analysis under formulation). These capacity -building programs are covered as the third step of implementation, below.

PPCs are typically implemented using productivity tools (such as TQM and 5S) to ensure consistency. Moreover, corporate governance, which is an essential part of the

42. Note that PPCs involve, at their core, establishing asymmetric positioning, accountability, responsibility and sequential activity, which embody the theoretical concept of Axiom 1 discussed in Chapter 1.

proper running of any business, can only be effectively implemented through proper processes and procedures. This is imperative, not only for private companies, but also for those publicly listed on equity exchanges.

Processes and procedures work together to define what to do, when to do it, the role responsible for doing it, and how to do it (Figure 20).

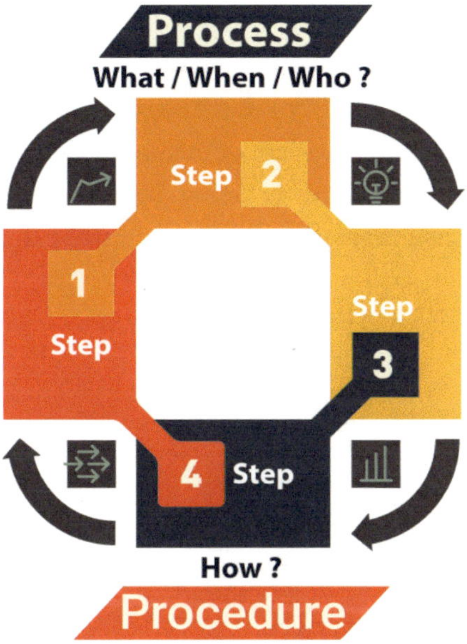

Figure 20: Processes and procedures go hand in hand: what to do, how often, by what function, and how

Processes

Processes describe what needs to be done (the activity), at what interval (the frequency), and by whom (the roles or functions within the organisation). Processes are typically represented by flow diagrams, and all have a dimension of time. Processes provide clear direction to ensure that various organisational functions complete the required activities within the required timeframe. They ensure the regular requirements related to Axiom 1 activities are completed on time.

Most businesses need generic processes to describe their routine tasks in areas such as finance, operations, marketing and human resources. For instance, processes describe financial reporting, operational and labour cost activities, and human resources performance reviews. These processes are common and will be used in many different types of business. Many businesses also require specific processes that are relevant to their particular work profile. Processes that might be commonplace for one business may not be needed in another. For example, start-up firms with a high requirement for innovation will need different processes than those used by firms operating in steady-state, mature industries.

As discussed in the *Communication* section below, processes require a standardised syntax to ensure they communicate clearly and precisely, and to ensure they can be implemented in the same way each time they are used. Processes allow for iteration over periodicity to create experience and feedback.

Processes are primarily sequential and time-based, and are composed by the organisation's more experienced personnel. Senior management is accountable for configuring processes and establishing the appropriate communication chain throughout the organisation. Processes can be understood as being introduced top-down organisationally. They remain a direct responsibility of management rather than of operational personnel.

The diagram below illustrates a typical business process.

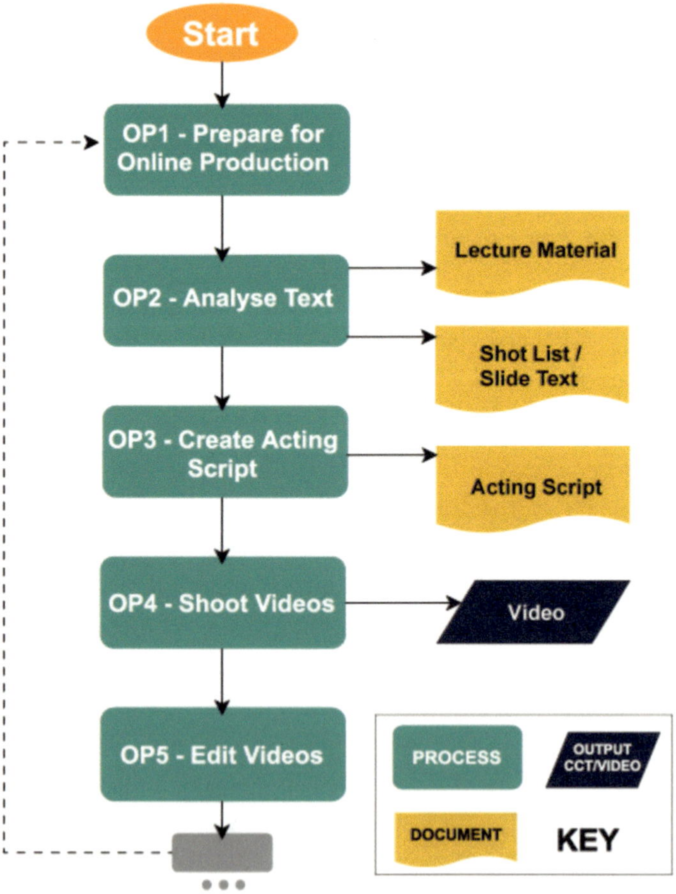

Figure 21: A typical example of a generic process with closed loop feedback and sequential steps

Procedures

Once processes have been configured (what, when and by whom), the question of *how* becomes relevant. This is the realm of procedures.

Procedures operate alongside certain steps of processes to explain how that step is undertaken and to ensure the process is completed effectively. Procedures may be written as numbered steps or as pictorial diagrams. They are usually written for clarity and easy reference, to ensure the procedure can be easily and repeatedly implemented by a wider group of candidates. In contrast with processes, which happen across time, procedures are mainly situationally based.

Procedures may be linked to a single process or may appear linked across several processes and different steps. For example, a staff review procedure or a procurement protocol could apply to processes for many different functions within an organisation. Unlike processes, procedures are best compiled by the individuals who are directly involved with the task. This will provide credibility and pragmatism into the question of how the steps and tasks should be undertaken. Procedures are, therefore, developed at the operational level, by the functions who are directly responsible for them. Procedures can be said to be compiled bottom-up organisationally. Senior leadership in the organisation are directly responsible for the accuracy and repetition of processes, and indirectly accountable for both processes and procedures. Operational staff are directly responsible for compiling procedures, which are situational, and which are appended to processes. Figure 22 illustrates a typical business procedure.

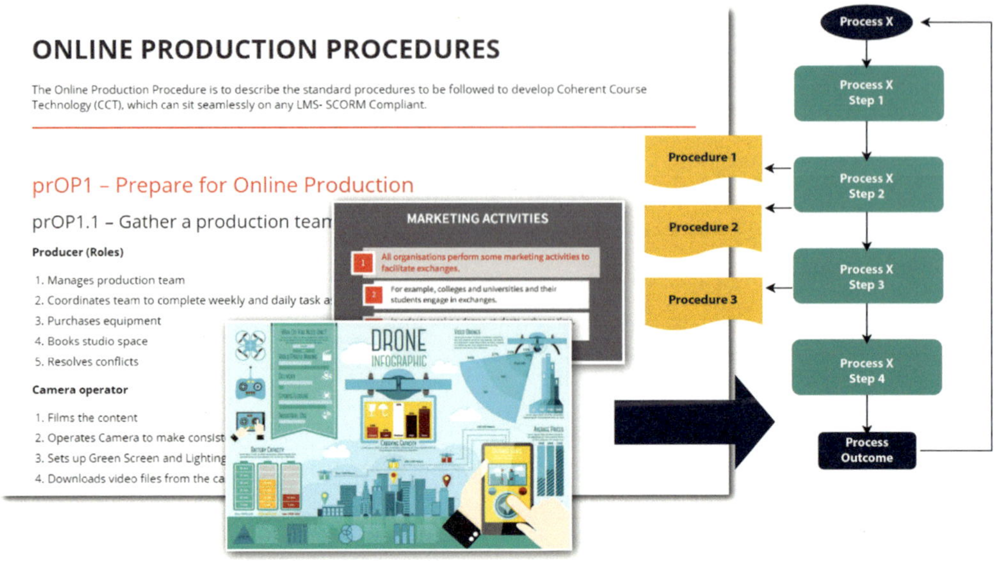

Figure 22: Generic procedures showing text and pictures to facilitate description of a situational nature[43]

Communication

Communication describes the way that information about processes and procedures is disseminated through the organisation. This is a critical element of PPC (recalling that PPC itself is the second element of implementation). Successful communication includes three elements:

1. A clear explanation of the outcome required, developed by functions with pre requisite experience and knowledge to explain it
2. Determination of skills and other resources needed to successfully complete the process within the specified timeframe
3. Appropriate monitoring and reporting (both in terms of frequency and intensity).

The first element of communication (a clear explanation of the outcome) involves an interchange between an instructor and a recipient. The scale and scope of the detail transmitted through communication is a function of the seniority and relative knowledge of both the instructor and recipient. Successful resolution of this element rests with the recipient: irrespective of how well the instructor may perceive they have explained the task, confirmation of full understanding can only come from the recipient. The recipient is responsible for confirming they understand the instruction (the interaction between accountability and responsibility will be discussed in more detail below).

43. The text in this diagram is not intended to be legible. It is included to show how a diagrammatic process may link to a textual and pictorial procedure.

The second element of communication (skills, resources and time) is a function of the recipient's experience and knowledge. The lower the recipient's level of experience, the more resources and longer time may need to be allocated to that recipient (for training, supervision and monitoring).

The third element of communication (monitoring and reporting) is a function of the comparative position between the instructor and recipient. In contrast with the first element (where the prerogative rests with the recipient to verify proper transmission of the message), in monitoring and reporting that prerogative shifts to the instructor to acknowledge that the outcome has been achieved as intended. The lower the recipient's experience, the higher will be the frequency of reporting (and vice versa).

The three elements of communication are interrelated. For example, if a new staff member with little experience or insufficient skill is required to complete a process, the timeframe may be extended or more regular reporting may be needed. In contrast, a highly experienced staff member may be able to work more independently, with reduced reporting and monitoring requirements.

A military example may demonstrate this point. At the most senior levels of the army, instructions will be broad and strategic – for example, an instruction to take control of a particular location. As the communication cascades down, officers require increasing detail about their role in the operation. At the most detailed level, the soldiers on the ground need to know the exact timing, location, formation and role of each unit.

These elements will vary in their degree (in terms of scale and scope) in consecutive parts of the organisation. Communication should cascade down (becoming increasingly operational) and integrate up (becoming increasingly strategic) through the organisation. As this occurs, the three elements above should be adjusted in scale and scope as needed. At the highest levels, communication should be broad, strategic and expeditious. It must cascade down through the organisation effectively (at lower levels, the scope of communication shifts, offering detailed discussion at a smaller, more focused scale). Communication then integrates back up through the organisation (higher levels of the organisation will require less detailed instruction and may include less frequent monitoring). Errors occur when the wrong degree of the three communication elements are undertaken at different levels of the organisation. This cascade of communication is illustrated in Figure 23.

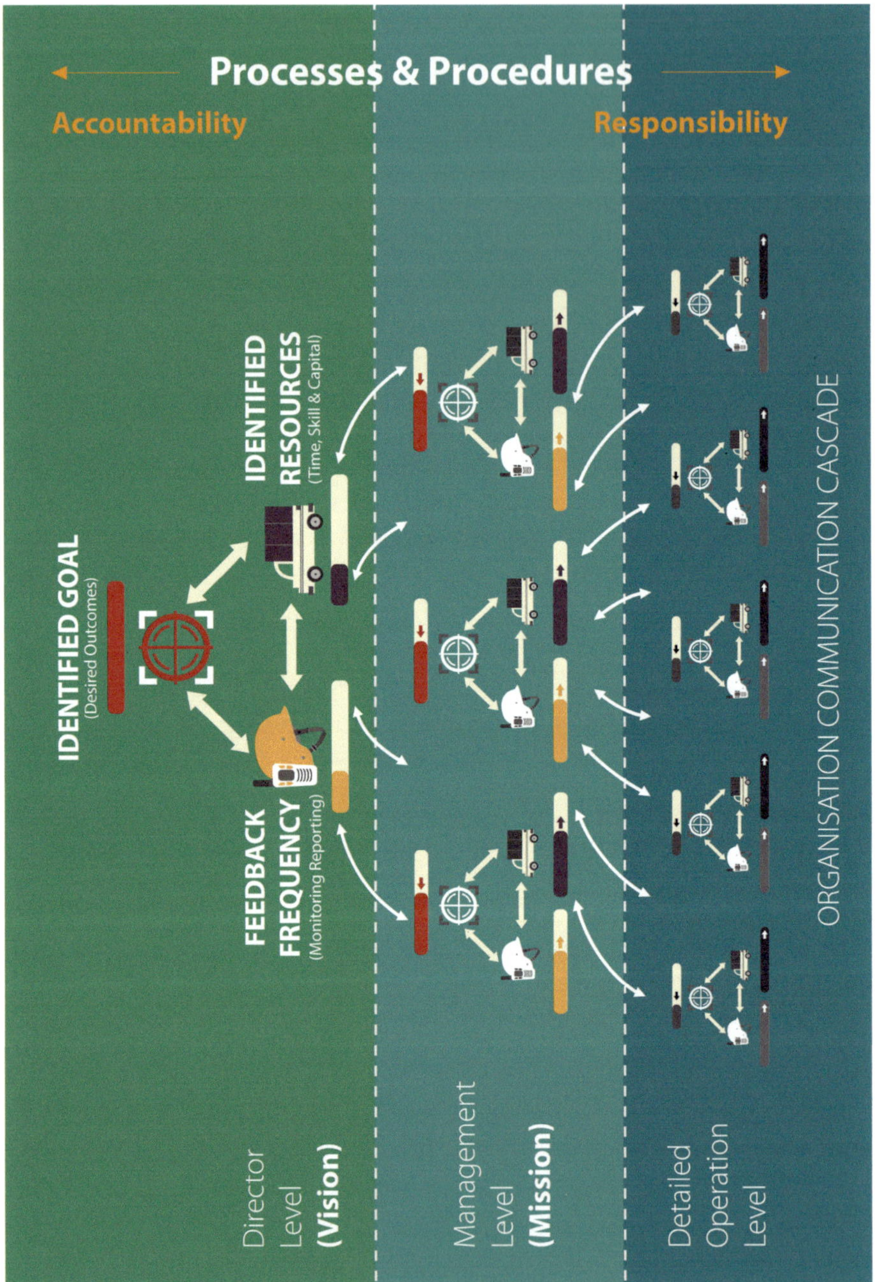

Figure 23: Communication cascades down through the organisation through processes and procedures, with linked accountability and responsibility (this figure is best viewed online; use the QR code for access)

The underlying reason why communication cascades down and integrates up relates to the difference between accountability and responsibility. Accountability is indirect: individuals accept accountability, based on their position, for tasks they do not undertake directly but which remain within their control span. Accountability is intertwined with leadership and senior positions within the organisation. Responsibility is direct: it is a characteristic of an individual's involvement in completing a direct task. Responsibility corresponds more with operational management.

In most organisations, with increased management seniority there is a corresponding increase in accountability and perhaps lower direct responsibility for completing individual tasks.

- Accountability is often associated with executive stress: the individual is accountable but does not have immediate control over the prescribed tasks. For example, if a soldier inadvertently shoots a person, it is the general who needs to resign, not necessarily the soldier. The general is accountable for the soldier's actions.
- Responsibility is often associated with job fatigue: the individual is operationally involved in completing the task and responsibility tends to reside at the operational levels of an organisation. In the above example, the soldier will still be reprimanded if they are found to have failed in their direct responsibility.

This continuum between accountability and responsibility plays an important part in determining the detail of communication required at different levels of the organisation. The three elements of communication help to determine whether the intentions of processes and procedures are organisationally understood, what resources are required to support communication (time, capital and training) and how monitoring and feedback should be conducted. The accountability of senior managers can only be effective if PPCs are well defined and operating properly.

This dichotomy of accountability and responsibility, therefore, straddles the organisational vision and mission.

- Accountability sits at the most senior levels, and is linked to organisational vision. The direct accountability of leadership feeds into the proper configuration of processes (as described earlier).
- Responsibility sits at the operational level, and is linked with management and mission. Direct responsibility of operational personnel feeds into the accurate compilation of procedures (as described earlier).

If any of the three elements of communication are not operating at the correct level, communication is likely to break down, resulting in an imbalance in accountability and/or responsibility. For example, if senior management does not put proper communication mechanisms in place and attempts to abdicate their accountability by becoming involved in every aspect of responsibility, the common over-control of micromanagement begins to manifest. This immediately increases the transaction costs (and entropy) of doing business. In this way, micromanaging by over-focusing on responsibility can be seen as the result of an inability to accept accountability. Conversely, where senior management fails to put proper communication mechanisms in place and passes its accountability down the organisational chain, the dysfunctionality of blame culture begins to appear. This also increases transaction costs (and entropy) within the organisation. In contrast, effective delegation that clearly cascades down the organisation is the successful implementation of accountability.

PPCs require clearly established guidelines for accountability and responsibility. Processes are time-based and procedures are situational. Combined with elements of communication and along the responsibility/accountability spectrum, together they form a powerful methodology. The business can reduce its transaction costs of doing business, both internally and externally.

Use this QR code to access a short video about the implementation building block of business strategy

Capacity-building programs

Following general operations and PPCs, capacity-building programs are the third step of the implementation block of strategic planning. These programs share the same format and characteristics of PPCs. However, in contrast to PPCs (which refer to the routine and regular activities of the business), capacity-building programs address the specific and selected issues that arise from the gap analysis and various risk, threat and opportunity identification conducted during the formulation stage. Capacity-building programs are intended to create a step-change over a finite period of time (as opposed to PPCs, which are of a continuous nature to provide consistency). They may be designed to develop a distinct capability or critical capacity within the organisation. Unlike general PPCs, they are not ongoing.

Capacity-building programs are an important part of the link between formulation (Axiom 2) and implementation (Axiom 1). For example, the business may identify gaps between its market opportunities and internal capabilities, or it may identify slack resources that need to be deployed across wider markets. Figure 24 shows the link between routine PPCs and capacity-building PPCs.[44]

44. These programs help to move the business towards the desired strategic outcome by ensuring the right cooperation games are resolved.

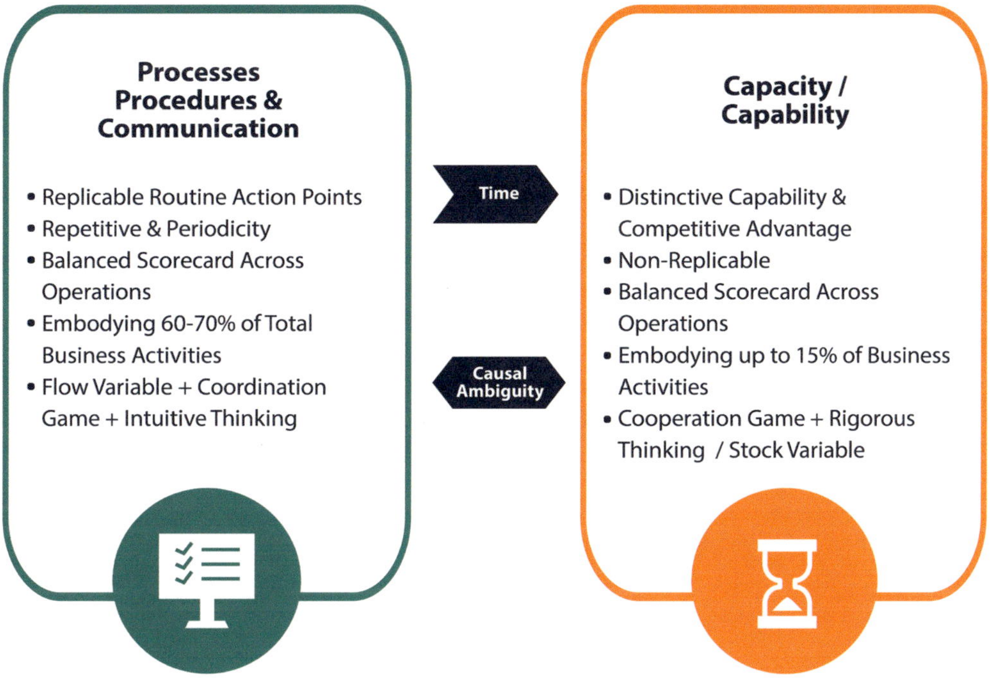

Figure 24: PPCs and capacity-building programs interact as part of implementation

Businesses need to ensure they do not undertake so many capacity-building programs that they cause prohibitive use of operational resources. Whilst the gap analysis undertaken during the formulation stage should identify sufficiently challenging business-capability targets, capacity-building programs should not consume more than 15 per cent of the business's resources.[45]

Implementation through the ongoing application of PPCs (Axiom 1) will achieve iterative, consistent signals. Over time, the combination of routine PPCs and capacity-building programs together contributes to the attainment of the goals identified in the formulation step (Axiom 2) towards developing competitive advantage (stock variables).[46]

45. This 15 per cent is part of the overall 70 per cent activity stipulated for PPCs in previous sections.

46. See the physical example of vehicle suspension systems at the end of the book.

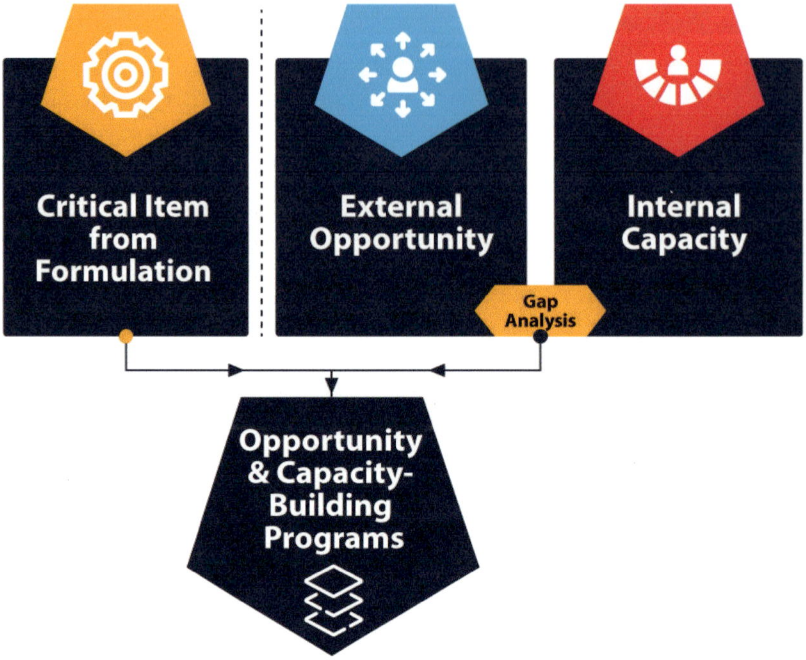

Figure 25: The justification for capacity-building programs can come from the gap analysis or other parts of the formulation stage

As noted previously, in the practical application of business strategy, the formulation stage (Axiom 2) occurs before the implementation stage (Axiom 1). Whilst it is most intuitive to theoretically describe the framework starting with Axiom 1 (flow variables, coordination games, intuitive thinking) and moving towards Axiom 2 (cooperation games, rigorous thinking, stock variables) (as undertaken in Chapter 1), the actual application starts with formulation (Axiom 2–style thinking) to determine the contents of implementation (Axiom 1).

Spot indicators primarily fit within the implementation stage and tend to include a discrete unit of time dimension. These provide information about current status and are better suited to operate the business. They often describe rates – such as the rate of production (number of units per day), the degree of service (complaints or returns per customer) or other rate KPIs. Spot indicators can provide useful information about how an individual business is currently performing in comparison with other parts of the industry (for benchmarking). Spot indicators typically (but not always) correspond to flow variables.

In the formulation stage, lead indicators were primarily used to drive the business (vision). Here, in implementation, spot variables are used to operate the business (mission).[47]

47. Lag indicators will be introduced in the next section for evaluation purposes.

Evaluation

Following formulation and implementation, evaluation forms the third block of strategic business planning. It is the link between formulation and implementation (in the same way as the interpretation stage is the link between Axioms 1 and 2 in Chapter 1). Evaluation enables the business to ensure the formulation and implementation blocks remain congruent and are moving towards the desired outcome. It is a crucial part of self-corrective, successful and closed-loop business strategy.

Evaluation should involve mainly financial (but also non-financial) monitoring and review elements. It should also monitor both flow variables (P & L and cash flow statement) as well as stock variables (balance sheet items). A balanced scorecard approach (described in the appendix) can help businesses to consider both financial and non-financial aspects as part of their evaluation. Actual business performance from implementation is reported for evaluation, which is then assessed against formulation goals over an agreed timeframe.

It is important that managers do not overly focus on the evaluation step and over-employ it as an operating mechanism for the business. Whilst evaluation is clearly important and many of the quantitative tools used in this step are valuable, they are skewed towards accounting and financial reporting rather than business operation. Much like the potential communication dysfunctions identified in the previous section, managerial errors occur when the business is operated (or driven forward) by over-relying on the monitoring parameters of the evaluation step. Evaluation should be used to examine corresponding modifications or refinements that may be needed to transpire through formulation and implementation. The evaluation stage (through lag indicators), therefore, helps to close the loop of business planning by allowing the business to reflect on its progress, return to the formulation stage and adjust the implementation steps as needed. The business is driven forward by formulation (vision), operated through implementation (mission) and only monitored through evaluation.[48]

Lag indicators monitor business performance at a particular point in time and follow on from lead (formulation) and spot (implementation) indicators discussed above. They are most commonly used for financial monitoring and reporting. For example, the balance sheet, which explains total assets and liabilities of a business at a particular point in time, is a key lag indicator of financial condition. Lag indicators typically (but not always) correspond to stock variables.

48. The old adage – *if you torture the figures long enough they will surely confess* – should be avoided as a mechanism for operating the business.

In this chapter we have referred to three different types of indicators: lead, spot and lag. As a useful summary:

- Drive the business with lead indicators
- Operate the business with spot indicators
- Monitor the business with lag indicators.

Business strategy – placing the building blocks together

Having defined the three main building blocks of business strategy (formulation, implementation and evaluation) and discussed their steps, we now combine these blocks to demonstrate the construct of business strategy, as shown in Figure 26.

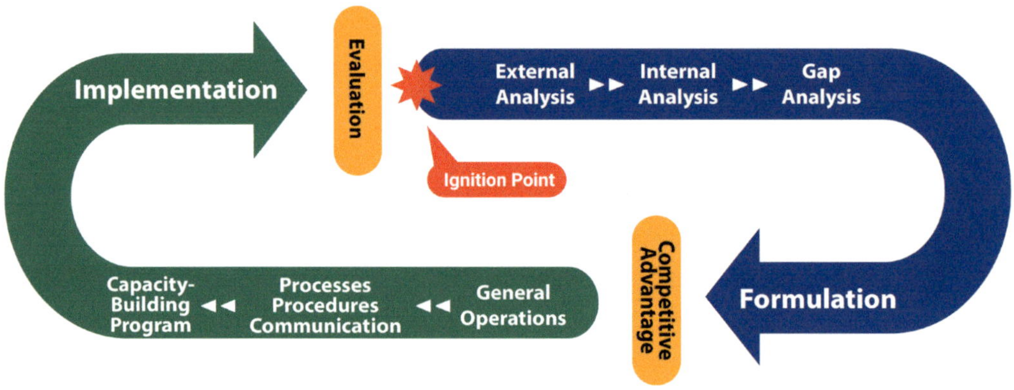

Figure 26: The three building blocks of business strategy (formulation, implementation and evaluation)

We now achieve our goal of applying the conceptual framework developed in Chapter 1 to the commercial business context developed in Chapter 2. It becomes apparent how the two axioms identified in Chapter 1 correspond with the applied version discussed in this chapter. As shown in Figure 27, there are discernible parallels between the three building blocks of strategic planning and the framework presented in Chapter 1.

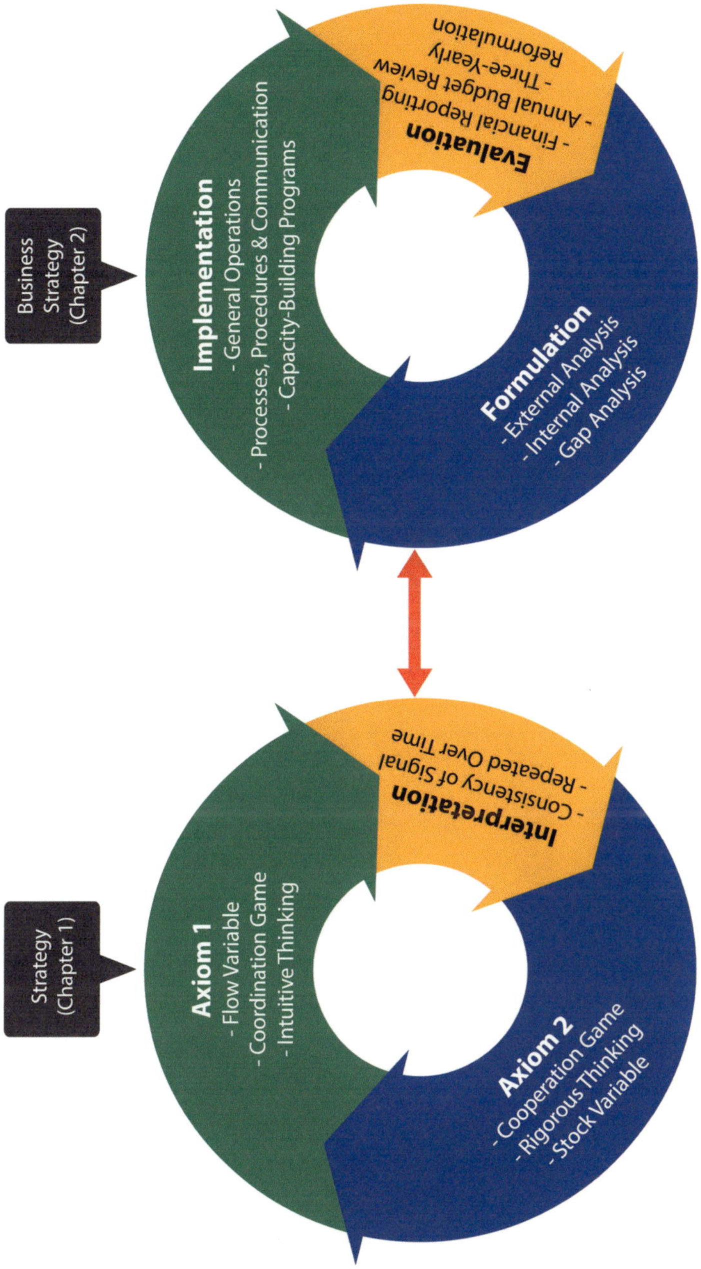

Figure 27: Strategic business planning involves three building blocks (formulation, implementation and evaluation) which correspond with the theoretical framework presented in Chapter 1 (Axioms 2 and 1, and interpretation)

The interactions shown in Figure 27 demonstrate why proper formulation, implementation and evaluation are essential components of successful business strategy. The material presented in Chapter 1 draws on real variables and elements to form the axioms, reflecting the physical applicability of the configured framework. Therefore, the building blocks in this chapter that correspond to these axioms are also themselves fundamental prerequisites – in this case – for business strategy. Unless such business strategy is based on an external–internal view and iteration for proper consistency, it is unlikely to create sustainable advantages of long-term value. The three building blocks provide a replicable, trustworthy method for generating stock variables and yielding competitive advantage. With competitive advantage, it becomes possible to create a localised system failure around an entity, attract above-normal accumulation of resources, and, therefore, create wealth. The case studies included later in this book show the degree of positive impact achievable through adopting these measures. Figure 28 shows this interaction in more detail.

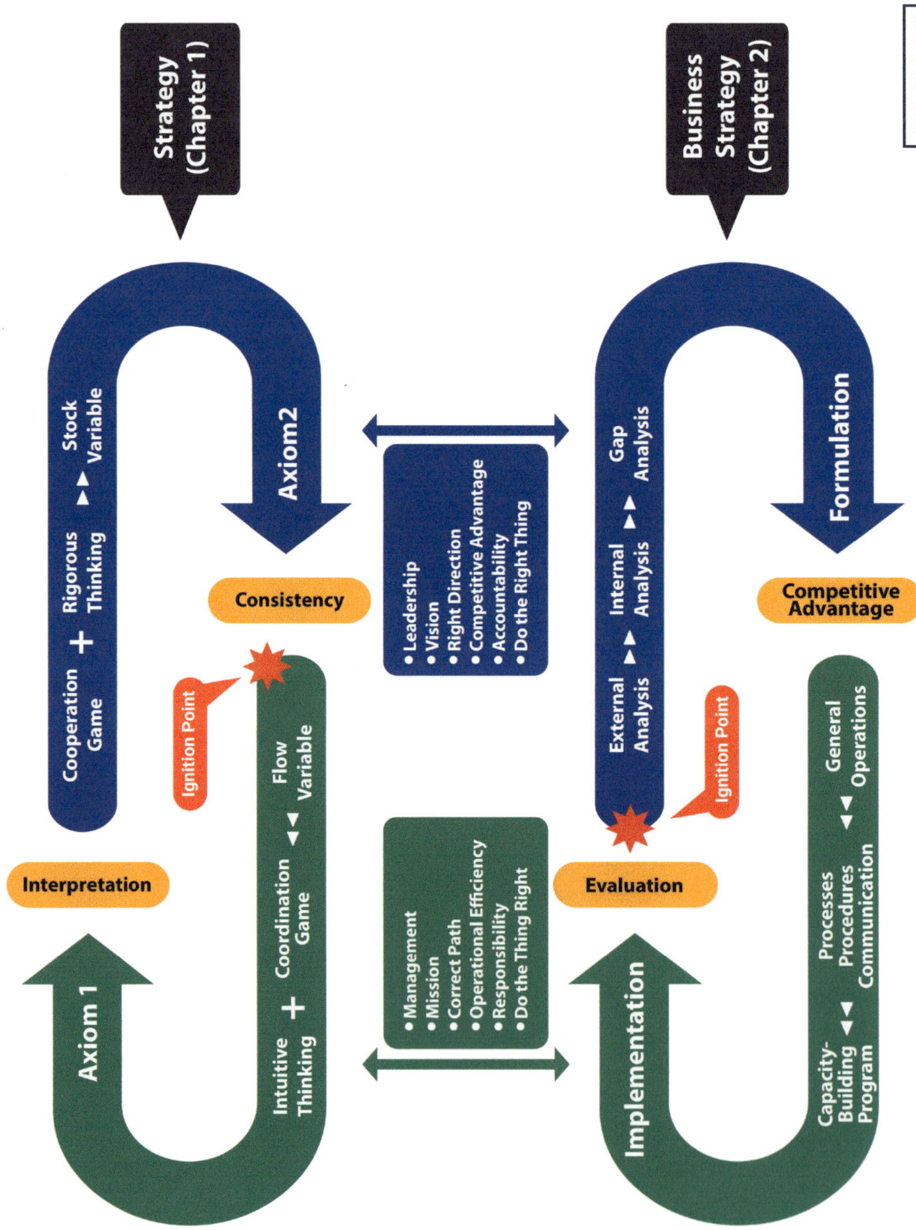

Figure 28: The corresponding interaction between the three building blocks of business strategy and the axioms introduced in Chapter 1; together these form the framework of the UTBS (this figure is best viewed online; use the QR code for access)

It is important to remember that business planning operates at the strategic level of the organisation. It embodies strategic aspects of marketing, operations and financial planning, without including their complete details. It is not a detailed marketing, operations or budgeting exercise. For such a strategic business plan to be useful and feasible, each subsection needs to be adequately scaled to fit within the planning process. In Chapter 3, we briefly look at how strategic business plans may be deployed later into annual budgets or specific operational elements.

Detailed plans for marketing, operations and accounting should be developed later, downstream of the strategic plan using appropriate tools and software. These may include customer management applications, project management tools and accounting packages. Each standalone plan will include significantly more detail than the strategic business plan. These downstream applications use outputs emanated from a strategic business plan to operate on a day-to-day basis.

Larger organisations may include complex and robust scenario planning within the formulation stage, using techniques such as the Monte Carlo method. This allows organisations to compare the strengths and weaknesses of different options within an overall business case. Whilst scenario planning is beyond the scope of this book, it is important to note that it still involves each of the activities discussed in this section. Each part of the plan (whether a flow variable or stock variable) is represented by a distribution rather than a single point (or event), to encompass many possibilities. The iterative running of the plan using different distribution points for various dependent (flow) variables, in turn yields a distribution picture for the desired (wealth) outcome.

In such large organisations, strategic business plans typically cover a three- to five-year timeframe. In the first year, the strategic business plan is used to develop detailed marketing objectives and tasks, operational tasks and budgetary targets. The first-year outcomes feed into an updated forecast for the second year. The second-year outcomes then feed into an updated forecast for the third year. Every three to five years, a complete review is undertaken, and a new strategic business plan developed. In Chapter 3, we will also briefly look at this discipline.

Use this QR code to access a short video about the evaluation building block of business strategy

Summary of Chapters 1 and 2

In order to provide the reader with a review of the material covered so far, this section summarises key points from Chapters 1 and 2. It shows the correspondence between the theoretical concepts developed in the framework in Chapter 1 and the applied version presented in Chapter 2. In Chapter 3, we look at detailed features of an actual strategic business plan.

Summary of Chapter 1

Strategy: We defined strategy as a series of correlated decisions, made at sequential points in time, based on an available information set and players' ability to interpret that information, in order to attain a desired outcome at a future point in time (or to reduce the likelihood of other outcomes).

In order to translate the correlated decisions of strategy into a causal strategic process, we introduced three sets of components. We then combined these into two interacting axioms.

1. **Variables:** We identified two types of variables that are acted upon and considered in strategic processes – flow (explanatory, independent) variables and stock (response, dependent) variables.

   1.1 **Flow variables** are used as inputs to strategic processes in our framework. Flow variables apply per unit of time.

   1.2 **Stock variables** result from an accumulation of flow variables. They are an output of strategic processes in our framework. Stock variables occur at a point in time.

2. **Games:** We then turned our attention to the activities within which these variables are engaged. Using game theory, we identified two relevant types of games.

   2.1 **Coordination games** are readily resolved by players accepting asymmetric positioning. Flow variables are the inputs to these games. Successful resolution of coordination games reduces transaction costs. The game must be repeated to keep transaction costs low.

2.2 **Cooperation games** are more complex to resolve and require a change in payoff structure or repetition of the game. The outcome of cooperation games has the attributes of a stock variable, which significantly reduces transaction costs on a longer-term basis.

3. **Modes of thinking:** We then introduced a human element, looking at how players think when dealing with variables within games. We introduced two modes of thinking.

    3.1 **Fast, intuitive thinking** (e.g., listening with the intent to reply) – operating in relation to flow variables and coordination games. This type of thinking is also referred to as intuitively subconscious (or right-brain).

    3.2 **Rigorous, in-depth thinking** (e.g., listening with the intent to understand and contemplate) – applicable to cooperation games to yield stock variables. This type of thinking is also referred to as analytically conscious (or left-brain).

Strategic axioms: We then placed these three components described above into two interacting axioms linked to construct a causal framework for the Unified Theory of Business Strategy (UTBS).

- **Axiom 1** operates at a tactical decision level, with flow variables as inputs and coordination games. Players use fast, intuitive thinking to resolve these games for tactics at each step along the strategic process.
- **Axiom 2** applies rigorous, in-depth thinking to resolve cooperation games. The outcome is a stock variable, based on cumulative iterations of Axiom 1 along sequential points of time.
- **Interpretation** serves as the link between the received signals from Axiom 1 and ensuing inference along Axiom 2 in order to arrive at a desired strategic outcome.

Together, these configure the fundamental structure of the UTBS. In this framework, tactical, flow variable inputs at various points in time are likely to produce strategic stock variable outputs at a future point in time. This process is based on correlation and causality. Figures 9, 10 and 11 in Chapter 1 summarise the above material.

Summary of Chapter 2

After constructing the framework in Chapter 1, we turned our attention to its analogous application in a business context. To show an applied version, in Chapter 2 we started at the end of the process and worked our way back along the framework.

Desired outcome (wealth): We began by discussing what is generally recognised as the desired strategic outcome by economic agents in the commercial monetary system – commonly called *wealth* – that is, risk-adjusted, superior returns on the resources allocated and the effort taken.

Risk: We first touched on elements of risk associated with wealth.

- **Systematic risk** is beyond operational control or diversification; it requires a correspondingly higher return on investment.
- **Non-systematic risk** can be feasibly mitigated or diversified; planning for non-systematic risk involves addressing likelihood and potential impact.
- We introduced frameworks such as VUCA as a system to identify relevant positions along the systematic and non-systematic spectrum.

We then turned our attention back to the attributes of wealth as a strategic outcome, noting that, in efficient markets, economic agents cannot extract above-normal profits. Above-normal returns (wealth) can only occur under certain conditions and market structures. For this outcome to occur, a localised system failure must be present. We identified two possible scenarios for this:

- **Structural market failure**, which involves privileged access to assets and positions. It is not necessarily replicable, and often has legislative compliance issues. We dismissed this as a one-off intermittent case
- **Natural (transactional) market failure**, which reflects the inability of the market to trade or deal with certain underlying entities. Once an economic agent possesses a particular advantage (such as specialised knowledge, extensive experience, intellectual property or brand), then they can attract above-normal returns. These conditions can result in the systematic creation of wealth.[49]

We then introduced three building blocks of strategic planning to demonstrate how these conditions can be replicably devised. These were correlated to the axioms presented in Chapter 1.

1. **Formulation** (analogous to Axiom 2) encompasses three steps:

49. In Chapter 2, we used an applied version of Chapter 1's framework to describe how this can be created.

1.1 **External analysis**, embodying macroeconomic, microeconomic, competitor and risk analysis and segmentation, including elements such as pricing, positioning and channels
1.2 **Internal analysis**, embodying evaluation of internal resources and capabilities
1.3 **Gap analysis**, comparing external opportunities and internal capabilities.

This formulation block has the characteristics of Axiom 2, with planners using rigorous thinking to formulate the strategic outcome. Lead indicators are primarily used in the formulation stage.

2. **Implementation** (analogous to Axiom 1) encompasses three steps:
   2.1 **General operations** (with degrees of freedom)
   2.2 **Processes, procedures and communication (PPC)**:
      2.2.1 Processes are a time-based mechanism and mainly an accountability of leadership (what to do – tasks, when to do it – periodicity, by whom – function)
      2.2.2 Procedures are a situation-based mechanism and mainly a responsibility of management (after the *what, when* and *who* of processes, these address the *how*)
      2.2.3 Communication, comprising three elements along the lines of accountability versus responsibility. These elements change in scope and scale as communication cascades up and down an organisation:
         — Clarification of objectives
         — Agreement on available resources
         — Feedback and reporting
   2.3 **Capacity-building programs**, which are identified through the gap analysis and other (risk or environmental) analysis components of the formulation stage.

The implementation block resembles Axiom 1 and is assessed mainly using spot indicators. Through the repeated, consistent approach of PPC plus capacity-building programs, the implementation block (Axiom 1) will induce operational efficiency and progressively translate it into a source of competitive advantage. Moreover, these advantages will be compatible with the stipulations in the formulation block (Axiom 2). These stock variables cannot be readily replicated or traded. They create an advantageous natural system failure around the agent with superior return on resources (i.e., wealth).

3. **Evaluation** (analogous to interpretation) is used to gauge the interaction between formulation and implementation, and is generally embedded in financial reporting mainly using lag indicators. The evaluation block has three elements:

3.1 Per unit of time measures (P & L and cash flow statements)

3.2 At a point in time indicators (balance sheet)

3.3 Corrective action recommendations (to feed back into the planning process).

Figures 26, 27 and 28 in Chapter 2 summarise the above material.

Use this QR code to access a short video about the framework of the UTBS

Chapter 3

Applied business strategy

Introduction

This chapter provides a practical method for developing a strategic business plan based on the theory and application presented in the previous chapters. We bring together the theoretical framework introduced in Chapter 1 and its business strategy concepts from Chapter 2 into a practical, day-to-day terminology for business planning. To facilitate planning, this chapter refers to general headings commonly used in a standard business plan and explains the content covered in each section. Readers can use this material and repurpose it for their own specific context as preferred.

A strategic business plan can be written for an entire business/entity or for a specific project within that entity. In this chapter, we use the term 'business' for ease of reading. If the strategic plan relates to a single project, the planner may elect to adjust the scope of the analysis. Whilst the information in this chapter is broadly applicable to all entities, its primary application is for medium-sized ones as scaled within different-sized economies.

Strategic business plans should preferably cover a timeframe that is long enough for the business to implement steps and realise outcomes, but sufficiently short to be responsive and flexible to the market and operating environment. The appropriate timeframe is frequently three to five years.

This chapter includes examples from Planium Pro, a proprietary business planning software tool developed by Levant Software Technologies Pty Ltd. The software uses practical, everyday language and syntax. The underlying composition of Planium Pro embodies the theories presented in this book. It provides an easy-to-use, intuitive interface for entering the details required in a business plan. It also includes a comprehensive section that explains the theoretical concepts and analysis tools in detail.[50]

50. A read-only version of Planium Pro is provided for readers via a QR code – with permission from Levant Software Technologies Pty Ltd.

Planium Pro has been configured with a consistent input pattern, with each section divided into three parts: 1) standard text to introduce elements related to that section, 2) quantitative inputs in a tabulated format, 3) free text for the user to add discretionary information. This input pattern cascades throughout the program, from the larger sections (e.g., formulation) to the focused sections (e.g., competitor analysis). The pattern is replicated for both input and output formats. The final output, whilst preformatted, can be fully edited by users as required.

The QR code below gives readers access to a free read-only version. More information and a free trial are available at www.planiumpro.com.au. Whilst this chapter includes screenshots to illustrate Planium Pro's input and output screens, we recommend that readers view the software directly using the QR code below to see dynamic samples.

Use this QR code to access a read-only version of Planium Pro

Strategic business planning is an exercise in forward thinking. Business plans need realistic analysis to guide the business forward. It is, however, possible that planners will not have ready answers to all the questions and issues raised in this chapter – if, for instance, the business is in the start-up stages. It is pragmatic to state in the plan that particular sections are not yet fully developed and answers may not yet be finalised. It may, therefore, not be necessary to fully articulate every proposed element of the business plan, and there is no concern in recognising that some elements are either unknown or under development.

The business planning literature is full of technical jargon (like USP, segmentation, VP, pricing, positioning, distinctive capabilities, accounting terms and so on). Effective plans provide a clear perspective of the business that looks beyond jargon to offer a pragmatic strategic direction and operational path. Table 1 provides an overview of the sections to be included in the business plan, aligned with the three building blocks described in Chapter 2.

Step	Strategic building block	Part of strategic business plan
1	**Background information**	• Executive summary • Context and general profile • Unique selling and/or value propositions
2	**Formulation**	• External analysis (marketing plan) • Internal analysis • Gap analysis
3	**Implementation**	• General (freehand) operations • Routine processes, procedures and communication • Critical capacity-building programs
4	**Evaluation**	• Financial analysis and plan • Revision

Table 1: Business planning stages and steps

Figure 29 illustrates the three building blocks of strategic planning to be introduced in this chapter.

Figure 29: The three building blocks of strategic business planning, to be introduced in this chapter

1. Background information

Executive summary

The executive summary is a short, concise, positive overview of the full business plan. It summarises the main points for readers, entices their interest and inspires them to read the full plan. For this reason, the executive summary must:

- Be concise and accurate
- Capture the key content from the plan
- Reflect the overall objectives of the plan
- Be consistent with the details of the plan.

The executive summary should be written last, after other sections have been compiled. It is described first here because it is the first part seen by readers. Many decision-makers (particularly board members and providers of capital) may only read the executive summary and use it to guide their decisions. They may then ask other functions to read the details of the plan and advise accordingly. It should be structured in a way that ensures readers can find more detail in the main body of the plan if they want it. It is important to see the executive summary as a compelling part of the document. It should, therefore, persuade readers of the plan's value and encapsulate the plan's main parts.

Plan context and general profile

The background information section provides enough detail about the business to demonstrate that the strategic intent of the business plan is justifiable, appropriate and well-conceived. It provides the context readers require to understand the plan, including the nature of the business, its industry and its market. Another important role of the background information is to also provide a conceptual framework for readers. This explains, for example, whether the plan operates relating to rapid growth and expansion, partial exit and divestment, distressed turnaround or steady state. The planner may consider the context of a first-mover advantage, locked-in situation or step-change. This type of prerequisite contemplation is paramount in developing the background of the strategic business plan.

- First-mover advantage: By being the first player moving into a market, a business may be able to capture a significant amount of the latent demand. Even though other competitors are likely to follow, having a first-mover advantage can enable the business to secure large parts of the market.[51] However, a first-mover advantage may not be possible when a locked-in situation prevails.

51. Microsoft, Uber and Tesla show attributes of first-mover advantage.

- Locked-in situation: This means that, in some circumstances, the expected benefits of a change to better products or services could be more than offset by the switching costs required to make that change. For example, it is recognised that cubic shipping containers are not the most practical way of moving goods (because the container shapes do not suit the objects they move). Most manufacturers also know that the QWERTY keyboard is not the best configuration for fast typing, or that existing mathematical notational calculators can be significantly improved using reverse (Polish) notation (not requiring the equal sign or brackets). However, potentially innovative but disruptive alternatives may not be economically viable because a locked-in situation applies in these examples. The massive existing infrastructure configured around the current shape of shipping containers (gantry cranes, ships, trucks, storage facilities, etc.) makes a switch unlikely and potentially renders any new system economically unviable. The same consideration applies to keyboard design and calculators' mathematical notation. Understanding whether a locked-in situation applies is important in the background of a business plan, particularly as more businesses seek to place themselves in the context of disruption, which has been commonplace in the last decade.
- Step-change approach: A step-change approach is a more pragmatic position, which enables businesses to introduce change at a smaller scale, rather than through a full disruption. In many cases, a step-change approach may, therefore, turn out to be strategically more feasible than disruption. It can provide lucrative economic benefits without attempting to completely disrupt the industry or market (and without, for example, facing the barrier risks created by locked-in positions).
- Start-up: Another common context for a business plan is the start-up situation. Business plans for start-ups need to explain the idea and manner in which the business will be developed and commercialised. It is important to recognise that most start-ups – up to 95 per cent – will fail. As a rough guide, around 75 per cent will fail simply because the idea is not well researched (and this, in part, explains why links to formal academic research centres are valuable, because of their background expertise). An additional 10 per cent will fail because, even though the idea may be a good one, it may not be commercially viable. As a hypothetical example, imagine that an inventor designs an engine that can run on air. This is a great idea and has the potential to offer non-polluting engines with no running cost. But to commercialise this idea, the inventor would need to take on large companies in the oil and car industries as well as potential aspects of labour dislocation. This great idea is risky because it is not commercially practicable to disrupt a large part of the system. Finally, around 5 per cent of start-ups will fail because they do not have the right people involved: an excellent, commercially viable idea may not succeed if it is not managed by individuals with the right profile.[52]

52. See Chapter 1 on the characteristics of game resolvers and modes of thinking. Also see the case studies, which follow Chapter 3.

Figure 30 illustrates some of the background contexts that may form the business plan's foundation.

Figure 30: The strategic business plan can encompass one or more background contexts that form the foundation of the plan

Other elements of the background information section may appear more mechanical and generic. However, these parts are also important as they will help to demonstrate what the plan seeks to achieve. These other sections may include elements such as:

- Description of the business – a general overview of the principal activities of the business and its markets, the business's legal structure, intellectual property, projected annual revenue and any other relevant detail (perhaps a business history or company profile)
- Business lifecycle stage – at what stage of a cycle the business has been operating and its goals for the future (for example, mature steady-state, new fast-cycle or sunset sectors)
- Industry – the industry in which the business conducts its main activities (this is the industry where value chain activities lie, not the market the business sells into)
- Market – a broad description of elements of the market and its growth opportunities[53]

53. Criteria for distinctions between industry and market were covered in detail in Chapter 2.

- Management structure – including information about key executives and critical personnel, and the ownership structure
- Vision and mission – future aspirations for the business (vision) and how it will be achieved (mission)
- Revenue model – the framework adopted to raise and generate capital and the overall use of financial resources with broad information on the opening accounting positions.

Value and unique selling propositions

Value proposition (VP) is linked to the unique selling proposition (USP). Both operate at the intersection of external demand opportunities versus internal solution capability, particularly in areas where competitors may have less capability and profile (illustrated in Figure 31). In business plans, VP is often incorporated in the background information section and the USP is covered in marketing. We discuss them together here to facilitate presentation. The VP or USP ideally includes two parts:

- External context – an existing (or latent) marketing opportunity requiring a solution
- Internal content – the business's offering to target customers that is either unique or significantly better than those currently available, and likely to be preferred as a market solution.

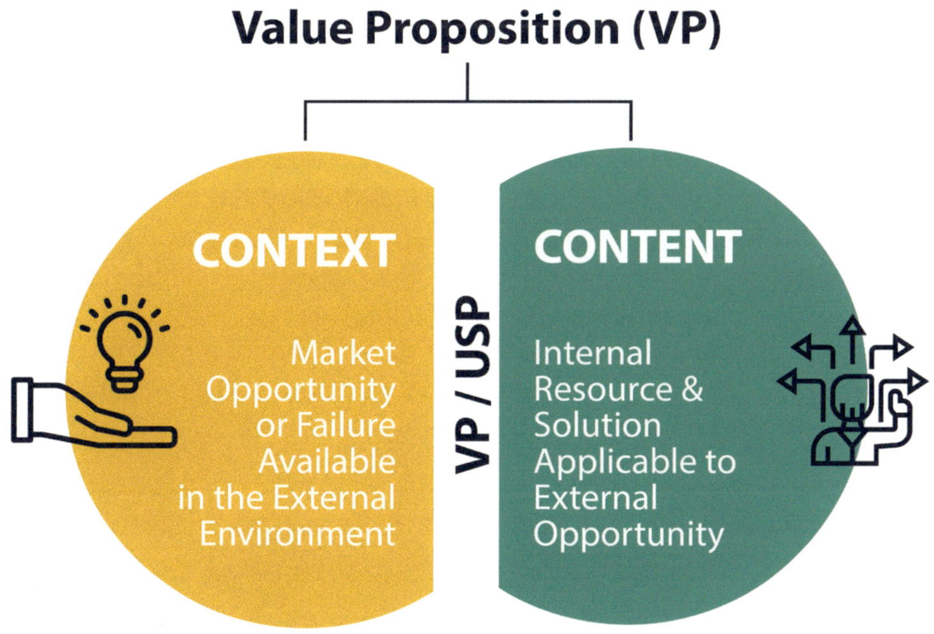

Figure 31: Both the VP and USP require attention to the external context and internal content

The VP/USP should respond to the business's external environment and its internal operating capabilities. These effectively combine market opportunities and possible latent demand with capacity for innovative ways for the business to address customers' needs.

Many managers and theorists suggest that a VP is a prerequisite for any successful project or business. Some successful businesses have, however, operated without being fully aware of their USP.[54] It is, therefore, important not to over-emphasise the validity of this concept for two reasons:

- Managers may not be able to fully or readily articulate or identify the VP (it may exist without being recognised)
- Managers may not have developed a VP, and it may indeed emerge from the planning process.[55]

Managers should, therefore, not be compelled to develop a VP simply because it is an expected part of a business plan. Slogan-driven VPs are unlikely to be useful. Planners should be confident to declare that they either do not currently know their VP or they expect to create it in the future.

The USP is also a unique benefit the business offers to the market: the thing that enables the company/product/service/brand to be differentiated from competitors. Being dimensionally equivalent to VP, it also considers market opportunity (existing, new or hidden) against potential superior solutions.

Both the USP and VP should address points of difference. Any attempt to over-rely on unique aspects, without first establishing the minimum requirements that the product or service is to meet, may be counter-productive. For example, a customer purchasing a luxury car first needs confirmation that the car offers the common features expected of the product, such as comfort and safety features. Luxury and performance elements are additional (point of difference) selling points, not replacements for the commonly expected features.

Figure 32 shows the interacting components of the USP. Business plans should focus on the point of overlap between what the market wants and what the company does well.

54. For example, it is unlikely that Bill Gates carefully considered or articulated the USP when he developed DOS in the 1970s.

55. The methodologies discussed in Chapters 1 and 2 describe how it is possible to create something of value and extend that value across to the external environment.

Figure 32: The interacting components of a USP: what the market wants and what the company does well

Use this QR code to access a short video covering applied definitions of components of the business plan

2. Formulation

This part of business planning involves using a series of analytical tools to understand the business's external operating environment, competitors, risk and market segments to develop a marketing plan.[56] Formulation comprises three steps: environmental (external), internal and gap analysis.

Environmental analysis

This step should look at the different aspects of the environment relevant to the business, including the macroeconomic level, microeconomic (industry/market) level and intramarket (market segmentation) level. In Chapter 2, we referred to this as external analysis.

56. More detail about these tools is included in the appendix.

Macroeconomic analysis

PESTEL is a useful tool for considering the external factors that influence business performance. PESTEL considers the political, economic, social, technological, environmental and legal issues relevant to the business.

Whilst PESTEL is useful for examining the macroeconomic environment, it is an explanatory tool that provides a static assessment based on a series of judgements. PESTEL may identify issues the business can address through critical capacity-building programs in the forthcoming sections. Alternatively, if no major issues emerge from PESTEL, planners should not unnecessarily create implementation steps corresponding to it.

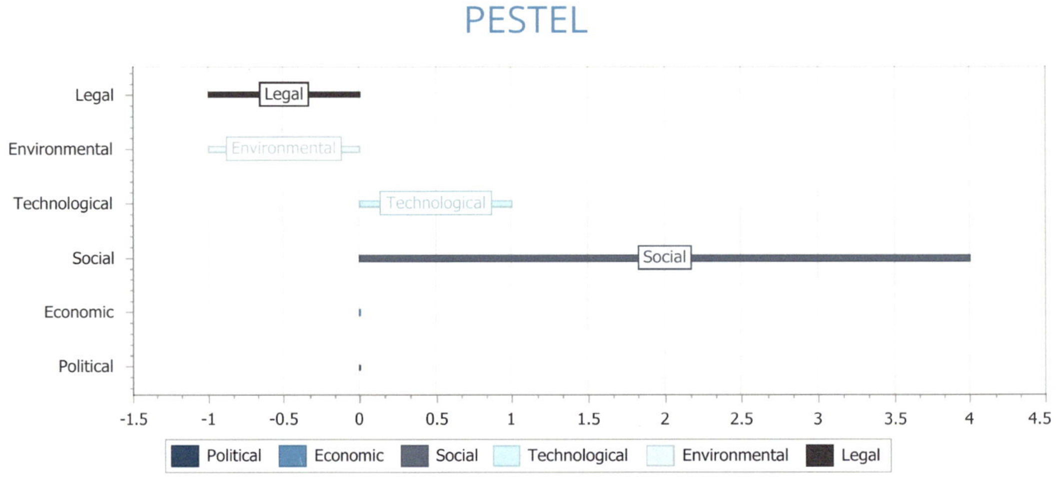

Figure 33: Sample PESTEL output for macroeconomic analysis

Microeconomic analysis

Porter's Five Forces framework is a useful tool for assessing and evaluating the competitive strength and position of the business. It helps the business to predict the likely profitability of the market. The Five Forces framework covers:

- Market and industry competitiveness
- Bargaining power of buyers
- Threat of substitution
- Threat of new entrants
- Bargaining power of suppliers.

Five Forces is one of the few models to offer a combined analysis of industry and market. (In Chapter 2, we described the significant differences between industry and market, and how confusing them can lead to inaccurate planning.) Like PESTEL, Five Forces is a descriptive, static model, which lacks dynamic linkages between its various elements. Five Forces may reveal important issues towards critical capacity-building programs in the sections below. However, it is also possible that Five Forces will simply serve as an informative tool that confirms the business plan's direction and does not have specific implementation steps attached to its outcome.

It is important to ensure that tools like Five Forces and PESTEL do not disproportionally overwhelm the general flow or size of the business plan. These models should apply at a proportional scale and not over-emphasise their role (in terms of quantum and impact) on the overall business plan.

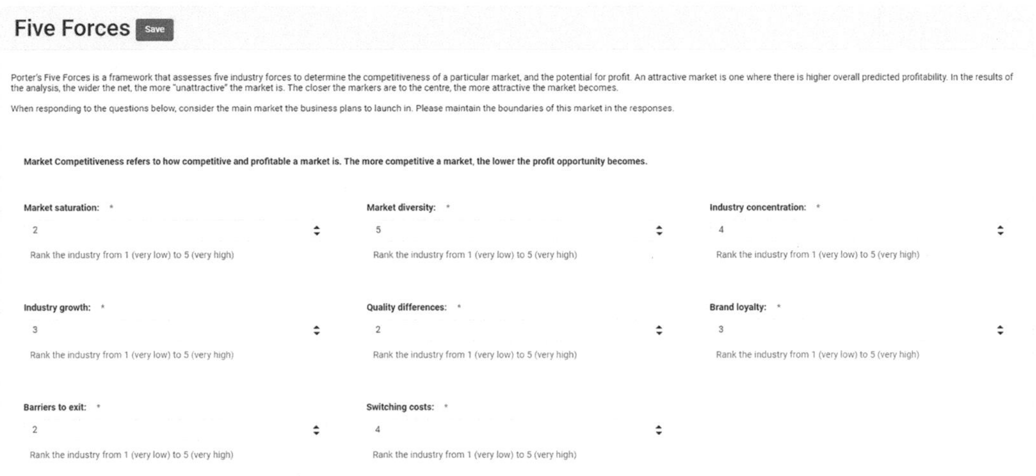

Figure 34: Sample input screen for Five Forces analysis

Competitor analysis

Competitor analysis involves assessing the relative positions of current and potential competitors. These should be ranked according to criteria such as price, quality, service, range and distribution.

The competitor analysis should consider traditional competitors (businesses that currently compete in the same market). In addition to this conventional approach, the analysis should address:

- Businesses in the value chain that are currently the main buyers of the product and who may decide to vertically integrate and produce the product and services in-house (backward vertical integration)
- Businesses in the value chain who are major suppliers and who may decide to produce the products or services themselves (forward vertical integration)

- Businesses with the capability to compete with the business even though they currently do not do so (horizontal or lateral integration).

Figure 35 shows an example of competitor analysis based on customer value dimensions.

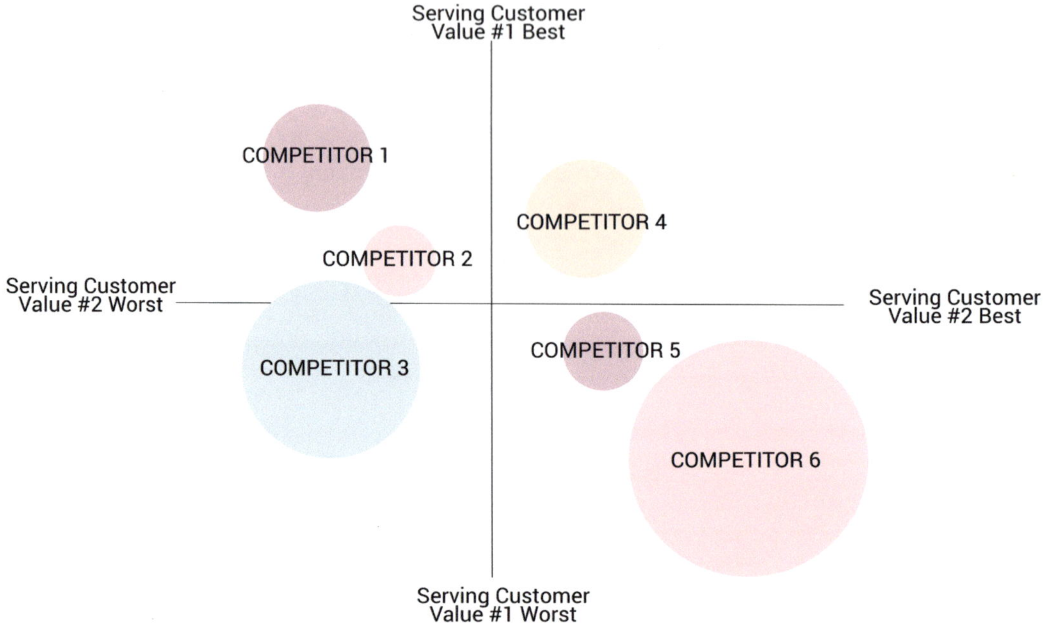

Figure 35: Consider competitors based on a range of direct and indirect factors that go beyond price, to include quality, service, range, distribution and market reach

A strategic business plan usually has a three-year timeframe. If a potential competitor cannot realistically become a competitor within three years, there is no imperative to include it in this analysis. The term 'competitor' frequently holds a negative connotation for business planners. However, if planning is occurring in the context of divestment or exit, the competitor analysis could also be critical in identifying potentially interested buyers or investors.

Figure 36: Sample input screen for competitor analysis

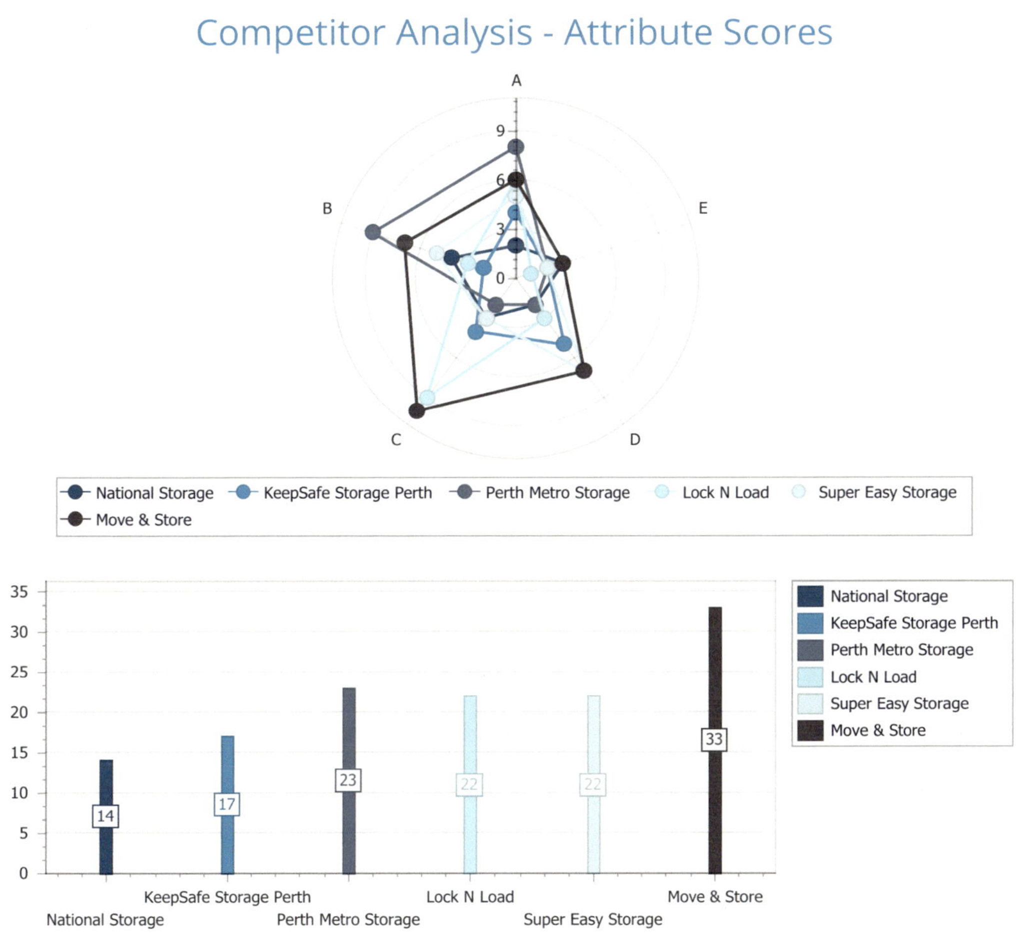

Figure 37: Sample output screen for competitor analysis

Risk analysis

Risk analysis involves identifying and analysing potential issues that could negatively impact the business, then considering ways to minimise those risks. Identified risks should be analysed according to likelihood, degree of impact, type (systematic or non-systematic) and mitigation strategy.[57]

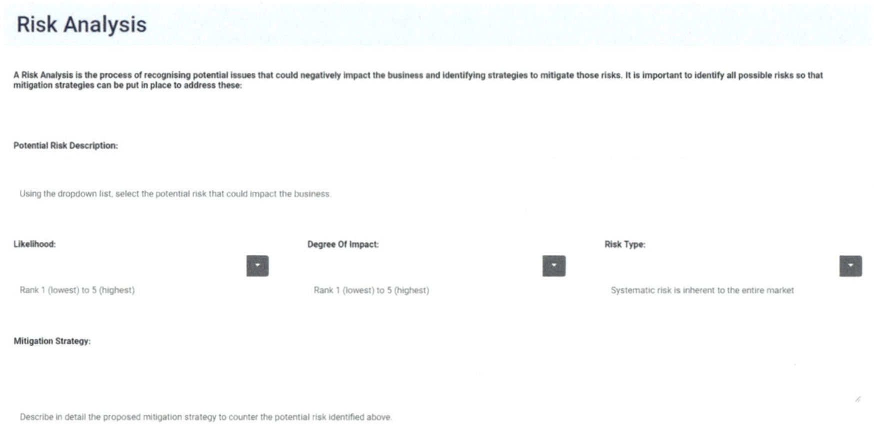

Figure 38: Sample input screen for risk analysis

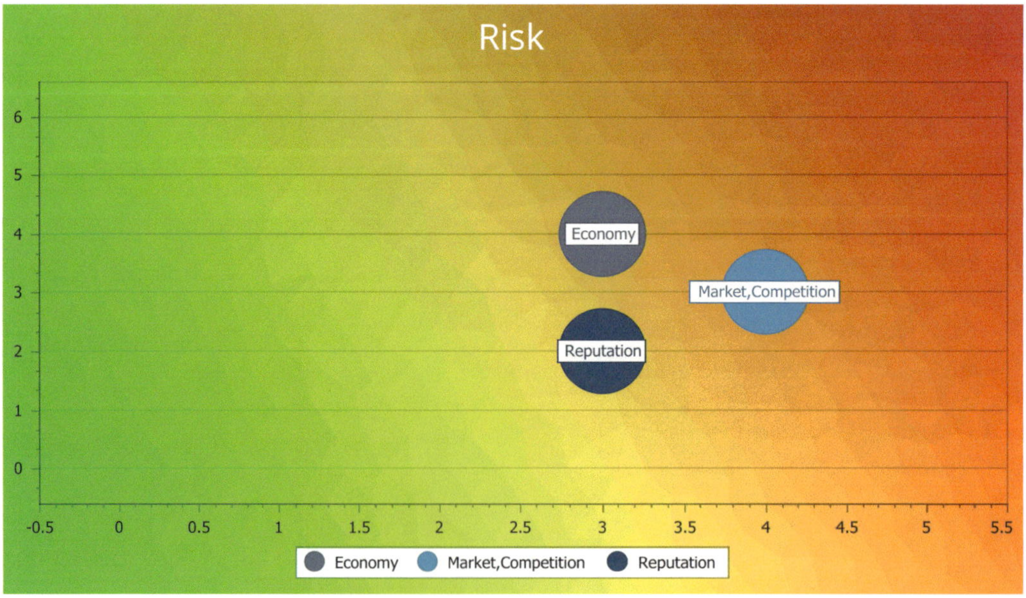

Figure 39: Sample output screen for risk analysis

57. Risk and its various types are discussed in more detail in Chapter 2.

Market segmentation

The strategic business plan includes an analysis of the market and its segments, and gives an overview of the marketing plan for each segment.[58] Note that the strategic business plan is not a detailed, full marketing plan; it operates at the broad, strategic level to summarise the business's future direction. Therefore, the marketing plan (as well as the operational and financial plans) should be proportionally scaled down to an appropriate size to fit inside a business plan.

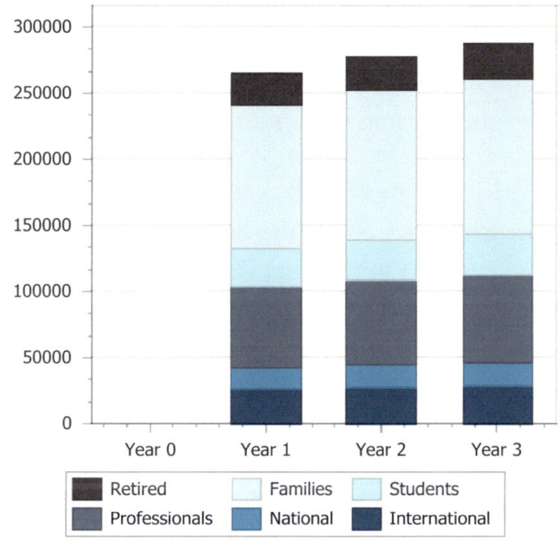

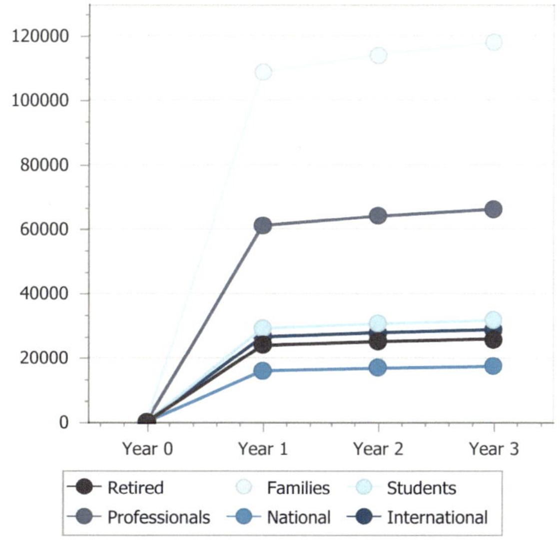

Figure 40: Sample output screen for market segmentation

58. Criteria for segmentation and subsegmentation are discussed in Chapter 2.

B2B or B2C

Prior to full segmentation, it is important understand whether the plan is being written in a B2B (business to business) context, a B2C (business to consumer) context, or a combination of the two side by side. This distinction will have important implications for pricing, positioning, advertising, distribution and sales tactics.

Whilst the distinction between B2B and B2C is typically understood as being a function of the nature of the buyer (corporate business versus individual consumer), it is more useful to understand the distinction in the nature of the interaction between the seller and buyer. This distinction relates to switching costs, type of the engagement, time, and other resources required to make a sale. Whilst B2B and B2C are most easily understood as a dichotomy, in reality they form a continuum with some overlap in the centre.

If the buyer has low switching costs and takes little time to become engaged in the sale, the context tends to shift towards B2C. If the buyer has high switching costs and needs extended time to become engaged in the sale, the context tends to shift towards B2B. In B2C, transaction costs for the buyer to shift suppliers are comparatively low. Conversely, in B2B, transaction costs for switching suppliers are comparatively high. This criterion is more relevant than simply the dichotomy of corporate versus individual profiles of buyers and sellers.

In a B2B context, industrial marketing parameters prevail. It usually takes some time for buyers and sellers to form an agreement, often as a result of a tendering process. For example, when a car manufacturer agrees to procure gear boxes for the next generation of its car, it would be both costly and difficult to switch suppliers part way through the production run. B2B situations typically involve higher upfront costs of association, high transaction costs of dissociation, long-term interactions and regular interface between the buyer and seller.

In a B2C context, mass consumer marketing parameters are more likely to prevail. Most B2C interactions involve low resource allocation for consumers and low switching costs. The purchase of fast food is a good example here. B2C situations may involve low upfront costs of association, low costs of dissociation, and short (intermittent) regularity of sales. Whilst individual consumers may be small compared to large corporate suppliers, their low transaction cost of switching paradoxically grants individual consumers high bargaining power. The B2B or B2C context is also relevant in microeconomic analysis (Five Forces framework) when considering the bargaining power of the client or supplier. At face value, it appears that B2C offers high bargaining power to the seller (e.g., a large supermarket chain selling to individual consumers). However, because the consumer confronts low switching costs, this example shifts the bargaining power towards the consumer. In B2B, on the other hand, a large buyer of products may be able to exercise pricing power by being the major customer in the market. Conversely, a supplier may have considerable bargaining power because of their access to patents or rare technology (which may give a small supplier significant bargaining power).

The distinction between B2B and B2C will also influence decisions about marketing and distribution. For example, B2B promotion may be focused on specific niche areas with long lead times and strong buyer–seller relationships may be relevant. In contrast, B2C promotion is likely to suit regular mass market advertising, needed to induct brand awareness for consumer engagement. B2C contexts require less face-to-face contact, but make widespread use of this type of advertising or social media promotions.

Segmentation

Markets are typically segmented according to criteria such as:

- Demographics (age, gender, family status, income, occupation)
- Behaviour (purchasing behaviour, product use, preferences, decision-making)
- Psychographics (lifestyle, activities, interests, opinions)
- Geography (location of potential customer base).

Initially, the market should be segmented on one criterion only. It is important not to mix the segmenting criteria at this level, as it may cause difficulties in determining other elements of segmentation such as price, positioning and distribution.[59]

Segmentation is a prerequisite for decisions about which markets to contest. The business may choose not to contest all the segments recognised. Identifying a segment is, therefore, not a rationale for contesting it. Decisions about which segments to contest may be based on various criteria, such as level of sales and potential margins available.[60]

Subsegmentation

As noted above, segmentation should initially be based on one criterion (such as geography). If the market analysis shows that market segments are complex, with significant differences between parts of the segment, it may then be appropriate to introduce subsegments. If a segment is not isotropic along the relevant dimensions (e.g., pricing, positioning, promotion, distribution), it may be appropriate to use different marketing tactics in different subsegments.

59. The theoretical criteria for segmentation were discussed in detail in Chapter 2.

60. For example, many car companies choose not to contest all segments – BMW does not make heavy trucks, whilst Mercedes Benz or Scania do.

For example, imagine that a business has segmented the market by geography, with a different marketing approach for each region. If some chosen regions are particularly complex or offer better prospects for sales, the business might subsegment those regions using other criteria. Subsegmenting enables the business to focus more tightly on relevant and specific parameters of each market. For example, whilst some parameters such as product packaging may be the same across subsegments, other specific parameters (such as pricing or distribution) may vary. Whilst the (first) top-level segments should all be based on the same criteria, subsegments can vary (so one region may be subsegmented according to buyer behaviour, with another region subsegmented based on product types).

Subsegmentation significantly increases the complexity of a marketing plan and tends to be more suitable for large companies. In businesses where subsegmenting is relevant, planning should include a full analysis for each subsegment. The costs associated with segments and subsegments should be translated into the financial plan as marketing overheads or variable commission costs.

Elements in each segment

We will now consider the various elements of each segment by describing them in more practical terms. As illustrated in Figure 41, the analysis should consider any special attributes relevant for each segment or subsegment:

- Product and packaging (what to offer, in what bundle and what format)
- Price and positioning (how much to charge, at what premium or discount)
- Promotion and advertising (how to signal or inform potential clients about the offering and pricing)
- Distribution (how to deliver the products and services to the point of sale)
- Sales tactics and funnel (how to get the actual sale transaction over the line after the above aspects have been implemented)
- Other (elements that might emanate from marketing analysis).

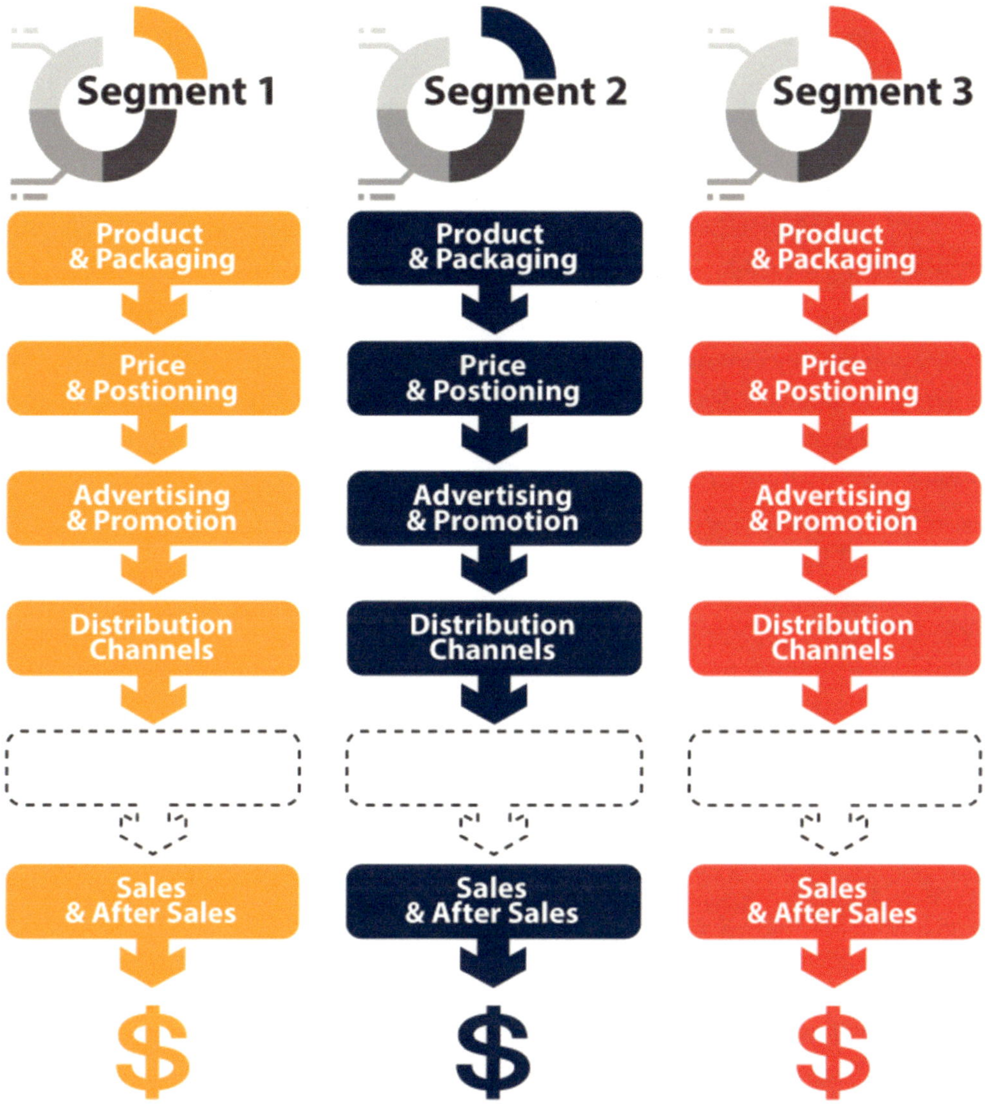

Figure 41: Each segment or subsegment will embody special attributes that need to be addressed specifically for that segment or subsegment (some may be the same across subsegments, but that is not necessarily the case for all)

Note that there is a logic to the sequence of these aspects of segmentation. It is important to determine the scope and scale of products and services within a segment (product and packaging) before establishing its price and positioning, which in turn should be established before considering promotion and advertising. Promotion and advertising should then be determined before decisions regarding distribution or channels. For example, premium positioning will mandate different advertising and different delivery modes compared with a low-cost positioning strategy.

Errors occur when there is incompatibility between these elements (for example, if the packaging does not align with the distribution strategy, or the positioning does not align with the advertising). Sales tactics also need to be compatible with the marketing elements that precede them in order to close the deal or secure the sale. Again, sales tactics for premium positioning will be significantly different from the sales tactics associated with low-cost, fast delivery.

Product and packaging

Whilst product and packaging embodies the physical presentation of the product or service, a more important aspect of this element is to describe the scope, scale, core features and ancillary features of the product or service offered in each segment. For example, a car manufacturer may decide to sell passenger vehicles in one geographical segment whilst selling utility vans in another geographical segment, each with different features and warranties. Product and packaging, therefore, relates to the core product and service as well its ancillary attributes. These elements may include free service, extended warranty, exchange offers or buy-back agreements.

Price and positioning

The price level appropriate for the market segment is related to where the product is positioned and how it is differentiated from those of competitors. For example, a premium pricing strategy to position a product as a (low-volume, high-margin) luxury good contrasts with economy pricing to achieve high sales volume (low margin), or break-even pricing to enter or become known in a segment.

The generic positioning strategy of differentiation indicates that the product/service commands certain features that can attract a premium price (e.g., a prestige consumer product). In contrast, cost leadership indicates that the product/service is available at a lower price than competitors (e.g., a low-cost airline or a category-killer furniture supplier). Alternatively, a niche (focused) positioning strategy concentrates on a particular attribute or functionality of the product/service. These decisions have on-flow effects on operational elements in the implementation stage.

Promotion and advertising

This is how the business intends to signal and communicate with the market about its products and services. Specific strategies and tools are likely to be best suited for this market segment (e.g., paid advertising, direct marketing, social and digital marketing, personal selling, public relations and sales promotion).

Care should be taken to distinguish between advertising and promotion, particularly as they apply in the B2B or B2C contexts. Whilst advertising is generally a continual signal to the potential client both in B2B or B2C contexts, promotions usually constitute finite-period initiatives. For example, promotions may include sponsorship, limited-time discounts or other special offers. In the context of B2C advertising and promotion, initiatives often occur on digital platforms. B2B advertising and promotion may also occur through tendering or by professional interactions. Paid digital marketing campaigns, particularly campaigns through social media, are now paramount in a business's promotional and advertising portfolio. These have their own expert requirements and need to be clearly identified and costed.

Promotion and advertising can be combined in push–pull marketing campaigns (discussed in more detail below in the section about sales tactics and funnel). In push–pull campaigns, advertising is pitched to the end user to pull the product by creating an overall interest, whilst promotion is used to appeal to intermediary channels (resellers) to instigate sales. Promotion and advertising here have specific roles in working together to close a sale.

Distribution

This element describes how the product will reach the market segment (e.g., direct to purchaser, third-party distribution, online orders or multiple channels). Decisions about distribution need to be compatible with decisions about product, pricing, position and promotion. Within the distribution tactic, the product/service may be sold directly to the end user, through a channel strategy that involves intermediaries, or through a combination of both.[61] In a channel distribution arrangement, it is common for the one reseller to hold multiple products within a product category (for example, a department store carries different brands on behalf of multiple suppliers). It frequently involves a margin or commission being taken by the channel player to compensate them for presenting the goods and acting as selling agent. In turn, the supplier of the product gains wider access to the market through the distribution channel.

The most relevant criterion here is to question where the point of sale occurs. In distribution directly to clients, the supplier of the product is compensated by the client at the point of sale (common in a B2C context). In distribution via a channel where the channel takes a commission, the link to the end client is done by an intermediary (such as department stores) but the point of sale still occurs with the client and hence the sales relationship shows characteristics of the B2C environment. In contrast, in distribution where an intermediary purchases the product and then on-sells it, the sale occurs with

61. Zara is an example of a company that sells directly to end users, through Zara retail stores (both physical and online). Apple uses a combination (multi-channel) distribution strategy, with Apple-branded retail stores combined with sales through electronics retailers.

that intermediary and here, effectively, no channel is being used. This distribution takes on characteristics of the B2B environment.

A further consideration is the relationship between distribution channels, logistics and the nature or value of the goods or services provided.

- In cases where the goods or services embody a high degree of added value, the cost of freight will be a small proportion of the final price. Under these circumstances, there is a strong case for a central (or international) supply chain where a product is shipped from one (or very few) locations to many different markets. For example, complex machinery typically includes highly value-added products which can be shipped from a single source. Conversely, when the added value imbedded in the products is low compared with the cost of freight, there is a case for distribution points along the value chain closer to the point of sale. For example, some basic metallic components are not feasible to transport over long distances because the freight component of the sale price becomes prohibitively larger compared with the underlying value of the product. In these examples manufacturing entities tend to have regional distribution networks and operations.
- Some goods and services are inherently freight inefficient – that is, they cannot be cost-effectively transported over long distances. For example, the shape and physical characteristics of a product may not suit the dimensions of main transport configurations (which are typically cubic). A situation can arise where the cost of freight is prohibitively high due to a great deal of empty space being transported with the product. For example, buckets or large containers that are not tapered may not be stackable, making them difficult to transport (indeed, the primary purpose of tapering in buckets is to improve stackability). In these situations, production and distribution will also likely be located closer to the end market.[62]

Sales tactics and funnel

The aspects discussed above are marketing activities that involve cost. The last step, sales tactics, translates those marketing activities (and their costs) into sales (and revenue). Sales tactics get the deal across the line, typically through expert personnel. These tactics are designed to close the sale (and therefore compensate for the marketing costs). Sales tactics should be compatible with segment characteristics (e.g., aggressive selling strategies, competitor-oriented selling, consultative selling or needs-oriented selling). For example, various marketing activities might bring a potential customer to a car yard, but it is the salesperson in that car yard and their tactics that propel the sale across the line.

62. Freight inefficiency explains the seemingly paradoxical situation where some low value-added products may be more cost-effectively supplied by domestic producers than from cheaper suppliers in low-cost foreign markets.

Sales tactics are important in both B2B and B2C contexts. In B2C contexts, common selling tactics include last-minute discounts, enhanced warranties, after-sales exchange options and complementary products included at the point of sale. In B2B contexts, selling tactics may also include extended warranties, after-sales service or inducements to buy within a particular timeframe. Some sales tactics are designed to encourage recurring purchases (such as guaranteed buy-backs or trade-in offers). Other volume-based tactics offer reduced price per item when higher quantities are purchased (this relates to the economic principle called price discrimination of the second order).

The process of marketing and selling a product can be equated with a sales funnel, which is somewhat different in B2B and B2C contexts. At the top of the funnel, advertising and promotion seek to make contact with a broad base of potential customers. Some of these potential customers are converted into further stages along the funnel, with a subset converted to confirmed sales (at the bottom of the funnel).

The marketing plan should consider cost to conversion along the sales funnel. This incorporates costs in achieving the sale. These costs need to be amortised against the revenue earned from actual sales. Three elements are important in ensuring that marketing translates into sales:

- Time to conversion
- Cost to conversion
- Expected revenue per client/unit of sale.

In considering these elements, both the conversion rate and the number of stages within the sales funnel become important. Conversion rate and time to acquisition need to remain within defined parameters to meet the expected cost of acquisition. Along the sales funnel, businesses should consider how their parameters compare with industry benchmarks. Business need to ensure that marketing funds spent in conversion are commensurate with actual sales, resulting in a reasonable cost of conversion at the bottom of the sales funnel. Whilst the terms 'marketing' and 'sales tactics' are often used interchangeably, it is important to note that marketing elements operate along the sales funnel whilst sales tactics apply only at the point of purchase.

In a B2B context, the sales funnel is likely to have a relatively smaller intake, more stages, a longer timeframe, and a relatively higher conversion rate (with the funnel showing attributes towards a cylinder). A B2B business may tender to small numbers of potential customers and invest considerable time and resources into converting them into actual sales. Compared with B2C, a higher proportion of fewer potential customers in B2B are aimed to be converted into actual sales. This type of lower-slope, narrow sales funnel is common in manufacturing, construction, logistics and intermediary providers of industrial goods and services. Selling tactics in this type of sales funnel are likely to involve extensive face-to-face interaction between sellers and buyers. The number of visits, method of follow-up and conversion after follow-up are of great importance.

In a B2C context, the sales funnel is likely to have a much wider intake, fewer stages, a shorter timeframe, and a lower conversion rate (with the funnel being relatively shorter but steeply sloped). This means that the business may approach a very wide group of potential customers, but comparatively a smaller number of the multitude of those potential customers translate into actual sales. Conversion may happen faster here. In this context, mass marketing campaigns are likely to be the most relevant selling tactics. The cost of acquisition needs to be amortised against a smaller conversion rate. In a B2C context, the revenue per unit sale is typically lower than in a B2B context.

Figure 42 shows the generic shape of the sales funnels common in B2B and B2C contexts.

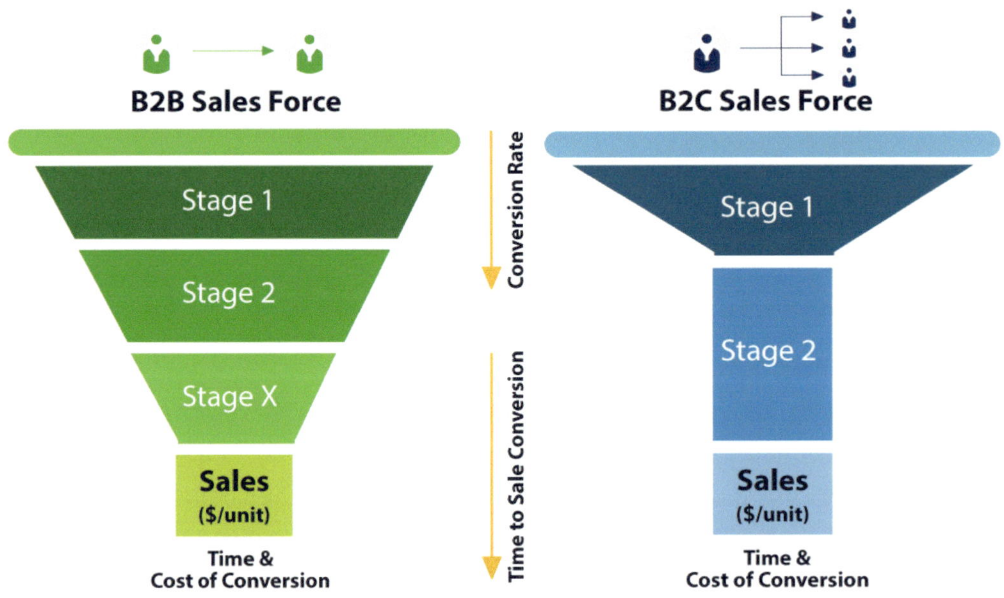

Figure 42: Generic shape of the sales funnels and stages for B2B and B2C contexts

Businesses in a B2B context often operate through an order book (particularly in manufacturing, construction and logistics). The order book manages accumulated forthcoming orders, which may be filled over months or years. In B2B marketing, businesses are likely to consider aggregate order book size, average margin, replenishment rate and rate of order intake per period of time.

Businesses will seek to maintain the order book within a controlled band and with a controlled margin, to achieve the strategic intent of the business plan. If, for example, order intake is high, the business can increase its tendering price because it does not require as much volume to be added to the order book. Conversely, if the order book is inadequate, the business may discount its products (reduce its margin) to boost order intake in an attempt to replenish it. As shown in Figure 43, by maintaining both order intake and margin within the control bands, the resulting volume of the order book will remain congruent with the sales targets of the business plan.

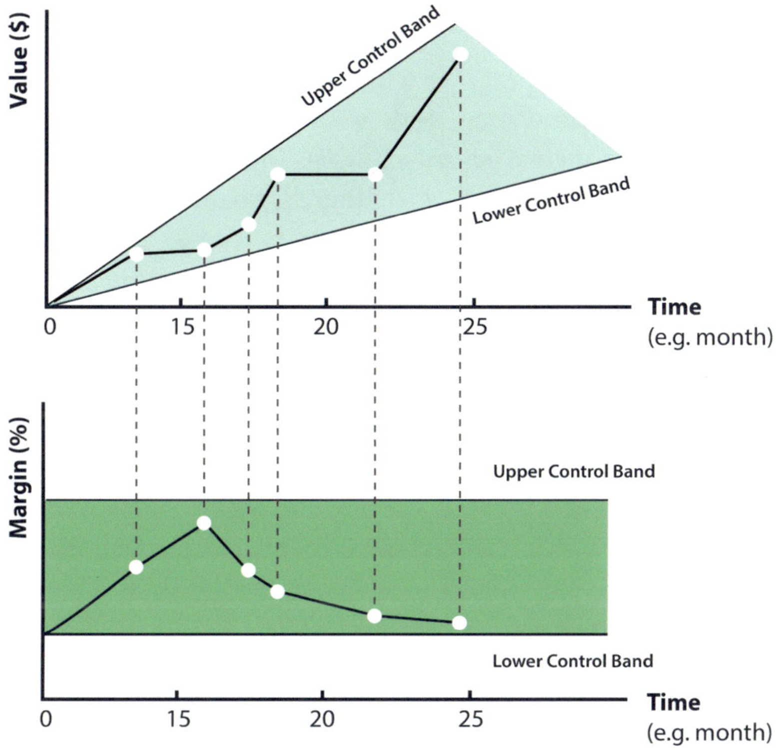

Figure 43: Representation of the order intake value and corresponding margin to keep the corresponding order book within a defined control band

The size of the order book should also be controlled from an operational perspective. If the order book becomes too big (compared to production capacity), the business is likely to experience cash flow and delivery problems due to overtrading (due to the working capital input required for raw materials, labour, logistics and so on). A thin order book, on the other hand, will put stress on the business due to the constant need to maintain the flow of work volume and spot sales to cover fixed costs.

In a B2B context, a push–pull approach to advertising and promotion is frequently used. In these circumstances, the supplier pushes the product to an intermediary reseller (often through promotion) whilst at the same time pulling the product towards end users (often through advertising). The promotion is designed to encourage the intermediary reseller to stock the product, display it prominently and on-sell it to end customers. The pull advertising is designed to create awareness and interest in the broader market. The advertising here does not by itself directly instigate a sale. Instead, it closes the loop to bring the end consumer towards the intermediary reseller. On the surface, consumer product advertising frequently appears to be designed as B2C advertising intended to sell a product. In practice, it is often part of a B2B push–pull strategy, intended to bring consumers to a reseller.[63]

Internal resources

The second element of formulation deals with in-house resources and capacity (in Chapter 2, we referred to this as internal analysis). The main aim of this step is to assess the internal attributes of the business – including the financial, organisational and innovative abilities that contribute to its strengths and weaknesses. It is possible that business profiles will shift over time, with issues identified as opportunities transforming into threats, and vice versa.

SWOT is one of the tools suitable for conducting an internal analysis and can be applied to any type of organisation. It involves identifying and analysing how internal factors may be affected by opportunities and threats facing the business, and considering activities for addressing them. Whilst SWOT is a strong and well-recognised model for internal analysis, it is a static model that is subject to potential error through the planner's judgements. SWOT is not the only model used for internal analysis. Other tools, such as the PROFIT model, for instance, offer an alternative. PROFIT identifies internal assets including physical, financial, operational and technology assets.

Figure 44: Sample (partial) input screen for SWOT analysis

63. In some situations, this type of push–pull is explicit, such as when advertising directly links a consumer product to a specific supermarket, hardware outlet or pharmacy.

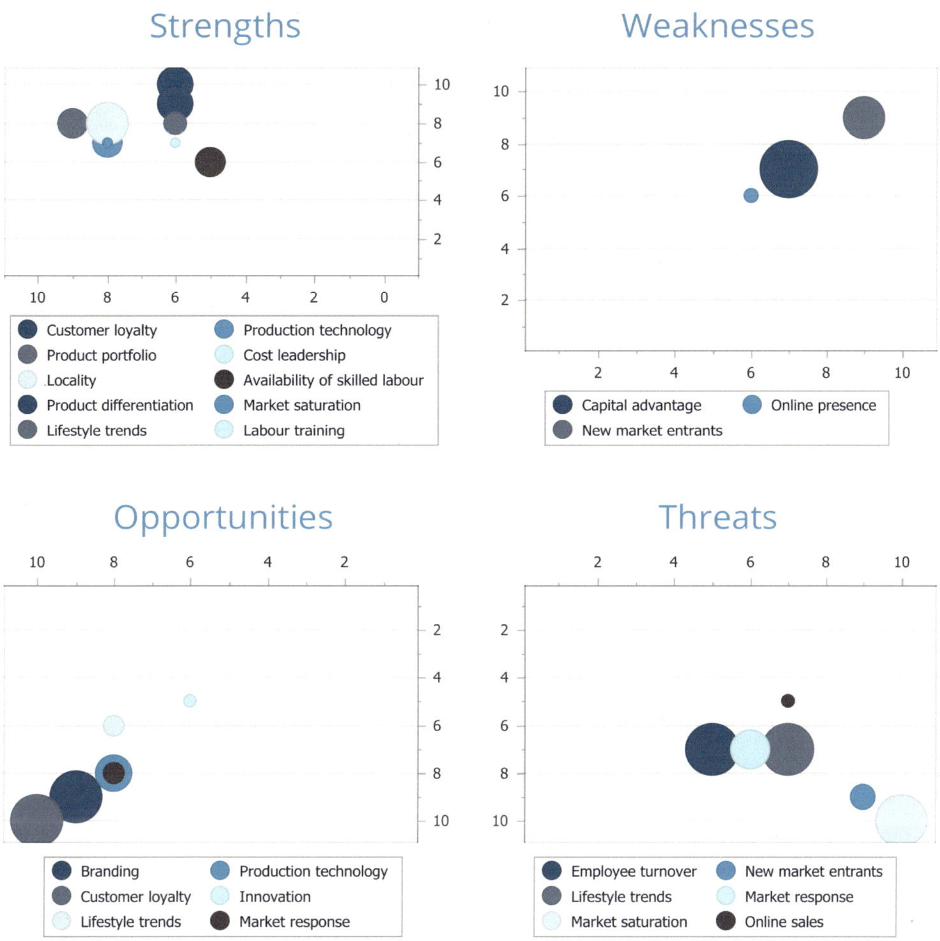

Figure 45: Sample output screen for SWOT analysis

External vs internal (gap) analysis

The third step in the formulation block is a comparison of the external environment and the business's internal capabilities (which we also referred to as gap analysis in Chapter 2). This step can identify opportunities in the market that the business aspires to but may not currently have the prerequisite capabilities to exploit. Conversely, the analysis may also identify capabilities that may not sufficiently be leveraged for external growth opportunities. Gap analysis leads into capacity-building programs in the implementation step (which will operate alongside routine business practices). Note that gap analysis is not a benchmarking exercise; instead, it compares the business's current environment and the business's internal capabilities.

Gap analysis can be performed at the macro or micro level and is used in all business areas (e.g., resource availability, costs control, quality improvement, processes applications, skill augmentation and financial performance). Useful tools for gap analysis include fishbone diagram, spreadsheets or questionnaires. Gap analysis involves defining:

- External prospects (identified through external analysis) – listed and ranked where uncontested market opportunities can be present
- Internal resources (drawn from internal analysis) – listed and evaluated as capacities or assets the business may possess.

As noted in Chapter 2, gap analysis will reveal:

- Whether there are current (or latent) opportunities in that market the business is unable to readily exploit due to a lack of internal resources and capacities
- Whether the business has internal capabilities that may currently be underutilised (or dormant) that can be deployed across broader market reach.

The outcome of the gap analysis will form the basis for capacity-building programs (as the third step of the implementation stage in the next section).[64]

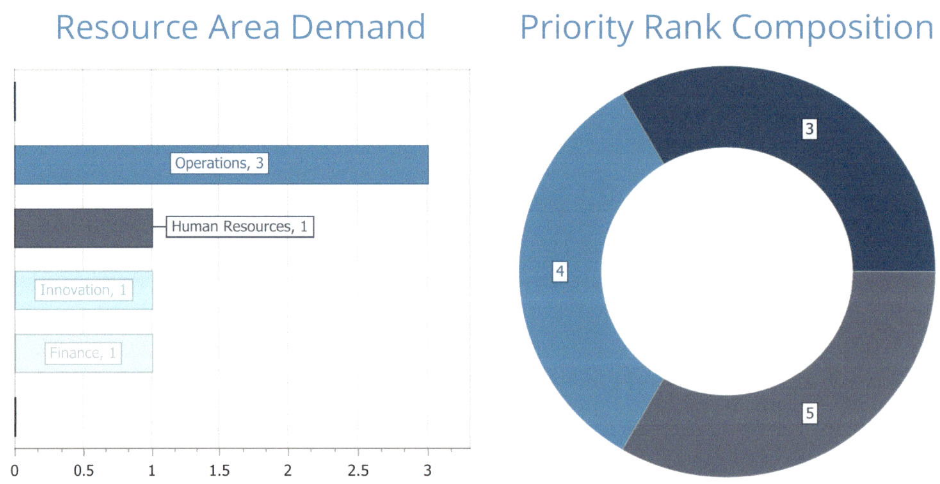

Figure 46: Sample output screen for gap analysis

3. Implementation

Implementation is the second stage of business planning, involving three steps:

- General operations
- Processes, procedures and communication
- Capacity-building programs.

64. Planium Pro greatly facilitates this step through simplified input screens for external prospects and internal resources side by side.

The implementation stage relates to the operations and running of the business. It involves translating the strategic goals into tactical objectives that will guide the business during the timeframe of the strategic business plan.

The operational plan included within the business plan should remain strategic and high-level. It documents the processes, procedures, communication and resources in a way that creates the most value for the business and its stakeholders.

General operational tasks

This part of the business plan is a place for planners to highlight any operational activities that do not fall into regular, structured, repeated processes and procedures. It relates to the general freehand operations discussed in Chapter 2.

Consideration should be given here to strategic decisions regarding operational formats and mechanisms relevant in B2B or B2C contexts. This is particularly in relation to fast-track (continuous) or step-by-step (intermittent) operations. Many B2C (and some B2B) supply relationships involve fast, continuous delivery of standardised products. On the other hand, various B2B supply relationships require step-by-step (intermittent) activity with staged approvals, project deliverables or site acceptance. These two categories require different operational configurations.

- Where there is fast-track, continuous delivery, care should be taken to ensure the operational process does not include too many stops and starts. Uninterrupted workflow in operations and agile internal approvals and decisions become important. For example, companies may measure the number of times a forklift's forks are put up and down before dispatch (to help minimise delays) or examine the number of times a document stops in an in-tray or is sent via email (to limit unnecessary stops and delays). A standard costing methodology is usually better suited for the continuous run of repeated similar products and services. These costing methods stipulate a standard contribution for sales and then assess material variances and overhead under/over recovery to arrive at the gross margin in a continuous manner.
- Where there is step-by-step (intermittent) delivery, the supply relationship involves project approvals or client authorisations. Under this scenario, the operations must not progress too far or too rapidly without those required approvals and checks. Detailed and specialist project management becomes critical. A project costing (or job costing) method is better suited in this situation, with revenue and expenditure captured in relevant stages and often submitted for progress payments. In contrast to a continuous standardised operation associated with standard costing, project or job costing relates to assessing the revenue and cost of each project as a discrete separate activity (such as in a construction company).

A common oversight in the configuration of general operations is to not clearly separate these two scenarios. Fast-track continuous delivery and step-by-step intermittent supply are not operated in series together. They should operate in parallel, each with the appropriate KPI measures and accounting set-ups. If they are not sufficiently separated, fast-track delivery is likely to be blocked by the recurrent requirements of projects. These may relate to any facet of the operation – including personnel schedules, production and logistics allocations.

An additional consideration is what activities in the value chain (if any) should be outsourced and subcontracted. Each business has an economic value chain that extends from its raw inputs to its final products or services output. The value chain has different stages characterised by value chain activities. Each of these activities can be done in-house or outsourced. Whilst detailed supply chain management is beyond the scope of this book, it is important to note that decisions about outsourcing should not be based purely on static accounting measures. Many businesses will outsource an activity if it can be offered more cost-effectively by an external supplier, thereby creating a less vertically integrated business.

This is generally a sound decision, particularly if the outsourced activity is undertaken by a specialist offering a superior service (such as specialised accountancy, legal or logistics management providers). It can also reduce internal working capital requirements and improve cash flow. However, this accounting assessment, whilst necessary, is not a sufficient basis for a complete outsourcing decision. In most circumstances, businesses should not outsource activities that contribute greatly to their *strategic* margin, particularly if it leads to dissipation of the economic value the firm generates.[65] Whilst the business will make a margin across the value chain, this margin is not uniformly divided between each value-chain activity. Some activities are likely to be responsible for the bulk of the economic margin. These activities may be costly, but they may also be the real source of the underlying value.

The decision about outsourcing is also related to a concept in economics known as *asset specificity*. Some outsourcing decisions cannot be readily reversed because these involve particular knowledge, resources or techniques. For example, a company that decides to outsource fleet management to transport specialised products (e.g., dangerous goods) may not be able to easily reverse that decision to bring back that activity in-house or

65. For example, when IBM outsourced production of the personal computer's operating system (believing the product's value was in the computer hardware itself) it shifted value outside the company to Microsoft and set itself on a path to losses. In the same way, when General Electric outsourced production of microwave ovens (conversely thinking that the value was in technology and not in the hardware itself), it shifted value to manufacturers such as Samsung. A strong example of correct outsourcing decisions is Toyota's keiretsu.

change suppliers. This is due to the specialist infrastructure assets inherent within that value-chain activity.

As part of planning, managers should, therefore, carefully consider how they configure their general operational activities to be compatible with and cater for different facets of the business. The operational plan should also include a balanced allocation of managerial time. For example, executives should allot around 30 per cent of their time to external aspects of the business (client markets) and around 30 per cent of their time to internal matters (operational and financial matters). In addition, managers should allocate around 10 per cent of their time to directly interact with the workforce (particularly in large organisations with multiple sites). The other 30 per cent of managers' time should remain indeterminate, to be applied as required. If managers allocate insufficient time to external issues, the business increasingly lacks information about clients' views and fails to meet market expectations. Equally, if managers allot inadequate time to internal issues, cost overruns and financial consequences can become dire.[66]

Procedural steps and processes

The second step of implementation relates to the development of processes, procedures and communication (PPC – as discussed in Chapter 2), which are relevant to all parts of the business including marketing, operations, human resources, innovation and finance.[67] Without them, it is not possible to deliver the product/service efficiently with consistent quality.

The strategic business plan should identify and outline only the main processes and their associated procedures. These may be under development or in need of review to be later implemented with relevant software (such as enterprise resource planning – ERP). Full details of the business's processes and procedures are included in these separate and detailed software applications.

Programs for building capacity

The third step of the implementation stage involves defining programs to build capacity – typically one-off, finite-term programs to support the business in achieving its longer-term external goals and objectives (see the discussion about capacity-building programs in Chapter 2). Capacity-building programs respond to issues identified during the formulation stage (such as the gap, risk or competitor analyses). Maintaining the same

66. There is a parallel between the time and resource allocations for internal and external activities discussed here, with the time allocations for routine PPCs and capacity-building programs (of around 70 per cent) suggested in Chapter 2. Around 30 per cent of time is left indeterminate.

67. Chapter 2 includes detailed descriptions of processes, procedures and communication.

general format of PPCs, the capacity-building programs are, however, one-off, limited-term equivalents.

Again, critical capacity-building programs should be discussed only in a broad, strategic way in the business plan. These can be then transposed into relevant software (such as project management). Combined with PPCs, these capacity-building programs create competitive advantage (stock variables) commensurate with the intentions of the formulation building block.

To avoid risking financial overburden, the business should not commit more than 15 per cent of its overall resources to capacity-building programs, spread across various areas of the business (under a balanced scorecard framework). The exception to this might be in cases such as a critical turnaround situation where, for example, it may be more appropriate to focus capacity building only on financial issues.[68]

4. Evaluation – Financial plan and analysis

The third stage of business planning involves evaluation, with particular focus on the financial plan. Financial analysis defines how the strategic intent uses capital and in turn how it contributes to bottom-line improvement of the business. It establishes the proper basis for comparison in order to determine and evaluate current financial performance and future forecasts, and ensure adequate cash flow caters for capital requirements.

The financial analysis in a strategic business plan is not a detailed budgeting exercise. It provides the information needed to help the business ascertain its current position and financial goals for the life of this plan. The financial plan typically covers four years – the three years of the business plan plus one additional year, with the fourth year being particularly important if the business is seeking a valuation.

Planium Pro offers a streamlined but powerful approach to financial analysis. It can help entities to forecast the balance sheet, profit and loss, and cash flow across the life of the business plan, offering both monthly and yearly forecasts.

Financial model

In setting up the basis for the financial model, inputs are:

- Sales, direct costs and overheads for income statements
- Opening position and general assumptions for the balance sheet.

68. Planium Pro supports users to identify capacity-building programs. The input and output screens used for capacity-building programs are similar to those used for routine PPCs. However, capacity-building programs exist for a finite time and respond to a specific strategic intent (emanating from the gap analysis).

Sales and direct costs

Sales figures include revenue for specific periods across the life of the business plan, either monthly or annually. Direct costs are involved in producing the product or service, across the life of the business plan, either monthly or annually. 'Direct costs' is an accounting term, broadly equivalent to what economists call 'variable costs'. These costs are proportionally related to the volume of work output (in the short- to medium-term). When production increases, direct costs increase (e.g., labour, cost of materials, energy). The type of direct costs incurred by the business will depend on the underlying nature of its work. For example, labour hire or professional services entities might account most of their staff costs as a direct cost, or manufacturers may account for raw material or workshop personnel as direct (variable) costs.

In considering gross profit, it is important to distinguish between mark-up and gross margin (a common point of confusion).

- Mark-up is the amount that a supplier of goods or services might proportionally add to its cost base in order to arrive at a price to charge a purchaser of those goods and services. Mark-up is typically relevant for trading entities (such as retail and labour hire), and is applied to the cost base to arrive at the sales figure. For example, a business might pay $20 per hour for labour, but charge a client $40 per hour for that labour, thereby applying a 100 per cent mark-up.
- Gross margin uses the difference between the value of sales (income) and the direct cost of the sale. It is calculated by dividing the gross profit (sales income minus direct cost) by the value of sales. Gross profit and gross margin are typically applicable to value-added entities (such as manufacturing or logistics), where there are larger fixed assets in the value chain. For example, a manufacturing company that makes a widget for $100 per unit and sells it at a price of $125 per unit, has a gross profit of $25 and a gross margin of 20 per cent (25 divided by 125). In this instance, a gross margin of 20 per cent corresponds to a mark-up of 25 per cent ($100 cost base versus sale of $125).

Overheads (operating expenses)

Overheads are a firm's costs of remaining in business, which are not directly linked to sales volume in the short- to medium-term (alternative terms include 'operating expenses' or 'fixed costs'). It is not feasible to rapidly change these types of costs because they are not directly related to the volume of sales.

In the long-term, almost all costs are variable. However, in the short- to medium-term, fixed costs cannot be readily changed. The costs included as overheads will vary according to the nature of the business. Because they are not readily adjustable, businesses aim to minimise overheads to extract higher profit from their gross margin (or mark-ups). Some overheads are ongoing, whilst others may be intermittent. Examples of common operating expenses include:

- Administration and HR
- Maintenance and depreciation
- Marketing (excluding commission included in direct costs)
- Research and development.

Care should be taken to include the correct overheads, as different industries may have varied critical expenses. For example, in the retail and hospitality industries, lease payments are typically a more significant consideration (as a percentage of sales) when compared with that of the manufacturing industry. In retail and hospitality, lease payments are likely to be critical, both financially and contractually. For example, it can be difficult for an established restaurant to change locations in the face of increased rent because its reputation could be linked to its well-known location. In the industrial value-added context, lease payments may be a less important consideration than, for example, depreciation of plant and equipment. In contrast, plant and equipment are less relevant in grocery retail because the majority of capital is engaged in the stock (working capital).

Measures of profitability

As noted earlier, gross profit is calculated from sales income minus direct costs. Gross profit is the starting point for various measures of profitability. Overheads (operating expenses) must be deducted from gross profit to arrive at useful measures of operating profitability. A number of profit measures are relevant to analysing the economic status and viability of a business.

EBITDA (earnings before interest, tax, depreciation and amortisation) is a relevant and equivalent indicator of operating cash profit. It expresses the profitability of the entity before it accounts for interest, tax payment, depreciation (a non-cash item) and amortisation (a non-cash item). EBITDA is useful as a ratio of sales to give a general indication of how well the entity is creating operating profits per unit of sales. Because interest payments are a corporate decision (management decides how much debt to take on) and tax is a regulatory stipulation, EBITDA is an important indicator of how strongly the underlying business is creating profit per unit of sales. EBITDA also has an important role when divided by the average capital employed (ACE) in the business to yield an indirect – but very useful – comparison with the company's opportunity cost of capital.

EBIT (earnings before interest and tax) is an equivalent operating profit measure, showing profitability after the entity accounts for depreciation (and amortisation) but before paying interest and tax. This is also expressed as an operating measure to indicate the real profit-earning capability of the entity. In businesses with low requirements for fixed assets, EBIT and EBITDA are typically numerically close (because depreciation does not impose a great difference between these two parameters when the underlying business is not asset intensive). Both EBIT and EBITDA can also be used with relevant multipliers to capitalise the enterprise value of the business – because they indicate the profit of the business irrespective of corporate and non-operational parameters.

PBT (profit before tax) measures profitability after the entity accounts for its interest payments. Comparing this measure with EBIT indicates the impact of interest payments (and hence the amount of debt) on the business. Large differences between EBIT and PBT highlight the severity of cost of debt (high gearing) to the business.

NPAT (net profit after tax) measures the profit distributable to shareholders or business owners after regulatory taxes have been deducted from PBT. Dividend payments to the owners can come from NPAT as this figure fully belongs to the owners of a business. NPAT is allocated progressively onto the retained earnings section of the balance sheet (as a profit or loss). NPAT is the indicator used with price-earning ratios to arrive at the market capitalisation or equity value of the company in external financial markets.

Opening position and general assumptions

The opening position is the starting point for a financial plan. It describes the main accounting and financial parameters at the time when the plan is being configured. In most cases, these numbers are transposed from the available corporate and regulatory information (such as management accounts or annual tax returns). Most of the indicators embody information found in the balance sheet, such as accounts payable, accounts receivable, level of debt, equity, cash position and any tax liability or prepayment.

With respect to the opening position, general assumptions then capture parameters that will affect the ongoing financial forecast. These include the expected interest rate, tax rate, dividend payments, debt retirement or capital raising. General assumptions combined with the opening position provide the foundation for the financial forecast. These also determine the level of capital structure and gearing for the business. Gearing is a financial ratio expressed in two different ways – either as the level of debt to assets, or as the level of debt to equity. Planners should be clear about which metric is used.[69] Gearing will change based on starting (opening) position, and on assumptions or projections to raise more capital from shareholders, pay down debt or take out new loans. This will

69. For reference, Planium Pro uses the level of debt to assets.

change the capital structure of the company (and hence its cost of capital) used as the discount rate for company valuation.[70]

Typical categories for general assumptions for input into the financial model are listed in the table below.

Borrowings/ shareholder equity **Shareholders' contributions and dividend payouts**	• New debt: anticipated new borrowings or principal debt repayments • Anticipated equity contributions by owners or dividend payouts to owners
Stock/inventory	• Raw materials, work in progress (WIP) and finished goods stock (often expressed as days of sale or days of cost of goods sold)
Depreciation rate	• Plant and equipment, motor and transport, buildings, IT, other
Accounts receivable	• Percentage of the anticipated proportion of receivables collected within a specific period (within one month, two months, three months or longer – often expressed as days of sale)
Accounts payable	• Percentage of the anticipated proportion of payables disbursed within a specific period (within one month, two months, three months or longer – often expressed as days of sale or days of cost of goods sold)
Other	• Tax rates: company tax rate, effective marginal tax rate and any applicable consumption tax • Interest rates and expected return on equity

Table 2: Typical general assumptions for input into the financial model; these will complement the (starting) opening financial position as the foundation on which other recurring parameters such as sales and costs can be input towards configuring the financial forecast

Some businesses use standard costing systems, particularly if the business provides recurring similar services or makes continuous products with standardised components. In contrast, businesses where goods and services vary from one project/client to another are likely to use a project or job costing approach. Whilst the detail of these decisions is beyond the scope of a strategic business plan, planners should be aware of these relevant parameters as they have significant impact on the configuration of operations.

The standard costing system attributes a predetermined standard contribution to the value of sales and then uses measurements within operations (or shopfloor) to identify

70. See the discussion about valuation later in this chapter.

material variances and overhead under/over recoveries. These are then attributed to the standard contribution by adjusting it to arrive at gross margin. The standard contribution data are regularly revised and updated so they remain accurate – to the point that material variances and under/over recovery of overheads become negligible. Examples of this include manufacturers of fast-moving consumer goods or suppliers of industrial components, where the companies make standard outputs with minimum variances. In contrast, project or job costing is appropriate when projects or jobs are not similar or closely related (e.g., the construction industry or jobbing fabrication). In these situations, each project or job needs to be separately costed for material, labour and overheads (allocation) and monitored specifically along the project.

Businesses also generally use two types of reporting formats. Financial reporting primarily adopts a structure suitable for monitoring by external (as well as internal senior) stakeholders. Cost accounting and reporting primarily focuses on activity within the business pitched at day-to-day operational management. Both financial reporting and cost accounting provide the same outcome in the bottom line, but the formatting and primary users are different.

Capital employed

Capital employed is an important measure that embodies the resources used in business operations mainly expressed as monetary parameters of capital. When this measure is averaged out over a certain period (e.g., from the beginning to the end of a particular financial year) it is also referred to as the average capital employed (ACE).[71] It includes working capital used for day-to-day business operations and fixed capital embedded in plant, equipment and buildings. Profit indicators such as EBITDA and EBIT (discussed in the section 'Measures of profitability'), when divided by the ACE, provide comparisons for the viability of the business's underlying value-added activities.

Working capital

Businesses require capital to cater for ongoing expenses. This is working capital, which covers costs prior to the receipt of cash from sales income. From an accounting viewpoint, working capital is the difference between current assets and current liabilities as stated on the balance sheet. However, it also has operational impacts on the business that extend beyond its accounting measure. From a pragmatic perspective, relevant elements in calculating working capital include:

- Cash in bank, *plus*

71. This averaging of capital employed is undertaken to better match this (stock) variable to other correlated (flow) variables such as sales and profit during a corresponding period.

- Accounts receivable (money owed by customers who have already received the product/service), *plus*
- Stock of raw materials held, work in progress (WIP) and finished goods held awaiting sale, *minus*
- Accounts payable (money owed to suppliers who have delivered goods but have not yet been paid).

Increasing working capital puts pressure on the cash flow of the business. Reducing working capital assists cash flow. For this reason, many managers pursue measures that reduce inventory, collect cash more quickly from customers (perhaps through incentives for fast payment), and extend terms for goods and services procured (though this must be done without damaging relationships with suppliers). Planners should consider the profile of the business's working capital, which will vary across industries. In retail, for example, accounts receivable is generally low because consumers pay at the point of sale, but the bulk of working capital is engaged in inventory and stock on the shelves. In contrast, manufacturing businesses may hold accounts receivable for 30 to 45 days, and may seek to optimise stock and inventory through a just-in-time system.

Understanding the profile of required inventory (based on particular business types) is also critical in managing this important element of working capital. The inventory, for instance, may include holding certain spare parts as critical components, the supply of which may involve long lead times. In this case, whilst these items may seemingly constitute slow-moving items in the inventory, they still need to be kept because of their critical nature or long supply lead time. Some businesses may not only require high levels of stock and inventory, but may also take longer to collect their funds from clients. Under these circumstances of larger working capital, correspondingly high sales margins should be factored into financial forecasts to compensate for the extra cost of cash allocation in that working capital. These correspondingly higher margins may be measured at gross profit level or at operating levels of EBIT. A low-margin business that requires heavy working capital (and possible expenditure on fixed assets) will always be exposed to prohibitive and cumulative cash flow problems going forward.

Capital expenditure

This section of the business plan summarises the forecast expenditure on longer-term assets across the life of the business plan (as well as potential acquisitions or divestments).

Capital expenditure can have a significant impact on the business's cash position. Often, major capital expenditure decisions are preceded by either raising equity capital from shareholders or by securing loans from debt providers (such as banks). The phasing of capital expenditure is, therefore, critical in business planning. Managers should remain cautious to approach capital expenditure in a reliable and controlled manner. Business plans for entities requiring heavy capital expenditure on fixed assets should yield corresponding profit margins to induce sufficient returns on capital to replenish future cash flows.

Capital expenditure profile also depends on the nature of the underlying business. For example, retailers often require significant expenditure on shop fitouts and outlet presentation. In contrast, manufacturers may require large expenditure on plant and equipment, or logistics companies may require expenditure on transport and machinery.

Whilst capital expenditure appears in cash flow statements, the underlying assets are placed in the balance sheet. Regular depreciation expense applied to these assets then appears in the profit and loss statement. When assets are obtained through a lease or hire purchase, these are not owned by the entity and not directly included in the balance sheet. The entries for lease payments appear in the cash flow statements and also in the profit and loss report.

Cash flow statement

The cash flow statement summarises the cash entering and leaving the business. It measures how well the business manages its overall cash flow position. Cash flow statements cater for all direct and indirect income and expenses (changes in working capital requirements), capital expenditure, tax, interest expense, dividend payments and equity or borrowing raisings.

Cash flow statements can be expressed in two ways.[72]

- The first format, most suitable for financial analysis, starts with EBITDA, adjusting it for changes in the level of working capital as well as capital expenditure, tax and other elements to arrive at the free cash flow.
- The second format, more suitable for operational work, starts with sales and captures operating expenses and various payments. This methodology does not report specific changes to working capital and relies directly on receipts and payments.

In addition to internally generated cash flows through revenue receipts net of cost expenditure, businesses can obtain funds from two sources: contributions from shareholders in the form of equity, or debt in the form of loan capital. These sources correspond to different contractual and financial obligations for the recipient entity.

- In the case of shareholder contributions, the business pays a dividend to shareholders if and when available (at the discretion of the board). If the entire business

72. Planium Pro provides both formats.

(or part of it) is sold at a higher price (compared to the book value), shareholders proportionally receive that capital gain.

- In the case of debt from loan capital, the business must make regular interest payments (and tranches of principal payments) according to an agreed time-frame. The providers of debt do not own the business and do not necessarily participate in any capital gain from divesting the business. However, they rank ahead of shareholders in the security over assets (as stipulated in their contractual agreement and covenants as a fixed and floating charge over the business). If the debt is not repaid according to the agreed schedule, debt holders can take over the business and trigger a wind-up to liquidate secured assets for the recovery of their funds.

There are also quasi-debt instruments, such as preference shares, convertible notes and other derivatives, that form what is generally referred to as mezzanine capital. These are outside the scope of this section and are relevant to more detailed discussions of structured finance.

A business's capital structure is influenced by decisions about how much ongoing equity and debt to acquire. In general, shareholders providing capital take on a higher degree of risk and, therefore, require a higher return on their investment. Debt providers, comparatively, have a more secure position and, therefore, (after tax) the interest rate of debt generally turns out lower than the cost of equity. The appropriate level of gearing, by increasing debt to a certain level, can reduce the business's overall cost of capital. However, too much debt can induce risk of bankruptcy. Conversely, too much equity can create a lazy balance sheet and require prohibitively high returns to shareholders, exposing the entity to external hostile leverage takeover (in turn using the entity's strong balance sheet to increase debt to cater for the cost of that predatory takeover). The decision about the most optimal capital structure is, therefore, a significant responsibility for finance directors and the board.

Cash flow profile should also cater for any relevant indirect taxes (such as a goods and services or value-added tax). The timing for collecting and dispersing these should be incorporated within the cash flow projections. The business must ensure there is no confusion between operating cash and indirect tax as part of cash flow management. Many businesses operate a separate account for this purpose. Indirect taxes are not readily apparent in conventional profit and loss statements and are typically only revealed through detailed cash flow statements. Indirect taxes should, therefore, be carefully managed to ensure that funds owing as tax are available when payments are due. Businesses must avoid using funds collected for indirect tax to temporarily bolster their working capital requirements.

The balance sheet shows current and long-term assets and liabilities, and hence the shareholder equity of the entity. It, therefore, provides a useful indication of the amount and type of capital that can be externally raised. For example, the accounts receivable (debtors) listing on the balance sheet may attract up to 80 per cent of their value in senior debt raising (depending on the quality and collectability of those debtors). If these debtors are mainly large, reputable organisations or government entities, the quality of the debtors would attract that higher valuation in loan raising. Equally, property, plant and equipment listed on the balance sheet could attract up to 70 per cent of its value in senior debt raising (depending on the age or location). Other elements of the balance sheet, including less marketable or less liquid assets, can also be used in gearing up towards debt raising. Entities should first assess this capacity to raise senior debt as it mandates a lower cost of capital than other sources. Many businesses, however, may already have debt facilities in place, so this further assessment may constitute a subordinated or secondary debt raising (which would rank behind senior debt already on the balance sheet).

Weighted average cost of capital (WACC) is a resulting measure based on decisions regarding the capital structure of the entity (decisions about the composition of equity from shareholders or loans from debt providers). It reflects the overall cost of capital to the company based on the proportion of injected equity by shareholders and the amount of loans advanced by debt providers. WACC applies expected return (cost of equity) and stipulated cost of debt (interest rate) to these corresponding proportions in the overall capital structure.[73, 74]

Figures 47–49 show sample output charts from Planium Pro related to the above material.

73. Planium Pro calculates WACC dynamically for every year of the operation, based on decisions about equity and debt (decisions to acquire debt, retire debt, retain more shareholders or pay dividends). Annual changes in the capital structure of the entity are used to refresh WACC for each year.

74. Further detail about WACC and its structure are included in the appendix.

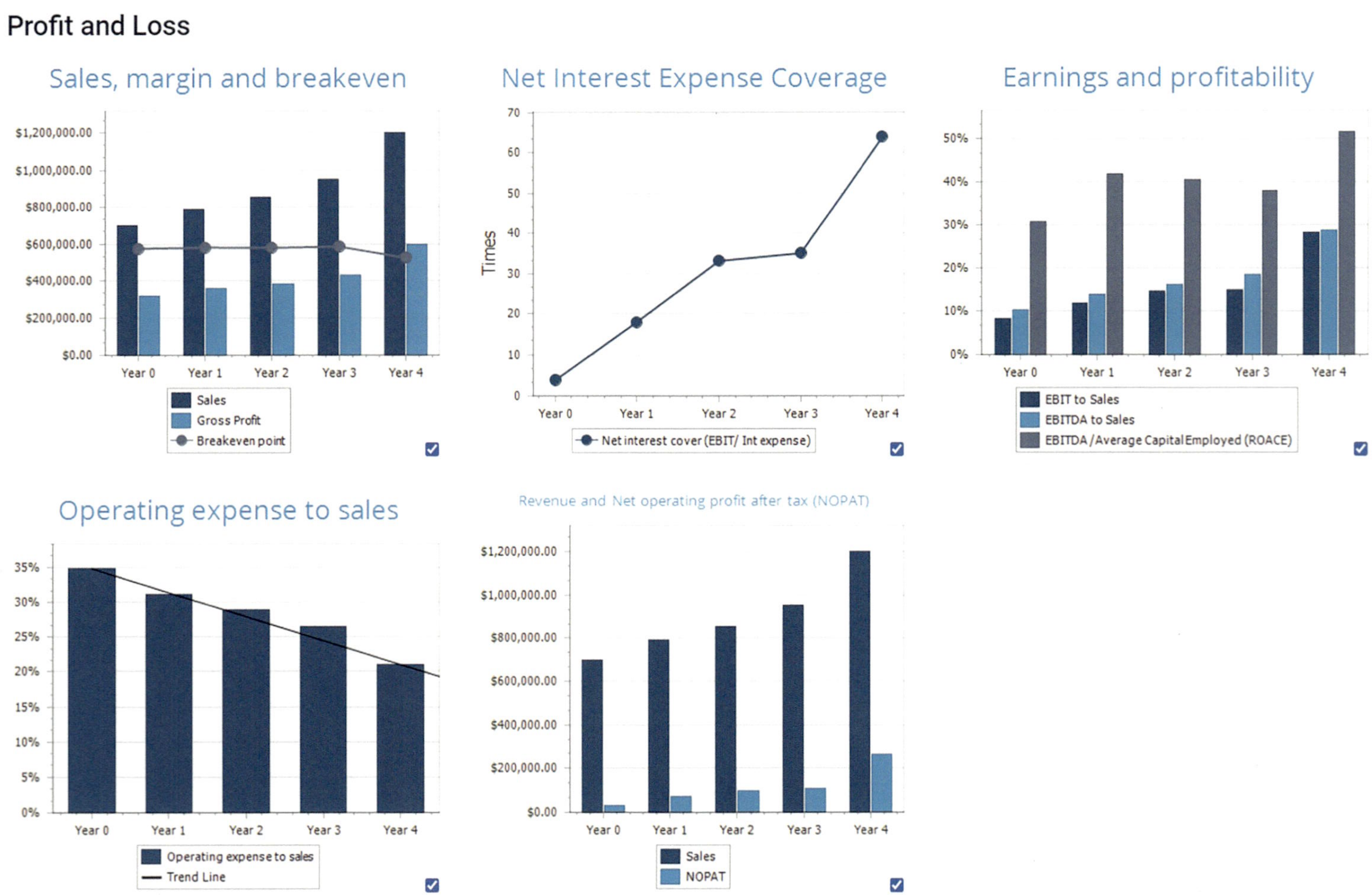

Figure 47: Sample profit and loss output charts

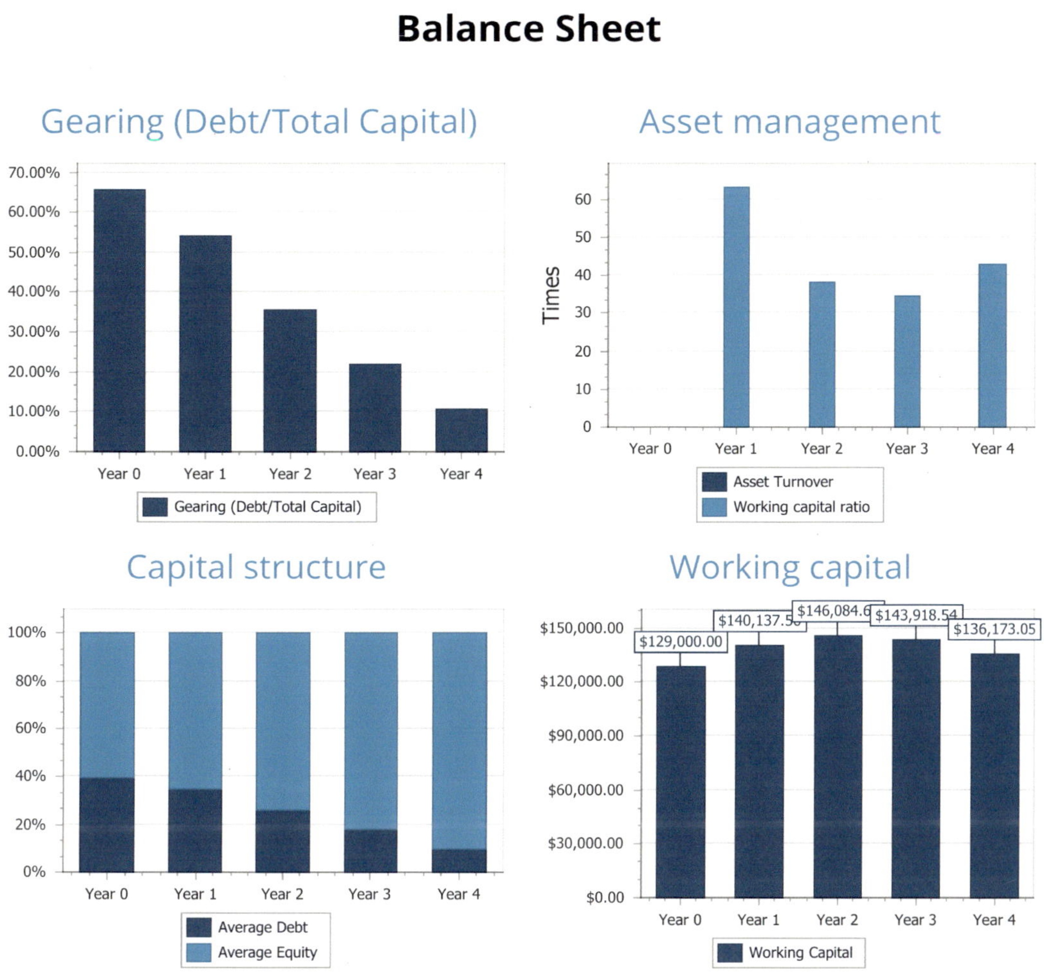

Figure 48: Sample balance sheet output charts

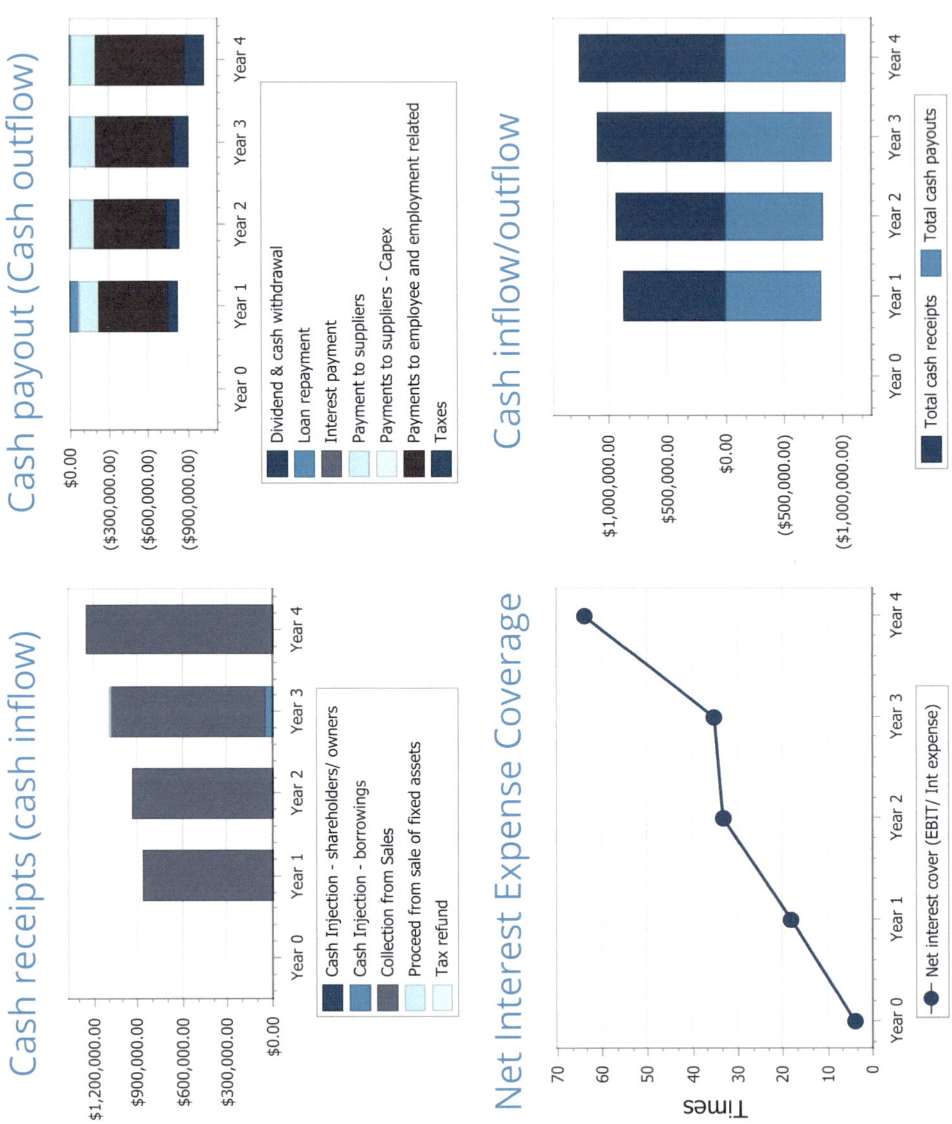

Figure 49: Sample cash flow and cash payout charts

Valuation

Valuation of an entity (or project) represents the worth of its ongoing earning capacity as described by its future cash flows expressed at a current or present value. This type of valuation can be described holistically as enterprise value (EV), comprising both equity and debt holding of the entity. Alternatively, an equity valuation represents only the shareholders' equity value, also called market capitalisation of the company. Broadly, two methods are commonly used for valuation: discount cash flow (DCF) and a multiplier method.

Discount cash flow

Discount cash flow (DCF) calculates the present value (PV) of the entity by applying a discount rate to the stream of its future free cash flows. The projected free cash flow is attained after receipts from sales, minus expenditure on costs and changes in working capital requirements and capital expenditure. This stream of cash flow is then discounted, using WACC as the relevant discount rate, to arrive at the sum of the present value of those cash flows. This provides the enterprise value (EV) of the entity, which embodies both the equity and debt value of the underlying business. The stream of future cash flows and WACC are critical components of the DCF method of valuation.

- Longer cash flow periods (10+ years) will inherently incorporate forecast inaccuracy. The further into the future the cash flow is forecast, the less will be the veracity and accuracy of the figures. However, there will be less emphasis on the final year.
- Shorter cash flow periods, whilst more reliable, place disproportionate emphasis on the final year of valuation (due to the mechanics of the DCF). Care needs to be taken not to incorporate any large, one-off capital expenses or other changes in the cash profile in the final year. DCF assumes that a steady state continues from the final year and mathematically encapsulates that value. Therefore, the final year of DCF should represent a steady-state composition.

Decisions made in the opening position and general assumptions of the company also create a significant impact on its capital structure and hence on its discount (WACC) rate. This, in turn, has a significant impact on valuation outcomes.

Capitalisation (multiplier) method

The multiplier method of capitalisation can run in parallel with DCF to provide a comparison. This method typically applies a multiple for capitalisation to a certain profit level of the business to arrive at its enterprise value (EV). The multiplier can be obtained from publicly available industry benchmarks or equity exchange markets.

EBITDA and EBIT are often employed at the relevant level of profit to apply across to a multiplier. For businesses that are not capital intensive (and therefore do not have great depreciation or amortisation), EBITDA and EBIT are generally very close. However, in cases where there are large depreciation expenses (such as capital intensive industries), care should be taken to select the most appropriate method compatible with the selected multiplier.

The capitalisation outcome for EV again captures both the equity and debt value of the entity (because the multiplier is applied before interest and tax, capitalising the value of debt as well as the value of equity). Whether EBITDA or EBIT is used, the resulting application of a multiplier provides an EV that is dimensionally comparable with the outcome of the DCF. Both DCF and market capitalisation methods are commonly used for comparison purposes.

An alternative multiplier method for valuing only the shareholder equity of a business (its market capitalisation) is undertaken by applying NPAT across to a PE ratio (price-earning ratio). This method is commonly used in the stock market.

- Share price is calculated from PE ratio multiplied by NPAT divided by the number of shares on issue.
- Number of shares multiplied by the share price gives the market capitalisation (equivalent to the multiplication of NPAT by PE ratio).

Typically, PE ratios are numerically higher than equivalent EBITDA or EBIT multipliers (because NPAT is comparatively a smaller number). PE ratios can be extracted for different types of industry and companies through publicly available information and the equity markets. Note that the market capitalisation method does not include the debt holding of the entity and is not dimensionally comparable with EV. To attain the EV of the business, the net debt can be added to this (market capitalisation) equity value. Another useful checkpoint could be to deduct the debt value of the entity from the EV (calculated using the methods described above); this result should be close to the equity value calculated using the market capitalisation methodology.

Figure 50 provides a sample of the input screens for capitalisation with multipliers used in Planium Pro.

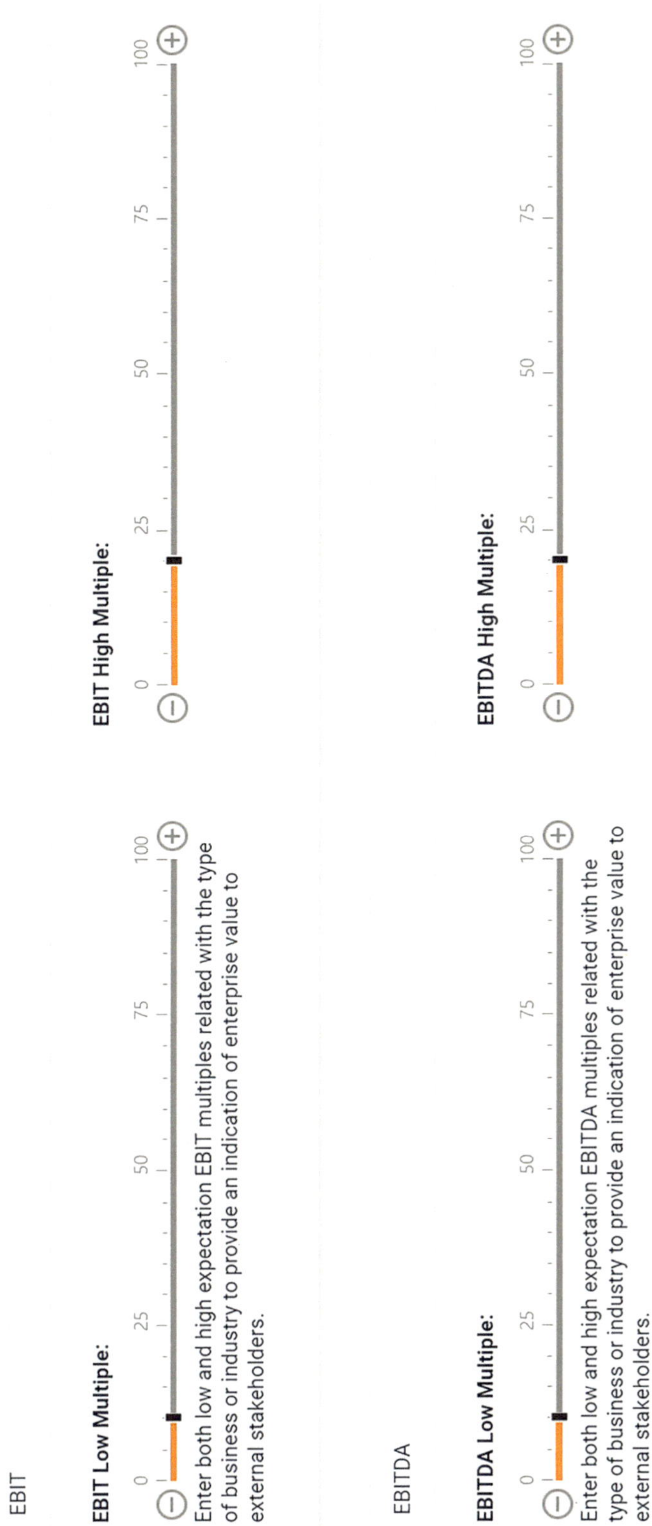

Figure 50: Sample capitalisation with multipliers from Planium Pro

Case sensitivity

Case sensitivity analysis helps planners to consider the impact of changes in certain variables on anticipated business outcomes. The initial financial analysis can be set on the base case, with alternative scenarios considered to examine the effects of possible future changes – such as sales, costs and margins.

In case sensitivity analysis, care should be taken not to change too many variables at once as part of the same analysis. If multiple variables are changed, the analysis can become ambiguous (creating difficulty in identifying the impact of each individual variable change). In Planium Pro, two methods are used for estimating case sensitivity: through the P & L statement (Method A), and through the balance sheet (Method B). Each method considers both the high-case scenario and low-case scenario.[75]

- *Method A:* Using the P & L statement method, the high-case scenario might involve an increase in sales and/or a decrease in direct costs and overheads. The low-case scenario might involve a sales decrease and/or an increase in direct costs and overheads.
- *Method B:* Using the balance sheet method, the high-case scenario might involve a situation where accounts receivable or debtor days decrease, combined with longer accounts payable and creditor days (improving cash profile). The low-case scenario might involve an increase in accounts receivable and debtor days, and a decrease in accounts payable and creditor days. A low-case scenario might also involve an increase in stockholdings (deteriorating cash position).

There should be a distinction between sensitivity analysis and scenario planning. Sensitivity analysis generally determines the impact on the financial model of movements in certain variables. This analysis shows how sensitive the underlying model might be to movements in those critical parameters. In contrast, scenario planning considers a completely different set of prevailing and underlying parameters for opening position, general assumptions, sales, costs and profit forecast.

75. This type of problem with concurrently changing numerous variables in an analysis can cause or exacerbate what is referred to as multicollinearity in econometrics.

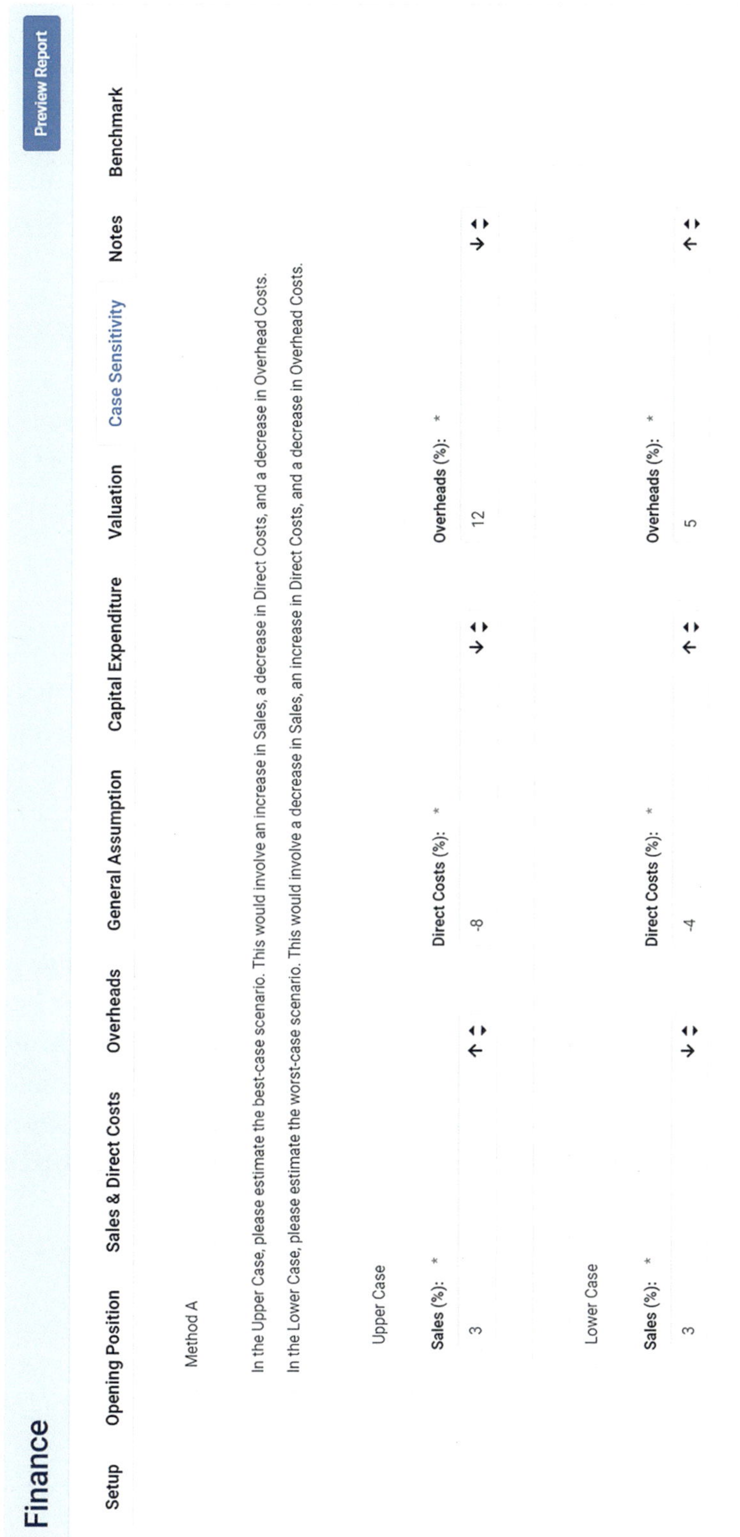

Figure 51: Method A input for case sensitivity analysis

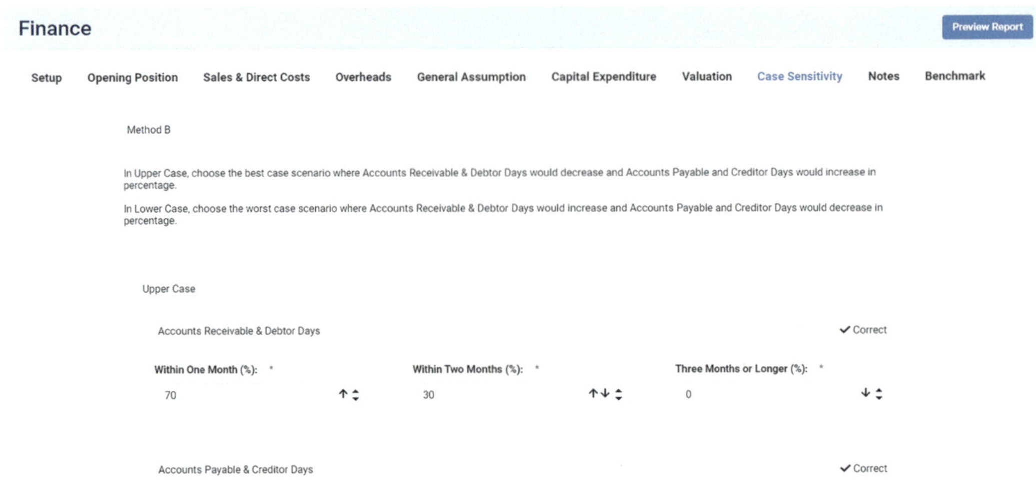

Figure 52: Method B input for case sensitivity analysis

Review (vision and mission) and modify

The final step in completing a strategic business plan is to review the content of each section and complete the executive summary. Business plans are high-level, strategic documents. As mentioned before, these are not a budgeting exercises, nor detailed operational undertakings, nor intricate marketing plans – though all these elements are incorporated into the plan at an appropriate scale.

It may be timely to update sections if operating conditions have changed. It is also prudent to review cost estimates, assumptions and calculations. Before final release, considerations may also be given to factors encountered and learned in the later stages of analysis, which may suggest review of earlier parts of the plan. Whilst the intent of this stage is not to repeat the full planning process, the review stage offers a valuable opportunity to refine and pragmatically improve the plan. In particular, the vision and mission may require slight adjustment and refinement in the light of the full analysis at hand (see Figure 53).

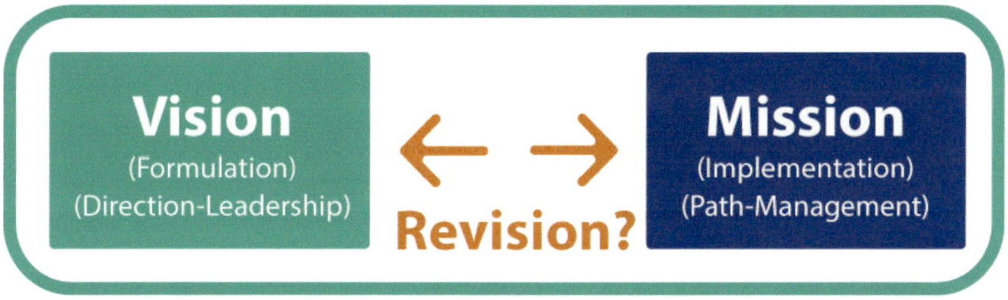

Figure 53: Both vision and mission may be revised after the business plan has been compiled to ensure they remain pragmatic, realistic and credible

Strategic business plans are not isolated documents. Most larger entities review their strategic business plan every three to five years. In a rapidly moving market, three years is the most common timeframe. Businesses generally translate the first year of their business plan into a detailed budget, then report against that budget on a quarterly or monthly basis. Depending on the direction of the business and its realised performance, the entity might report actual figures against forecast for the first year. Again, depending on performance, the entity might adjust and fine-tune its forecast throughout the year (as a reforecast).

Towards the end of the first year, the entity will translate the second year of the business plan into a budget, and use actual results from the first year as the new opening position. In this way, the second year will go through the same cascading effect as the first year – actual/forecast then actual/reforecast, based on the new opening position (the actual figures for the first year). At the end of the third year, it is timely to revise the full strategic plan.

In a three-yearly review of the plan, businesses should pay particular attention to the vision and mission statements. The vision and mission are the overarching statements that guide the plan; every part of the business should be focused on achieving these. For this reason, they must remain clear, concise and up-to-date. Without an adequate vision and mission, the business will lack the necessary direction and foundation for operating.

As mentioned in Chapter 2, relevant indicators should be factored into different parts of the business plan (see Figure 54).

- The formulation stage typically uses lead indicators to drive the business forward.
- The implementation stage typically uses spot indicators (which features rates) to operate the business.
- The evaluation stage uses lag indicators to report on comparative performance.

Care should be taken not to drive the business with lag indicators and, therefore, over-emphasise reporting elements. Similarly, care should be taken not to use lead indicators (which are not sufficiently concrete) in monitoring and reporting activity. Whilst these separations are not always strictly valid and there might be slight overlaps, it provides a useful guideline for selecting appropriate key performance indicators for relevant stages.

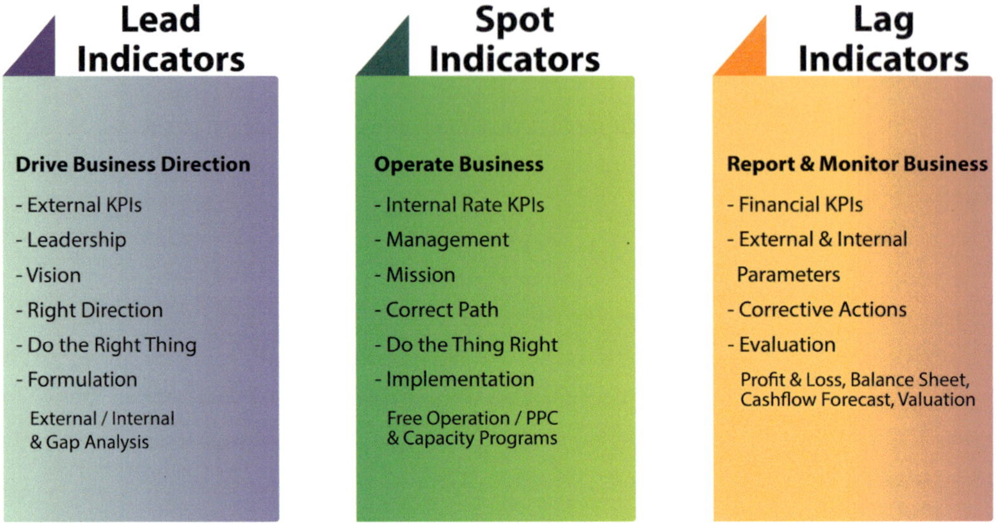

Figure 54: In a strategic business context, managers drive the business forward with lead indicators, operate the business with spot indicators, and report on performance using lag indicators

In addition to an annual review cycle, triggers that may suggest the business plan needs to be reviewed include:

- Current mission has been achieved
- Stakeholder dissatisfaction with direction (vision) or path (mission)
- Significant step-change or disruptive changes in the economic, market or political environment.

Target programs within the strategic business plan should cascade to lower-level, detailed plans that are developed in the most appropriate software (such as accounting, customer relations management, project management and enterprise resource planning software). This type of cascading from the strategic plan into detailed marketing, operational and budgeting activities is pragmatic. It also forms part of the compliance requisite for entities trading on the equity markets due to requirements of continuous disclosure to various stakeholders.

Physical examples and case studies

Physical examples

To assist in explaining the concepts introduced in the Unified Theory of Business Strategy (UTBS), we draw parallels here between business concepts and examples from physical engineering. Our purpose is to show the real and practical nature of these concepts at work. Intangible concepts from the social sciences (such as business theory) frequently have tangible (but not readily observed) parallels in the physical sciences. Many people perceive that 'being in business' is an intangible, esoteric occupation, particularly when compared with the practical experiences of working with engines, bridges or electrical circuits. It is commonly assumed that the physical world is inherently different from the business world, and that business is somehow more complex and less predictable. But this distinction is a fallacy. The concepts may look different, but the underlying principles are the same. They are all part of the same reality framework within which we operate. If a mechanic operates a business in the same way as they fix a car, their business is likely to be a success. In the physical sciences, outcomes are more predictable. It is possible, for example, to use mathematics to design a bridge that will not collapse, or to design a vehicle with a superior suspension system. These same principles can be applied in business. In this section, we show that the UTBS can be equivalent to a first-order physical system.

Business strategy meets vehicle suspension

In Chapters 1 and 2, we defined our theoretical framework and noted that PPCs (processes, procedures and communication) work in conjunction with capacity-building programs during the implementation building block of business planning (Axiom 1). We also noted that capacity-building programs yield stock variables (a source of competitive advantage) commensurate with the requirements identified through the formulation building block (Axiom 2).

PPCs work with flow variables to provide the underlying consistency of business operations and governance. Through PPCs, stock variables are yielded as the mathematical integration of the PPC flow variables over time. Alternatively, the flow variables of PPCs can be described as the first derivative (differentiation) of capacity-building programs with respect to time (this was shown in Chapter 1). The combination of these produces superior and relevant outcomes of implementation (Axiom 1) commensurate with the requirements of formulation (Axiom 2).

We now use a vehicle suspension system as a clear physical analogy of the above mechanism. An electro-mechanical suspension system is something that many people interact with every day – every time they drive a car or ride in a vehicle. Suspension systems are designed to create a comfortable ride for passengers (called critical dampening) by attenuating movement from the road (called platform motion, created by potholes, bumps and corners) and reducing the movement experienced by passengers. A suspension system includes the following components:[76]

- The first component has the characteristics of a spring, and is made of either a coil or leaf spring (in heavier vehicles) or an air bag with pneumatic pressure inside. This component shows (or accumulates) an opposing force based on the amount of its displacement. If the spring is compressed or extended, it resists the movement. The amount of its resistance depends on the spring rate coefficient (or constant) and on the amount of compression or extension. The induced force is, therefore, based on both the spring rate and how much the spring has been compressed or extended. The force is in the opposing direction of the displacement.[77]

76. The full corner assembly of a vehicle also includes other components (such as ball joints or knuckle arms). Here, our attention is focused on the two main components – the spring (coil, leaf or airbag) and the shock absorber (sometimes called the dampener). The analogy presented here could be extended further, but for ease of description we limit the discussion to these two components of the suspension system.

77. Displacement is the vector version of distance (distance is a scalar or amount-only entity). The combination of a scalar with a specific direction creates the vector version. Other examples are mass (scalar) and weight (vector), speed (scalar) and velocity (vector). Scalars are sometimes referred to as tensors of the zeroth kind, whilst vectors are referred to as tensors of the first type. Speed is (a scalar) rate of change of distance (scalar) with respect to time. Velocity, on the other hand, is a (vector) rate of change of displacement (vector) with respect to time. Speed and velocity are both derivative (differentiation) of their underlying movement

- The second component is a shock absorber – a hydraulic cylinder with viscous fluid inside. In contrast with the spring described above, a shock absorber exerts opposing force depending on how *fast* it is either compressed or extended. The rate of the induced opposing force is a function of the viscosity of the fluid it contains. It exhibits *inertia* – the faster one tries to move it, the more opposing force it generates.[78] Here, it is not displacement, but the first derivative of that displacement with respect to time (velocity) that determines the induced force.[79]

The two components of a shock absorber are installed side by side (see Figure 55). As the vehicle moves, the weight of the vehicle on top coexists with vibrations (incoming from below) received from the road (platform motion – as used in the test laboratories). Depending on the type of road (smooth freeways or bumpy conditions), the combination of the spring-dampener effect *attenuates* those vibrations and provides a better ride.[80]

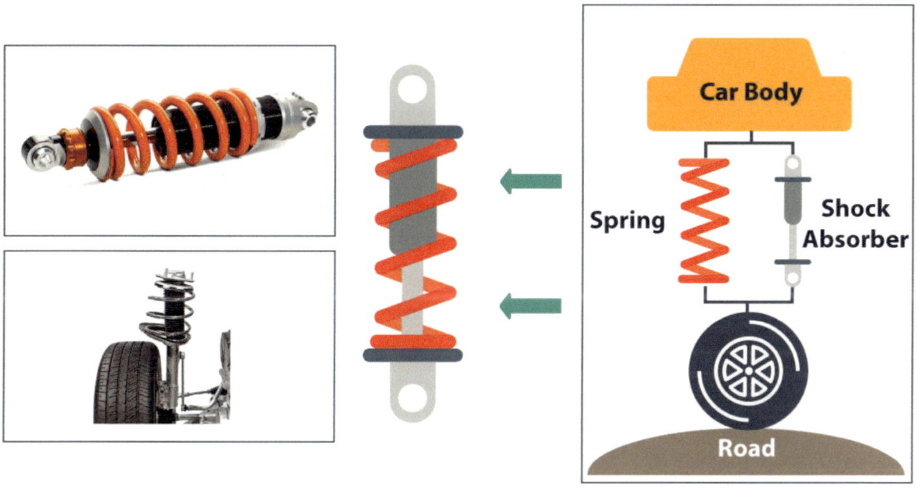

Figure 55: Components of a vehicle suspension system: the spring and shock absorber create a comfortable ride for passengers. This is analogous to the workings of formulation (Axiom 2) and implementation (Axiom 1) in the UTBS

counterparts, but one without direction (speed) and the other with predetermined specific direction (velocity). This distinction of a variable being without or with direction (being scalar or vector) is critical in understanding causal (direction-based) processes such as the UTBS with a clear unidirection between the axioms.

78. In Chapter 1, we referred to this type of inertia as diseconomies of time compression for stock variables, such as knowledge, character or competitive advantage.

79. Parallels are discernible between stock variables, being a mathematical integration of a corresponding flow variable, and flow variables, being the first derivative (differential) of stock variables with respect to time. Displacement-induced and velocity-induced forces in springs and shock absorbers carry this underlying connection.

80. This becomes together a first-order system – as defined in the mathematics of non-linear dynamics systems. This is analogous to the workings of the two axioms introduced in our framework.

If the suspension assembly (through the spring rate and dampener rate) is set to move up and down more (absorbing more vibration), it can provide a smoother ride for passengers, but will compromise corner stability at high speeds (such as in a family SUV). In contrast, a stiff arrangement (with little movement) will not create such a comfortable ride (by not attenuating so much of the incoming vibration from the road) but will provide better corner handling (such as in sports cars and racing cars). This off-setting of performance provides a compromise towards a suitable outcome based on the average weight of the vehicle and the typical input (platform motion) encountered from the road. The combination of the pre-selected spring constant and shock-absorber rate (set in the design process) provides a suitable generic average outcome. It provides safe cornering and a relatively smooth ride for the type of vehicle application.[81]

In a dynamic suspension system (which uses airbags for springs in parallel with dampeners), the weight of the vehicle is continuously measured (by load sensors) and the (platform motion) vibration received from the road is also measured in real time by sensors. Through resolving differential equations, an onboard vehicle computer rapidly determines the most effective spring rate (selecting it by changing the pneumatic pressure in the airbags) in conjunction with the most effective pressure of the viscous fluid in the shock absorber. This combination yields an optimal set-up for the vehicle's weight, type of road and cornering. Critical dampening is achieved, not based on static pre-set parameters, but based on continuous measurements of external inputs, internal capacity (weight) and their interpretation. Through this closed-loop control, system parameters are changed to suit the environment.

When working well, PPCs and capacity-building programs are like a dynamic suspension system – operating not simply in a static way, but with intermittent modifications based on received signals from formulation (through gap analysis and risk assessment) and identified internal resource capabilities (such as the spring and dampener types). The existing realities of the business are like the vehicle's weight, whilst external market signals act as vibrational inputs (road types).

A limited set of information may still produce acceptable business performance (in the same way that a static suspension system can produce acceptable vehicle performance). However, such limited external information is unlikely to produce a superior outcome. Optimal outcomes (competitive advantage commensurate with external opportunities and internal resources) can only be achieved by dynamically adjusting PPCs and revising both the scope and content of capacity-building programs. In the physical example of the shock absorber, the direction of the movements (and ensuing forces) are critical to

81. Tyre pressure, profile and composition as well as vehicle body shape, centre of gravity and other parameters also have a bearing on the overall outcome, but are beyond the scope of our discussion here.

the functioning of the system. The UTBS provides a directional, causal path that aligns external elements and internal capabilities with implementation efforts.

The critical dampening of dynamic suspension systems requires rapid data (per second). The analogous strategy system in business requires yearly inputs with three-yearly revisions (the business plan). The business can then move ahead, 'humming forward' under those conditions in much the same way as the dynamic suspension system's critical dampening provides a comfortable ride for passengers.

The UTBS fundamentally relies on the elements of system dynamics in its axiom sub-components and for the configuration of Axioms 1 (implementation), Axiom 2 (formulation) and the interpretation link (evaluation). The concepts introduced in Chapter 1 and the applied business version discussed in Chapter 2 directly relate to the analogy of the first-order system presented here.

Competitive advantage meets power transfer

Competitive advantage gives a business superior returns on its resources, towards accumulation of economic value added wealth. Once attained, such competitive advantage, therefore, bestows wealth-generating *power* on the underlying economic agent or entity. This power can be carefully transformed to manifest itself in different ways.

Contrary to commonly advanced viewpoints, businesses do not necessarily need to continually produce more (sources or types of) competitive advantage, or even replicate their existing competitive advantage. If businesses properly sustain the source of their competitive advantage (through processes similar to those described in our framework), they transform existing competitive advantage into various outcomes and expressions. These outcomes and expressions may be more suitable for the prevailing external circumstances. Converting competitive advantage in this way comes at a small transformational cost. We provide a physical analogy below to show the underlying reality of this concept.[82]

In physics, power is generally defined as the ability to undertake physical work (or the rate at which work is done on an object). Power is measured in watts, and is closely related to energy (energy is itself the ability to create change). Essentially, power is how much energy is used per unit of time (power = energy / time *or* energy = power x time).[83] In the industrial world, energy is converted to power in certain electrical, mechanical and nuclear devices, to then provide an ability to undertake work.

An example of this, which many people interact with daily, is the conversion of chemical energy in fossil fuel to produce a power output using an internal combustion engine (petrol or diesel). These are commonly used in cars, industrial equipment and heavy vehicles. Through the internal workings of the engine, fossil fuel is compressed and combusted within the cylinders to release its inherent chemical energy. The power output first shows itself in the combination of two components – the ability to turn (called torque) and the angular velocity of rotation coming out of the engine (power = torque (newton meters) × angular velocity (radians/second)).

When a vehicle first moves from a stationary position, it mainly uses higher torque and ability to turn its wheels. It does not need high velocity when starting. As the vehicle becomes mobile and gathers higher velocity, it requires less torque (because it has

82. The three case studies included in this book show how some of the most successful companies (in terms of both size and profitability) have progressively shown elements of superior logistics, low-cost but quality production, and strong brand name. The underlying source of their advantage has been translated and transformed to show these various outcomes.

83. Energy (in joules) = power (in watts) × time (in seconds). Commonly used units of kilowatts and hours are, for example, used in electricity bills to charge for household or industrial energy consumption in kilowatt-hours (kWh).

momentum going forward). This change is achieved in practice by using a transmission device (gearbox), either manually or automatically. The transmission device incurs a small efficiency loss (through its workings) in making these changes. Heavy vehicles (such as trucks or earth-moving machinery) generally do not have high-speed requirements, and hence focus more on turning torque ability. This explains why heavy vehicles use diesel engines more suitable for low-speed and high-torque applications. Conversely, racing cars use higher velocities with less need for turning (torque). The critical point here is that the vehicle's power output is progressively changed (using gearing mechanisms) into different combinations of its components, suitable for the status of vehicle and the relevant application. Whilst we see different manifestations of it, the underlying *power* generated by the engine is unchanged in its essence.[84]

Once a power output is produced, the velocity and torque combination may not be themselves required for practical application. In these circumstances, for example, an electrical generator-motor can be connected to the end of the internal combustion engine. These electro-mechanical assemblies are commonly used in large trains and ships. In this way, power (through wire windings inside the generator) can be translated to its electrical version and manifest itself as voltage and current (power = potential (voltage) × current (amps)). The electrical power can be transmitted (by copper wire) to achieve the suitable combination of voltage and current (for the devices used). This change occurs using intermediate transformer devices. As with all transformations, there is a small efficiency loss in the electro-mechanical conversion and the later change to the combination of voltage and current. Once again, the underlying power remains of the same essence (released from chemical energy in this example) but it can be witnessed in a different manifestation.

Conversion to fluid power (as used in hydraulic equipment or car brakes and steering) is another, similar example. This may be achieved by connecting a hydraulic motor to the engine (or electric motor) in order to change the torque–velocity (or voltage–current) combination into a more suitable combination of pressure and flow rate (power = pressure (pascals) × flow rate (m^3/second)) as needed. The trend of this analogy can then also continue to describe the power output of hydraulic machinery into the two components of force and linear velocity (power = force (newtons) × velocity (metres/second)). That is, indeed, how construction machinery or cranes use force to shift earth or heavy materials.

84. For mathematically minded readers, both velocity and torque are vector entities (i.e., scalar entities with a directional element). Power is, therefore, the vector multiplication of those two (with scalar amounts multiplied by the sinus of the angle between the two vectors' directions). In this example (and examples such as voltage × current, pressure × flow, or force × velocity), the relative directions of these vectors are perpendicular to each other. Because the sinus of the 90 degree angle is 1, it has, therefore, been eliminated (but not ignored!) from our discussions earlier, to facilitate clear description. Direction remains a critical component of causal systems, as it is in configurations of the UTBS.

Again, aside from small efficiency losses, the power remains the same in essence but is different in its presence and effects.

In each of the given examples, power is transformed to yield different outcomes and manifestations that best suit the context at hand. It is not simply transmitted (or in business context, extended). It has also been selectively transformed as well as transmitted.

In a business strategy context, competitive advantage has the attributes of power, and the entity can show varied aspects of it in response to new external realities. The consistency of operations and governance, as defined through steps in the implementation stage, can deliver a reliable brand name. This approach (in conjunction with freehand operations introduced in Chapter 2) can be transformed into a sustained ability to innovate. This is illustrated in our case studies: Toyota extended its source of competitive advantage (its keiretsu network) to produce reliable and high-quality products whilst being cost competitive (and Toyota's brand name was a manifestation of underlying power); Zara's source of advantage is embedded in attributes of its supply chain management, translated into rapid design changes and superior brand name; Amazon achieved similar transformations. All three entities transformed their competitive advantage into different expressions directly relevant to the contexts they faced. As with all such conversions, there is a small economic cost (transaction costs and entropy) to each of these transformations. The net effect, however, can be disproportionality lucrative by realigning the original competitive advantage to representations more relevant to the context and circumstances at hand.

The power analogy shows that successful businesses are not compelled to create more competitive advantage (as proposed by some literature). Indeed, our stipulated constraint for capacity-building programs is to ensure they absorb no more than 15 per cent of company resources – this, itself, postulates such limitation. Instead, businesses sustain the source of their competitive advantage and use strategic business processes to transform their source strengths across different contexts and outcomes. These do not then become mere extensions of the same features to further contexts. These are *transformations* that increasingly constitute the content of capacity-building programs (backed by the consistency of PPCs), based on the revision of the external environment in the formulation stage.

Case studies

This section includes three case studies – Toyota Motor Corporation, Zara and Amazon – which embody the elements discussed in the first three chapters of this book. The case studies, which we have compiled from various sources, reflect the businesses' real experiences and practical attributes to represent links to the concepts we have presented in this book. Each case study includes certain aspects of our theoretical framework and illustrates how powerful these measures can be when successfully and effectively implemented.

Toyota Motor Corporation

Toyota Motor Corporation was founded in 1937 by Kiichiro Toyoda. It started as the automobile division of Toyoda Automatic Loom Works, the loom business owned by Toyoda's father, Sakichi Toyoda. Toyoda was encouraged by the Japanese government to begin an automotive industry in Japan. Toyota initially struggled and, in 1950, was on the verge of going out of business. Production of vehicles for the US military during the Korean War helped to revitalise the company. In 1982, the Toyota Motor Company and Toyota Motor Sales merged into one company, creating today's Toyota Motor Corporation.

Toyota primarily conducts business in the automotive industry, but also conducts business in finance and other industries. As of 31 March, 2018, Toyota operated through 606 consolidated subsidiaries (including variable interest entities) and 199 affiliated companies, of which 57 companies were accounted for through the equity method.

Toyota Motor Corporation operates in over 170 countries and regions, and has more than 60 manufacturing facilities in 27 countries and regions. Toyota's automotive operations include the design, manufacture, assembly and sale of passenger vehicles, minivans, commercial vehicles such as trucks, and related parts and accessories.

Toyota is clear and concise in its approach to market segments. Given the company's global reach, it first segments its markets in geographical terms. Toyota then primarily subsegments geographical markets along product lines. Where possible, it uses common platforms across subsegments, with different branding and positioning, and some minor adjustments. This has been a very effective and successful strategy for Toyota. Until recently this made it difficult for competitors to fully comprehend Toyota's allocation of its range in various international markets. Toyota Motor Corporation is broadly divided into three main groups, as shown in Figure 56.

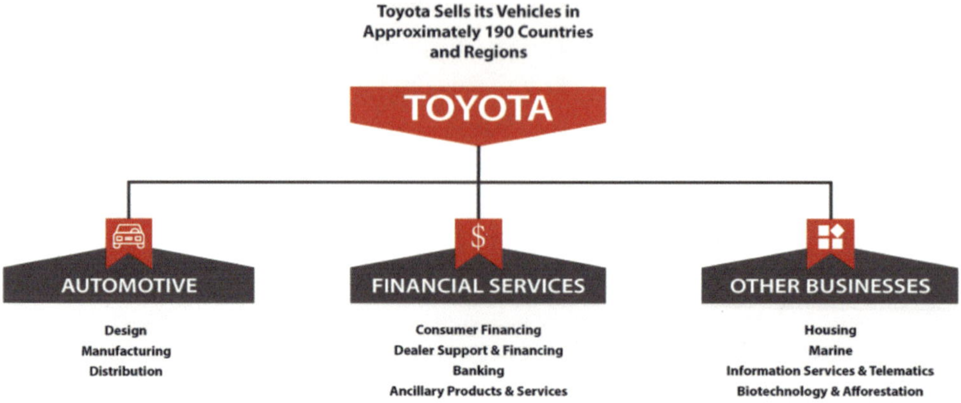

Figure 56: Main divisions of Toyota Motor Corporation[85]

Toyota's Global Vision

In 2018, Toyota unveiled its Toyota Global Vision, a corporate outline for the future which gives direction to Toyota employees and conveys Toyota's vision to the wider community. Toyota is working to achieve sustained growth through the following ideals:[86]

Toyota Global Vision

- Toyota will lead the way to the future of mobility, enriching lives around the world with the safest and most responsible ways of moving people.
- Through our commitment to quality, constant innovation and respect for the planet, we aim to exceed expectations and be rewarded with a smile.
- We will meet challenging goals by engaging the talent and passion of people, who believe there is always a better way.

'The safest and most responsible ways of moving people'

- Safety is Toyota's highest priority, and Toyota will continue to provide world-class safety.
- Toyota will also continue to contribute to environmental quality and to human happiness by using leading environmental technology and by deploying that

85. Toyota Motor Corporation, 2018a.
86. Toyota Motor Corporation, 2018a.

technology in a growing line of vehicle models. At the same time, Toyota will work through the provision of products, sales and services that exceed customer expectation to offer a rewarding experience for customers.

'Enriching lives around the world'

- Toyota has been consistently true to its founding spirit of serving society through conscientious manufacturing, and it will continue working in that spirit to contribute to enhance the quality of life wherever it has operations.
- Toyota will strive to continue contributing to economic vitality wherever it has operations by generating stable employment and by participating in mutually beneficial business relationships with dealers and suppliers. It will also strive to continue to actively engage in initiatives for human resources development and the promotion of cultural activities of its host communities.

'Lead the way to the future of mobility'

- Toyota will lead the industry in technological development that will spawn next generation mobility. For example, it will explore possibilities in personal mobility and in the convergence of information technology for automobiles and 'smart grids' for optimizing energy generation and consumption. Toyota will strive to offer products and services that match the needs in each market.
- Toyota will strive to advance environmental technology and develop low-carbon technologies and technologies for maximizing safety through interaction with the transport infrastructure to lay a foundation for sustainable and amenable future mobility.

'Our commitment to quality, constant innovation'

- Toyota is committed to providing quality vehicles that are highly reliable and driven with a sense of safety and reliability.
- Toyota will constantly reinvent itself and continue to engage in cutting-edge technology development. Toyota will work towards offering vehicles around the world that address the needs of today and of tomorrow at affordable prices.

'Respect for the planet'

- Toyota will continue working to minimize environmental impact in its manufacturing and other operations, as well as in its products.
- Toyota's activities will include conserving energy and reducing output of carbon dioxide, as well as conserving material resources through recycling; it will also include establishing mindsets and production methods appropriate for coexistence with nature.

'Exceed expectations and be rewarded with a smile'

- Everyone at Toyota will continuously maintain a sense of gratitude to customers and will strive to earn smiles with products and services that are stimulating and inspiring and exceed customer expectations.

'There is always a better way'

- All Toyota employees will share the recognition that there is always a better way and share a commitment to continuous improvement, which are fundamental to The Toyota Way.

'Meet challenging goals by engaging the talent and passion of people'

- Toyota will nurture a corporate culture where teamwork and individual creativity thrive and where people will approach their work with pride and passion.
- Toyota will honour the spirit of diversity in recruiting, training and promoting capable individuals around the world. Human resources development at Toyota will continue to promote the transfer of the company's monozukuri spirit of conscientious manufacturing and related skills and know-how from one generation to the next.

Keiretsu system

In Japanese, the word *keiretsu* can be translated to mean 'group' or 'system'. The Japanese keiretsu system refers to a grouping of organisations – that is, formal and informal links between organisations, customers, suppliers and financial institutions that reduce agency costs and provide financial and strategic flexibility.[87] A keiretsu generally involves a conglomeration of businesses and organisations associated with cross shareholdings that are formed around their own trading companies or large banks. However, equity ownership is not a prerequisite for keiretsu formation; a keiretsu can form on the basis of a business network comprised of manufacturers, supply chain partners, distributors and even financiers, who are all financially independent but who work very closely together to support and ensure mutual success. The Japanese keiretsu systems of formal and informal links between firms, customers, suppliers and financial institutions reduce agency costs and provide financial and strategic flexibility.

There are essentially two types of keiretsu systems: 1) horizontal (also known as a financial keiretsu), characterised by the cross-shareholding relationships formed between businesses that are centred around a major bank (the bank provides these companies with a variety of financial services); and 2) vertical (also known as a jump-style keiretsu

87. McGuire & Dow, 2002.

or an industrial keiretsu), characterised by the tying together in partnership of suppliers, manufacturers and distributors of an industry. Both horizontal and vertical keiretsu systems somewhat differ from the market model found in North America, which is characterised by market-based corporate control mechanisms and discernible distinctions among financial stakeholders.

Toyota's large size enables it to show elements of both vertical and horizontal keiretsu. It is best classified as vertical, because it displays a typical manufacturing pyramid that focuses its attention on the assembly and design of motor vehicles. It purchases most of its components and other input requirements from firms that have earned a connection with Toyota (keiretsu membership) on the basis of performance ahead of ownership. In contrast to the zaibatsu (integrated business conglomerates), Toyota's vertical keiretsu is achieved by networking amongst separate organisations rather than by internalising more and more activities within one organisation.

Toyota's success is based on multiple, complex links: with suppliers and manufacturers for parts and components, with employees for production, and with real estate owners/managers for dealerships. These links extend beyond automotive manufacturing to include dealerships and finance. All ancillary companies operate within the vertical keiretsu of Toyota (that is, suppliers, manufacturers and distributors within the automotive industry) but are members of a larger horizontal keiretsu (with some cross-shareholding relationships across entities).

Toyota accurately identified its long-term resource shortages and effectively implemented a vertical keiretsu to form a solution. This structure emanates from successful resolution of cooperative behaviour, resulting in reliable, cost-effective products for the market. The vertical keiretsu became a source of competitive advantage, gaining Toyota superior returns on its capital (demonstrated through increasing share price and market capitalisation). Toyota grew from a small company into one of the world's largest automotive companies.

Toyota built these resources using an intense focus on continuous improvement of routine tasks and objectives. Its methods became globally commonplace from the 1990s. Toyota's keiretsu suppliers cooperatively develop technology and create its potent competitive advantage. Joining Toyota's keiretsu represented a discrete change in the payoff structure for smaller organisations: potential benefits were sizeable and players gradually filled the gap in Toyota's resource shortfall. The company, as a result, experiences a low transaction cost of doing business. This is a direct outcome of its ability to coordinate across the keiretsu and provide incentives to all participants (both short-term and long-term incentives). Toyota thus ensures cooperative behaviour across the keiretsu. This gives Toyota an enormous competitive advantage over its international competitors.

Strategy implementation: The Toyota Way

Toyota grew from a small, industrial company based only in Japan into the largest and most successful automotive company in the world. This type of growth does not happen by accident. Toyota manages every aspect of its business with regular processes, procedures and communication. Over time, this has lowered Toyota's transaction costs and created a more efficient way of doing business. Toyota has implemented regular improvement of its processes through continuous review and refinement.[88]

The Toyota Way encompasses Toyota's strategic values and business methods, summarised with the following five strategic principles:

- Challenge (ask questions, identify threats and opportunities)
- Kaizen (continuous improvement – standardised processes and procedures)
- Genchi genbutsu (go and see – understand the problem)
- Respect (develop organisational culture)
- Teamwork (coordinate and cooperate).

Consistent implementation of workflows has enabled Toyota to provide superior coordination across its network, leading to cooperative behaviour both internally and externally. One example of this is Toyota's inventory management system, based on the just-in-time principle. The Toyota Way is a clear illustration of how Axiom 1–style activities, demonstrated through implementation of routine processes, procedures and communication, can create improving and superior returns for a business.

Supply chain efficiency

Just-in-time (JIT) manufacturing was promoted by Toyota in the 1970s, and is also known as the Toyota Production System. Just-in-time manufacturing is an integrated strategy that satisfies customer demand efficiently by linking all production activity to current and forecast market demand. Its production relies on finely tuned processes in the capital-intensive assembly sequence, using only the quantities of items required, only when they are needed. Just-in-time manufacturing optimises workflow whilst minimising production time, material and cost. It enabled Toyota to offer tailored solutions to customers long before its mass-production competitors could do so. Just-in-time manufacturing enabled Toyota to create long-term competitive advantage (a stock variable) by implementing rigorous processes, procedures and communication. It focused on the

88. Edwards & Samimi, 1997.

ongoing resolution of coordination-style games to create progressive improvement and financial gain by resolving those games across its keiretsu network.[89]

Cost-base, quality and safety

The traditional keiretsu involved relationships of obligation, based on trust and goodwill, in order to keep costs down and provide flexibility in product sourcing. Toyota mostly buys from companies with which it has long-term relationships, but also looks at the prices offered by other sources whose streamlined operations allow them to offer low prices. For example, at the bottom of the Toyota keiretsu are many smaller companies, which outsource to other contractors that in turn supply to Toyota. Whilst the lower-level companies have no official associations with Toyota and their exact number is not accurately known, it is estimated to be several thousand companies.

To develop high-quality products, Toyota encourages suppliers to provide integrated systems of components and become involved in product development at the planning stage.[90] Because Toyota's keiretsu generally has more than one supplier for most components, threats are credible. Toyota does occasionally discontinue working with suppliers, but not suddenly and only after a period of consultation and attempts to rectify quality control incidents. The consistency of Toyota's operations through processes, procedures and communication mechanisms (including Kanban and team incentivisation) has resulted in significant reductions in quality incidents. In turn, this translates to lower transaction costs for the consumer.

Toyota has established an occupational safety and health management system to prevent accidents at work, including ongoing efforts to avoid near-miss accidents and accidents that may lead to lost workdays, bodily injury or fatality. Toyota is involved in various activities to improve safety and health, such as training its employees to behave safely in the workplace, improving the safety of machinery and establishing occupational safety principles. Toyota has a health management system for its employees, including fitness-focused preventive action against lifestyle disease in the form of initiatives to promote healthier diets and exercise, and action on mental health through information for employees on emotional health. Toyota is expected to lead the way to the future of mobility with the safest and most responsible ways of moving people. Toyota is successful because of its philosophy and reputation of commitment to quality and constant innovation.

89. This is closely linked to Axioms 1 and 2, as discussed in Chapter 1, and corresponds to the implementation and formulation building blocks discussed in Chapter 2.

90. Edwards & Samimi, 1997.

Culture of continuous improvement

Toyota constantly endeavours to increase the quality of everything it produces. This attitude can be expressed by 'kaizen', a Sino-Japanese word for improvement or change for the better, meaning continuous improvement. Kaizen is key in working towards perfection by optimising routine and repetitive tasks. It is an integrative methodology, which means a cross-functional, gradual improvement with direct involvement of all staff.[91]

Toyota's leading global role in adopting lean operation production techniques demonstrates its focus on using rigorous processes, procedures and communication to implement routine tasks. At Toyota, all employees, from executives to shopfloor workers, are challenged to use their initiative and creativity to experiment and learn – to explore ways in which processes, procedures and communication can be improved.

Toyota's philosophy of continuous improvement involves fine-tuning its processes and procedures, which allows Toyota to build knowledge and quality, eliminate waste, reduce costs and achieve competitive advantage (stock variables). Toyota's strategic principles align with the vertical keiretsu system, which focuses on relationships based on trust.

Toyota's approach to regular examination of issues and to continuous improvement includes:

- **Genchi genbutsu** (go and see – understand the problem): Toyota always examines suppliers' physical workplaces and products to ensure it receives only the highest-quality products. The supplier relationship is collaborative, because suppliers know they are members of Toyota's vertical keiretsu and their success depends on the success of Toyota vehicles in the marketplace
- **Kaizen** (continuous improvement – standardised processes and procedures): Toyota aims to build suppliers' tacit knowledge through long-term sharing of work experiences, including attempts to solve problems together through trial and error (teamwork). Toyota recognises that training and workshops are crucial for building cooperation with suppliers towards a gradual affiliation, preferably with repeated business. Toyota provides subcontracted workshops with a single market outlet for the bulk of their output and the opportunity to earn a place as a repeat business supplier.

Toyota's long-term capability-building approach across organisational culture, research and development, operational improvement, marketing and sales, and information technology is superior to any of its competitors. Toyota focuses on routine processes and procedures, clear market segmentation, and close attention to the interface between the

91. Edwards & Samimi, 1997.

external environment and internal resources. As a result, Toyota has become one of the largest and most profitable entities in the world.

The company's accurate understanding of its market's requirements in the 1970s, and particularly Toyota's understanding that it could not incorporate resources into the organisation with the approach used by its main competitors, encouraged it to implement a step-change program. Through this, Toyota achieved two key outcomes: 1) continuous improvement of the accuracy and replicability of its processes and procedures and its ability to communicate these effectively, and 2) development of an external network that became its vertical keiretsu to replace resources that would traditionally be vertically integrated into the firm.

Conclusion

Central to Toyota's success is its vertical keiretsu system, which is difficult for competitors to replicate. Toyota's vertical keiretsu has a simple objective: to outperform any rival. Toyota's success depends on strong organisational links between suppliers, whose fortunes are tied to the success of Toyota in general rather than to the success of any particular firm. Each supplier's interest is best served by cooperating as much as they possibly can to support the market success of Toyota. The keiretsu became Toyota's key source of competitive advantage and could not be easily replicated by its competitors. The keiretsu matched the external elements of Toyota's business environment with its internal capabilities.

Throughout its history, Toyota has successfully understood what internal resources it lacked compared to the requirements of the external environment, and developed processes and procedures that allowed for enhanced quality and continuous improvement. In its early days, Toyota lacked production know-how. In its gradual transition to the world's most successful automotive manufacturer, Toyota developed world-leading production know-how and invented business methodologies that have been adopted by many industries. Through consistent, rigorous application of iterative quality improvement processes, procedures and organisational communication, Toyota became a company synonymous with quality and reliability. It built relevant capacity and capability through specific programs alongside its routine improvements. Toyota's world leadership did not happen by chance. It is in illustration of the power of Axiom–1 style activities (implementation), supported by critical capacity building and creative thinking (Axiom 2–style formulation activities) to create long-term superior returns and other successful business outcomes for all stakeholders.

Inditex – Zara

Zara was established by Amancio Ortega Gaona and Rosalia Mera, who opened their first store in the Spanish coastal city of Arteixo, Coruña, in 1975. Zara is a high-fashion retailer offering clothing, accessories and footwear for women, men and children. Zara's business model is unique: it combines affordable prices, vertical integration and quick response time. Products designed at Zara headquarters in Arteixo reach stores quickly, usually just three weeks after they are designed. The Zara business model led to Ortega being named one of the richest individuals in the world.[92]

Zara is the main brand of the Inditex fashion group, which is one of the largest fashion retailers in the world with over 7,000 stores (both online and shopfront) operating in more than 100 markets. More than half of the Inditex factories are located in Arteixo (Coruña, Spain). The company works with over 1,000 suppliers and over 7,000 operational facilities worldwide. Figure 57 lists Inditex's eight brands.

Figure 57: Main brands of Inditex[93]

92. Forbes, 2019.

93. Inditex. Available: https://www.inditex.com/about-us/who-we-are

Business model

Zara's key business model is to sell quality fashion at affordable prices, with vertical integration and very short lead times. Zara's entire business process has four fundamental success factors: 1) short product cycle, 2) small batches per product, 3) extensive variety of product every season, and 4) heavy investment in information and communication technology. Around the world, Zara stores receive deliveries twice a week. These factors have contributed to Zara's competitive advantage over its rivals.

Zara's segmentation strategy is based on its customer demographics: gender, age, psychographics and preferred fashion style (e.g., classic, contemporary, Latino). It seeks to provide its customers with trendy, hip, high-fashion products at competitive prices. Zara markets directly to women and men aged 15 to 45 and to children. Their customers are fashion-conscious, educated, middle-class, working people who are interested in the latest fashion trends. Zara's marketing positions the brand as a product that democratises fashion: a high-fashion, low-cost strategy.

Zara spends little on direct advertising – just 0.3 per cent of revenue. Most traditional retailers spend 3–4 per cent of revenue on advertising.[94] Zara reaches the target market by investing funds in new stores in prime town-centre locations instead of investing in advertising. The marketing strategy is based on exclusivity, experience, differentiation and affordability. Zara's products are only available in Zara's retail stores (high-street stores or online). This creates exclusivity for the brand. This decision (whilst an expensive choice for Zara) is an example of successful critical capacity building based on strategic thinking (reflecting Axiom 2–style activities).

Design capability

Zara's designers each create around three items of new clothing a day, and their pattern makers cut one sample for each design. In total, Zara's internal processes enable designers to create approximately 40,000 new designs annually, from which around 10,000 are selected for production. Zara operates three parallel but operationally separate product families for its women's, men's and children's lines. Each product family has separate teams for design, sales, procurement and production planning.[95] This is unusual for a fashion designer and retailer: most would streamline what could be considered as redundant roles across the product families.

This integrated approach creates a successful product design framework for Zara. Trained commercial sales specialists from each region form close relationships with customers

94. Ferdows, Lewis, & Machuca, 2005.

95. Denning, 2012.

and identify changing needs and emerging trends. This information is then passed on to Zara's designers who seek to respond by delivering new designs for their customers at the right place and at the right moment.

Zara's approach to product design is difficult for other companies to copy. This is reflected through the leadership's vision (rigorous thinking) in its formulation of strategy, complemented with their management mission (fast thinking), resulting in superior returns on capital. Through creating non-replicable competitive advantage, Zara is able to allocate programs that replenish and sustain its competitive advantage and its distinctive capabilities.

Retail fashion consumers have a propensity towards new products. Zara capitalises on this by producing 10,000–12,000 new styles every year. In comparison, the average fashion retailer may produce 3,000 styles. Zara's approach means that new fashion trends reach their stores quickly. As a result, Zara's customers visit stores frequently, with an average customer visitation rate of 17 times a year, compared with the average of three times per year for other retailers.[96] This means that Zara has more opportunities to engage with customers, whilst offering a wider range of choice and enjoying a higher chance of offering what customers want. The wide range of styles means that each store offers more opportunities for customers to find a winning style, giving Zara a competitive advantage. The company's deliberate excess capacity strategy in its manufacturing means that it can always respond quickly to unexpected demand.[97]

Zara's recognition that it required improved forward architecture (connection with its consumers in the market) and superior distribution channels were critical factors in developing its external environment. Staff in Zara's stores report on sales frequently. Sales information is captured through sophisticated information processing. This enables the company to target its products to the places where they are most likely to sell. Different products are sold in different parts of the world. If a product does not sell well in one store, it can be moved to another store.

Supply chain and competitive pricing

Zara designs most of its products in Europe and uses low-cost factories (mainly in Asia) for production. Before committing to production, Zara tests samples. This facilitates rapid product replacement, and enables Zara to sample many different designs. Zara's internal processes of manufacturing and supply chain capabilities allow it to maintain low levels of inventory across the supply chain and replenish as often as twice a week.

96. Harbott, 2011.

97. Toyota has a similar strategy of retaining some excess capacity by running only two shifts in some manufacturing plants.

This is an important part of Zara's business strategy because holding large volumes of inventory is risky and can lead to heavy discounting or outright waste.

Critical to Zara's competitive advantage is its efficient, rapid-response supply chain management. Zara delivers customer orders within approximately 24 hours in Europe, the Middle East and much of the United States, and within 48 hours in Asia and Latin America. The company can design, produce and deliver a product, and display it in its worldwide stores within 15 days. This pace is unknown is most fashion businesses, where designers typically spend months planning for the next season.[98]

Zara also uses a just-in-time (JIT) inventory system management strategy to ensure that material orders from suppliers arrive in stores on time.[99] This system implements and supports a certain amount of its production in-house and ensures its own factories reserve most of their capacity for in-season adjustments. Zara fulfills orders centrally, which enables the company to maintain efficient processes from initial design right through to delivery. The supply chain is coordinated to ensure deliveries are systematic. Trucks leave at scheduled times with all garments fully labelled and priced, ready to be displayed immediately on arrival.

Zara implemented processes and procedures, and communicated these both internally and externally to provide fast-tracked links with customers directly through its retail network. The company decided not to rely on distribution channels such as department stores and other avenues, and instead invested in its own direct retail outlets. This decision enabled it to have on-time and rapid understanding of trends in its different markets. Zara implemented internal communication mechanisms that achieved two outcomes: 1) to integrate information about fashion trends and customer preferences from retail outlets back to the headquarters in Spain, and 2) to cascade information and products to its retail outlets.

The combined impact of the company's ability to forecast demand accurately, use in-house production, achieve high-quality workmanship and maintain relations with long-term material suppliers allows Zara to be flexible in the number, frequency and variety of new products to be launched. Whilst this just-in-time model is highly effective, it does bring some risks: Zara's production may suffer if it experiences unanticipated delays due to weather events, labour strikes, terrorist disruption or machinery breakdown, and this could have a serious impact on sales as it has no alternative supply centres in Europe. However, Zara controls the quantity of each style. Through this, it creates the perception of scarcity in customers' viewpoints, which increases the desirability of its products.

98. Denning, 2012.

99. This has similar features to Toyota's approach in the automotive industry.

Scarcity means that customers must buy quickly, as the item may not be available after a short time. This lowers the risk of unsold stock and leaves little stock to be disposed of at the end of each season. Zara only discounts around 18 per cent of its stock in sales, approximately half the industry average.

Conclusion

The fashion retail industry and market are competitive and difficult. Few companies have the privilege of sustained profits. Zara's model of 'fast fashion' creates a competitive advantage in three ways: 1) by giving customers what they want (a constantly changing choice of apparel and accessories at attractive prices, closely following fashion trends), 2) by getting products to customers faster than competitors (a centralised supply system with short delivery windows), and 3) by creating product scarcity with small product runs and limited editions (increasing product desirability).

Zara is well known for its high-fashion, cost-effective business model, making its products attractive for the young market who pursue fashion with little disposable income. Zara provides consumers what they want at a low price, resulting in a competitive advantage over its competitors due to its successful internal capabilities.

The company's value proposition is facilitated by an internal and external value chain configuration that involves a creative team of designers and strong collaborative ties with textile producers. The foundation to these success factors is that Zara uses its flow variables (processes, procedures and communication) in a combined coordination and cooperation tactic that builds its own stock variables (knowledge, efficiency, quality) resulting in a competitive advantage. The result is a system that is difficult for competitors to copy.

Zara's sales and distribution networks and its ability to understand fashion trends are difficult (if not impossible) for its competitors to replicate within a reasonable timeframe. The cost and resources required for replication in a short timeframe are likely to render any benefits redundant. Moreover, a takeover of an entity like Zara would require a premium to be paid, which would bid away the future economic gains of such a move. The company, therefore, continues to attract superior returns based on its competitive advantage through its strategic process. This involves understanding its desired strategic outcome, then formulating and implementing the relevant steps whilst constantly evaluating its position.

Careful sales and supply chain management (Axiom 1–style implementation activities with clearly defined processes, procedures and communication) are a prerequisite to Zara's success. Very little is left to chance (an Axiom 2 formulation that provides clear vision forward).

Amazon.com Inc.

Amazon was started as an online bookseller by Jeff Bezos and his wife MacKenzie in 1994, and rapidly expanded to sell other products. Today, Amazon is the largest online retailer in the world with very high levels of customer loyalty and profitability.

From the beginning, Bezos's vision was to create an 'everything store' – focusing on selection, price and convenience to revolutionise the way people shop and to dominate e-commerce. He began by selling books. His rationale was that books would sell well online because of their global market, low unit price and large number of available titles. By 1997, Bezos promoted Amazon as the world's largest bookstore. Amazon also had a significant impact on the e-book market, with its Kindle e-book reader launched in November 2007. Since the early 2000s, Amazon has developed into a retailer of nearly every product imaginable.

Amazon gradually developed into a retail website to create an online community of consumers, where people could help each other to find and rate products. This was achieved by adding personalised features that enabled customers to add reviews and by developing a system of recommending products based on customers' purchasing history.

Bezos has always been a 'game resolver' – an individual who successfully resolves logistical issues and business processes whilst also maintaining an ability to innovate and recognise the best ways to move the business forward.[100] As Amazon's leading entrepreneur, Bezos seems able to continually improve and refine his overall ability to apply the most relevant mode of thinking. He adopts fast, intuitive responses where needed, interchangeable with rigorous, in-depth thinking as required. This ability to synthetically judge the most appropriate mode of thinking for a specific context is, itself, significantly linked to positive outcomes in Amazon.

Business philosophy and structure

Amazon's 2018 financial report included a reprint of a 1997 letter to shareholders where the company emphasised Amazon's goal to move quickly – to solidify and extend their current position whilst pursuing online commerce opportunities in other large markets they were targeting. Bezos noted the strategy was not without risk: it required serious investment and crisp execution against established franchise leaders:

> ... to continue to solidify and extend our brand and customer base. ... This requires sustained investment in systems and infrastructure to support outstanding customer convenience, selection, and service while we grow.[101]

100. Demonstrating Axiom 1–style implementation activities and Axiom 2–style formulation perspectives.

101. Amazon, 2019.

Amazon's successful philosophy is guided by four principles:

- Customer obsession rather than competitor focus – through a generic strategy of cost leadership and low prices to attract consumers
- Passion for invention (such as Amazon CloudWatch, a cloud-based monitoring and observing service)
- Commitment to operational excellence
- Long-term thinking, focused on online retail, global growth and leadership.

These elements:

- Demonstrate a clearly selected strategic direction based on external markets and internal resource requirements
- Reinforce Amazon's application of formulation activities – rigorous, creative, thoughtful problem solving that builds stock variables and changes the way work is done (with their implementation achieved through Axiom 1–style activities)
- Show Amazon's commitment to operational activities and continuous improvement through the rigorous application of processes, procedures and communication.

Amazon progressively established a forward architecture (links with customers) to extensively assess its external environment as part of its strategy formulation. The company's mission is linked to the first principle mentioned above: customer focus. Bezos has spread the customer focus philosophy to every corner of the business. This drives Amazon to relentlessly gather customer feedback and offer very high levels of customer service. Amazon's customer service centres provide 24/7 support, and customers are offered a replacement on any problematic product. This customer focus creates loyalty and encourages clients to return to Amazon for their next search and purchase.

Amazon's products, services and divisions are vertically integrated to create internal synergies. Department names and structures are dynamic and change often. Amazon operations are divided into three segments: 1) online retailer in North America, 2) online retailer internationally, and 3) Amazon Web Services (AWS). These segments reflect the way the company evaluates its business performance and manages its operations, with strategic e-commerce goals based on the economic conditions of each geographical market.

Amazon's organisational structure is flexible, designed to adapt to changes in the external marketplace. It is structured into eight function-based groups: office of the CEO, business development, AWS, consumer business, international consumer business, finance, accounting, and legal and secretariat. Amazon's product categories are divided into four groups, as shown in Figure 58. Whilst Amazon began as a retailer of books and became a retailer of any product, it is now a retailer of 'everything', with its retail interests moving into web services and online content delivery.

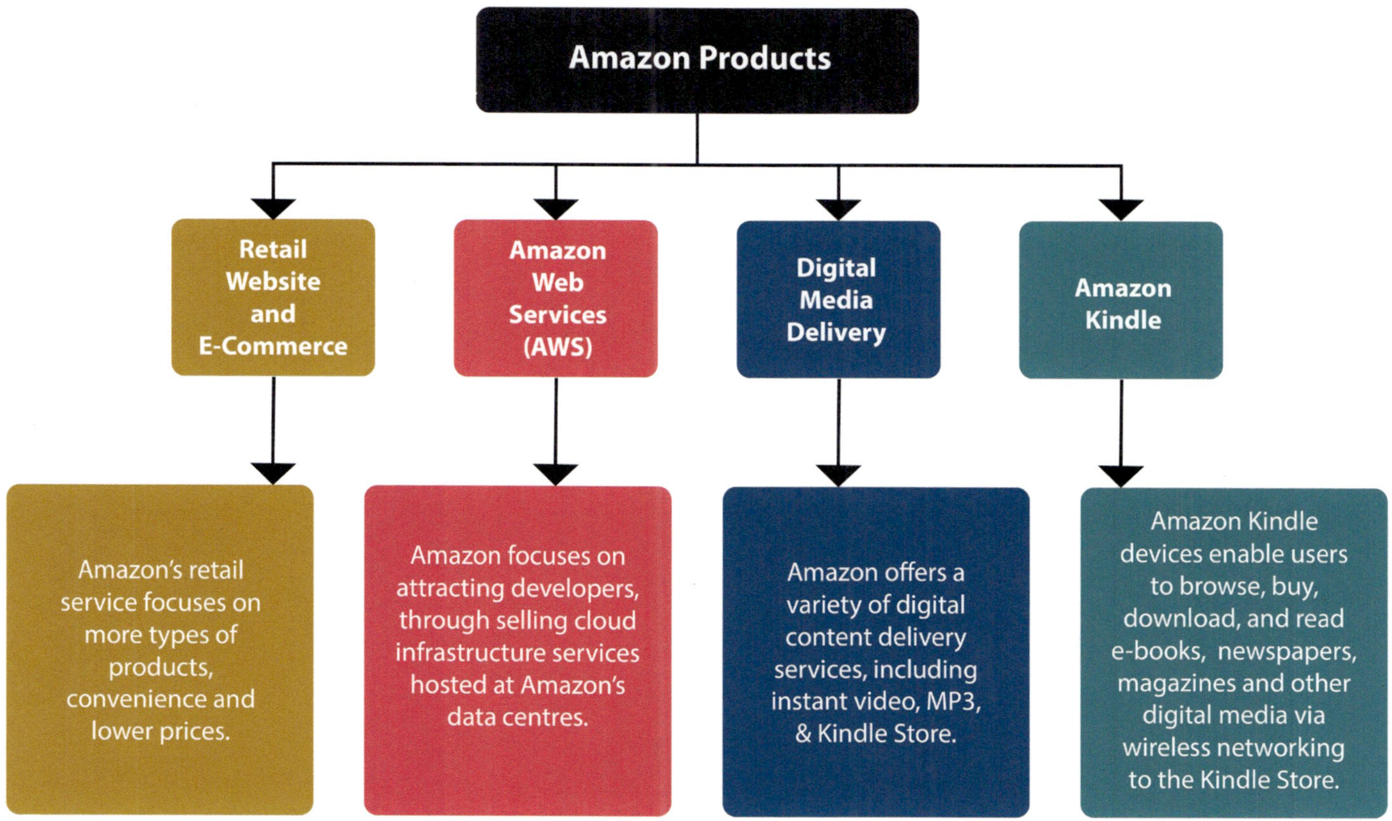

Figure 58: Main divisions of Amazon[102]

102. Chart developed by Sentinel 9 using information from multiple sources.

Amazon CloudWatch is a component of AWS. It is a monitoring and management service for developers, system operators, site reliability engineers and IT managers. It is the web-based service that provides monitoring for AWS resources and applications. CloudWatch's functions are described in Figure 59. CloudWatch provides users with online monitoring and management through a single platform – including visibility into resource utilisation, operational performance and overall demand patterns (including metrics like CPU utilisation and network traffic).

Amazon's move into CloudWatch resulted from its gap analysis of external opportunities versus available internal capabilities. The company identified internal resources and capabilities (from its book and online delivery system) that could be extended into a newly contested, external market. More recently, Amazon has achieved this with TV streaming and database management.

Amazon maintains competitive advantage in cloud computing through its consistent application of its underlying philosophy – including its customer focus, commitment to operational excellence and long-term thinking. The effect for CloudWatch is the same as the effect for retail products: capacity building and resource building have generated economies of scale, allowing Amazon to reduce up-front costs to customers and create a competitive advantage.

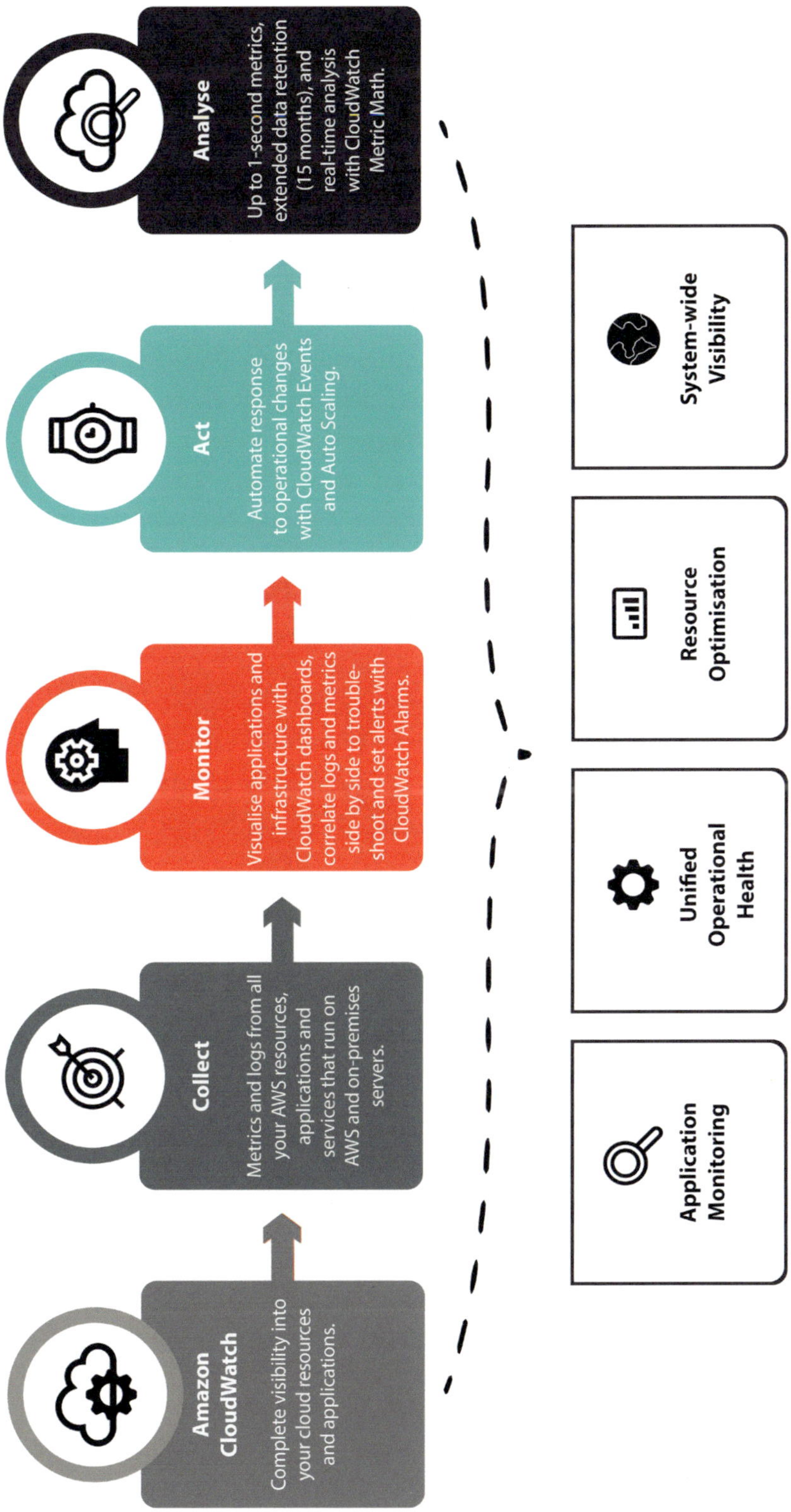

Figure 59: Amazon CloudWatch – How it works[103]

103. Amazon CloudWatch. Available: https://aws.amazon.com/cloudwatch/

Capacity for low-cost delivery

Amazon has accumulated competitive advantage through continuous improvement of its information technology infrastructure. Its processes and procedures use advanced computing and networking technologies for maximum operational efficiency across all aspects of the business. By fine-tuning its processing, scheduling and operational processes, Amazon has built stock variables – such as a reputation for reliability and efficiency, a trusted brand name and customer loyalty. It has achieved these stock variables through cost minimisation and continuous improvement of its processes and procedures.

Amazon has massive warehousing facilities and processing capability. It holds a wide selection of products and services, operates an efficient supply chain to fulfil orders, and provides excellent customer service. Its processes and reputation have allowed Amazon to benefit from (fixed assets) economies of scale, which give it a cost advantage. Amazon's success has been enhanced by efficient capacity planning and building, particularly related to the IT resources needed to ensure customers' orders are met and service providers' costs are recovered. It has a strong reputation for investing in research and development as part of its strategic objective to enhance efficiency, reduce costs and, as a result, reduce prices to attract consumers.

Amazon, therefore, has built distinctive capabilities with critical capacity commensurate with the requirements of its external environment. These latter requirements, Amazon identified successfully in its formulation stages during its formative years.

Conclusion

Amazon started as an online book seller. Bezos's strategic approach built Amazon into the world's largest e-commerce company because of his ability to understand and deliver on the requirements of the external environment: low price and reliable delivery service. Consumers choose Amazon because it has resources to cater for these criteria better than other suppliers.

Amazon's competitive advantage comes from its combination of product range, competitive prices, customer service and continuous innovation. Amazon's business philosophy has built strong strategic resources (stock variables) – of customer trust. These strategic resources help Amazon to sustain its competitive advantage by lowering the clients' transaction costs of procuring online goods and providing suppliers with a platform for selling their products.

Amazon understood the requirements of its external environments and proceeded to build corresponding capabilities internally that could directly cater to these requirements. This was evident in the formation years of Amazon, when its general online sales of books and other products were successful. However, its original offerings had limited scope, particularly with the entrance of other online portals such as eBay.

Amazon's regular take-up of new business opportunities reflects both leadership vision and a rigorous approach to thinking, translated into formulation and well-matched with an iterative fast-thinking approach to mission. This trend is discernible along Amazon's history. The company seems able to allocate resources for building capacity and programs that replenish and sustain their position. Moreover, they are careful not to overburden the business with new programs. They achieve sustainable growth by pitching capacity building at the right level, to benefit the business without overburdening it. Amazon then extended its internal resources and applied them across new markets. By extending its markets whilst retaining the consistency of its internal operations, Amazon created competitive advantage and achieved superior returns, rendering it one of the largest corporations in world history.

Appendix: Concepts and theories

This appendix summarises key theoretical concepts, tools and theories employed in configuring the Unified Theory of Business Strategy (UTBS) discussed in the main body of this book. It also provides references that offer additional detail. The appendix is structured into three sections:

1. Theoretical concepts in economics and business
2. Strategic tools used in developing a business plan
3. Background theories of business strategy.

Part 1: Theoretical concepts in economics and business

Balanced scorecard

The balanced scorecard (Kaplan & Norton, 1996) is a management system used to identify and improve various internal business functions and their resulting external outcomes. Data collection focuses on providing quantitative results as managers and executives gather and interpret the information and use it to measure performance, provide feedback and make better decisions for the organisation. A mix of financial and non-financial items are measured, often divided into four perspectives (financial, customer, internal process, and learning and growth). This assists in focusing on the firm's big-picture strategic goals. It also helps the firm choose the right things to measure.

Bounded rationality

The concept of bounded rationality (used in social sciences) recognises that decision-making is limited (or bounded) by a range of factors including access to information, knowledge, capacity and time. Decision-makers are facilitators, who see an adequate solution rather than an ideal one. Both the decision-making process and the individual decision-maker will influence the decision that is made. Rationality is bounded and limited due to the cognitive constraints of decision-makers. They may adopt short cuts in dealing with complex information that could result in suboptimal decisions.

Business costs

The goal of an organisation is to maximise profit, which is equal to revenue minus costs. Three types of costs are relevant in decision-making:[104]

- Explicit costs, related to direct payments made in the course of running a business, such as wages, rent and materials
- Implicit costs, related to an organisation's resources, which are used to calculate economic profit but are ignored when calculating accounting profit
- Opportunity costs, related to a benefit or value of something that is given up when acquiring or achieving something else.

Economic costs are equal to explicit costs and implicit costs. Explicit costs can be further broken down into fixed and variable costs, which combine to equal total costs.

- Variable costs (direct costs) are costs determined by the level of production, which will (in the short- to medium-term) vary according to the volume of activity.
- Fixed costs (overheads) are the costs associated with running businesses that must be paid (in the short- to medium-term) regardless of the level of production.

Capital Asset Pricing Model (CAPM)

The Capital Asset Pricing Model (CAPM) describes the relationship between systematic risk and expected return. The model caters for pricing risky securities and generating expected returns on assets, given the systematic risks involved and the cost of capital. CAPM uses a formula to calculate expected return whilst accounting for the time value of money (called the risk-free rate) and the risk the potential investment will add to a market portfolio (via the *beta* volatility measure of the underlying investment). It helps investors evaluate whether an asset is fairly valued when its risk and the time value of money are taken into account and compared with the expected return. Even though CAPM is not a perfect model, it is widely used because it is simple and facilitates comparative analysis.

Correlation and causation

Correlation and causation refer to the relationship, if any, between two variables.

Correlation

Correlation means that two variables are related. The correlation coefficient measures the strength of the relationship between movement of two variables. A coefficient value greater than zero indicates a positive correlation; a coefficient value below zero indicates

104. See also the discussion of transaction costs in this section.

a negative correlation. Generally, it is only when the value is at least 0.8 (or -0.8) that the correlation is considered strong (1.0 indicates a perfect positive correlation and -1.0 indicates a perfect negative correlation). A correlation coefficient of zero indicates no relationship.

Causation

Causation means that one variable directly results in another (cause and effect). Causal relationships between variables can be further described as either unidirectional or bidirectional. In unidirectional relationships, one entity affects another. For example, smoking cigarettes increases the risk of lung cancer. In bidirectional relationships, the effect flows both ways. For example, deforestation leads to decreased rainfall, and decreased rainfall negatively affects forest regrowth.

A spurious causation can be incorrectly perceived when variables only appear to have causal interactions. For example, imagine that sales of sunscreen increase in summer each year. During the same period, the incidence of jellyfish stings also increases. Any connection between sunscreen sales and jellyfish stings is caused by a third variable (in this case, the number of people going to the beach). There is no direct causal relationship between sunscreen and jellyfish and it would be incorrect (spurious) to conclude otherwise.

Economic value added (EVA) and cash flow return on investment (CFROI)

Economic value added (EVA) is a measure of a company's financial performance that focuses on the value generated by the resources invested. It is calculated by deducting the cost of capital from the operating profit. A positive EVA shows the company is generating economic value from the capital employed in it. Conversely, a negative EVA indicates the company is not generating economic value from its capital.

Cash flow return on investment (CFROI) is a valuation model based on cash flow (rather than on corporate performance and earnings) related to the cost of capital. It is calculated by cash flow divided by average capital employed. CFROI can be compared to a hurdle rate to determine whether the business is performing adequately, giving insight into a company's internal operations and its earning capacity.

Externalities

An externality can be defined as the impact of an economic agent's actions on the status of another agent where the first may not receive full compensation and the second may not pay for the effect. An externality can either be negative (costs) or positive (benefits).

Positive externalities are usually when other parties benefit for free. For example, society may benefit from the new knowledge generated by a company's research and development activities. Negative externalities occur when effects are costly to other parties. Examples of negative externalities are organisations that produce air pollution or spill contaminants, which have a significant adverse effect on other parties.

Game theory – concepts

Game theory was invented by John von Neumann in 1937, and further extended by von Neumann and Morgenstern (1944). Game theory is a method of analysing strategic decision -making. It considers strategic interactions – that is, the ways people act when they take into account the expected behaviours of others and the mutual recognition of interdependence. It is relevant for understanding political, military and general business strategy.

A game is any situation in which players make strategic decisions – that is, decisions that take into account each other's actions and responses. Game theory has three important concepts:

- Rules: The game assumes players are rational (they think through the consequences of their actions)
- Strategies: Games involve a strategic plan of action (players maximise the expected payoff), strategic decisions (which involve longer-term commitments) and tactical decisions (short-term responses to the current environment). A dominant strategy is an optimal action no matter what an opponent does. It always gives a better payoff to the player, regardless of what the other players do. When all players have a dominant strategy, the outcome can be described as 'equilibrium in dominant strategy' – each player does the best they can, regardless of what competitors do
- Payoffs: A utility or monetary value that reflects the desirability of an outcome to a player. When the outcome is random, payoffs are usually weighted with their probabilities. The expected payoff incorporates the player's attitude (i.e., coefficient of risk aversion) towards risk.

Threats and rewards

Threats and rewards are used to instigate and influence the actions of players. Making a threat indicates that deciding to oppose a given instruction will result in a (punishment in the form of) a negative payoff. Offering a reward promises a positive payoff in return for compliance.

Threats and rewards can be used to induce or deter players' actions and must be credible and proportionally scaled in the given scenario. If these are not credible or scaled to the game, they will not influence players' responses. A classic example of a non-credible threat is parents who threaten to turn the car around on the way to a family holiday in response to children's poor behaviour. It is highly unlikely that parents will cancel the holiday. The threat is out of scale and unlikely to work more than once – with low credibility.

Player's information set and asymmetry

A player's information set is available to them when choosing their game strategy. Information may be perfect (complete) or imperfect (incomplete). With perfect information, players know everything that has happened in the game so far at the time of choosing their action. Chess is an example of a game with perfect information at each point of the game.

Information asymmetry occurs when individuals or organisations lack some of the information held by the other party. Having access to more information allows a business to gain a relative advantage and a stronger market position. There are positive kinds of information asymmetry, such as internal organisational knowledge to produce a unique product or develop a new process that is difficult for others to replicate. There are also dishonest or illegal forms of information asymmetry, such as insider trading. The prisoner's dilemma and poker are examples of games with incomplete information (Peirson, 2017).

Zero-sum and negative-sum games

A game is said to be zero-sum if, for any outcome, the net sum of the payoffs to all players is zero. In a two-player zero-sum game, one player's gain is the other player's loss, so their interests are diametrically opposed.

In a positive-sum game, all players receive a positive payoff no matter what the outcome is. For instance, imagine a carnival game where players compete for the top prize, yet all entries receive a participation reward. The goal is to win the top prize and gain the largest payoff, but all players nonetheless enjoy a gain by taking part.

In a negative-sum game, all players make a loss in any outcome. Despite their comparative wins or losses, all players are left with less than they had before. An example of this is an organisation which makes company-wide budget cuts. The commonly referred to condition of 'damage minimisation' is another example of a negative-sum game (Barron, 2013; Turocy & von Stengel, 2001).

Repeated and sequential games

Repeated games involve actions and payoffs happening over and over again. In a repeated (or multiple-shot) game, players have opportunities to amend their strategy and respond to the other players' moves There are two types of repeated games: infinite repeated games (where the game is played for ever) and finite repeated games (where the game is repeated for a set number of rounds).

Games offer players different numbers of moves or chances. The consequences of players' decisions vary, depending on the number of moves players can make. In a one-shot game, players have only one chance to formulate and implement their game strategy; they win or lose based on that decision. In a multiple-shot game, players have opportunities to amend their strategy and respond to the other players' moves. The prisoner's dilemma is a one-shot game. Chess is a multiple-shot game, where players generally formulate a strategy ahead of time, but make decisions move-to-move depending on the actions of the other player.

A sequential game involves players moving in turn, responding to each other's actions and reactions. Sequential games can be visualised as a decision tree (an extensive form of a game). Whilst both players are making moves, one will outperform the other. For example, the first mover has an advantage (in the same way that a business entering a new market gains an advantage over its rivals) (Owen, 2013).

Nash equilibrium

Nash equilibrium proposes that, in strategic games, each player will act for their best advantage with respect to other players. A Nash equilibrium exists when each player adopts a strategy that cannot be improved, provided that other players also follow the overall recommended strategy. Players are assumed to be rational, so they will not deviate from this recommended strategy because there is no way for them to benefit individually through such deviation. A key property of a Nash equilibrium is stability: players can be expected to follow the recommendation because it is in the best interest of each player.

Market structure and possible failure

Economists hypothesise different market structures: perfect competition, monopoly, oligopoly and monopolistic competition. These market structures are defined and distinguished from each another in terms of the number and size of buyers and sellers of the product, and the type of product bought and sold. Market structure is relevant to an organisation because it influences business decisions in order to form price setting, advertising strategies and profitability.

Perfect competition

In a perfectly competitive market, there are many buyers and sellers. All participants have complete knowledge about traded products and prices. As a result, the actions of any single buyer or seller have a negligible impact on market price. Entry to and exit from the market is unrestricted, resulting in numerous competitors, none of which can influence the price of the traded product. These market participants become price takers. Firms in a perfectly competitive market tend to only generate normal (expected) returns.

Monopoly

A monopoly is an industry where one supplier produces a product or service with no close substitute and there is a barrier to new suppliers entering the market. Since there is only one supplier, that firm has the ability to influence the market price. Barriers to entry are an important feature of a monopoly. Legal barriers to entry can create monopoly, where competition and entry are restricted by the granting of a monopoly franchise or government licence. Natural barriers to entry may also create a monopoly, where one organisation can supply the entire market at a lower price than two or more organisations (e.g., an electricity utility) or where one firm owns the essential resources (e.g., raw materials).

Oligopoly

An oligopoly is a market with only a few sellers, each offering a product similar to or slightly different from others. An oligopoly can be identified by determining the concentration ratio, which means the percentage share of the total industry accounted for by the few largest firms in the industry. The characteristics of oligopoly include high barriers to entry, a small number of organisations each with large market share, firms with an ability to be price-makers, interdependency, and the temptation to cooperate/collude to increase joint profit. Many theories have been developed to explain and predict oligopolistic pricing behaviour (such as game theory).

Monopolistic competition

Monopolistic competition suggests the market contains elements of both monopoly and competition. In monopolistic competition, barriers to entry are relatively low, so new organisations can enter the industry. There are enough sellers for competitive behaviour, so sellers need to compete in order to stand out from the rest. The main characteristics of monopolistic competition include a large number of firms, where products are slightly differentiated from each other. Firms compete (on quality, price, marketing and branding), and are free to enter and exit the market. Examples include the clothing or computer retail industry, car dealerships (not manufacturers) and petrol stations.

Market failure

A market is a place where two parties can gather to exchange goods and services. In this theoretical, optimal, perfect market structure, a reallocation of resources within the market cannot make one person better off without making someone else worse off (called Pareto optimality). However, this may not always occur, and the result is market inefficiency.

Market failure refers to the inability of an unregulated market to achieve allocative efficiency under a free structure. Key reasons for market failure include government interventions (taxes, subsidies, quotas and price controls) and information asymmetry. Pareto optimality assumes that producers and consumers have perfect information regarding market behaviour. However, in the real world, there is asymmetric information, creating uncertainty on the part of buyers and sellers, rendering decisions that have to be based on incomplete information.

Multiplier effect

The multiplier effect occurs when a given change in an input to the economy (by government and/or consumer expenditure) results in a greater change in real economic output (GDP). For example, a government may fund an organisation to revitalise a dilapidated piece of land. In turn, the organisation employs architects, engineers, construction workers and designers. Each of these source goods from other businesses to complete their work. The government's original injection of cash into the local economy has multiplied into income for a range of businesses and workers, who will, in turn, spend their funds towards other entities (multiplier spending).

Profit maximisation

Profit maximisation is an assumption of classical economics and, all things being equal, profitability becomes the main driver of businesses. Profitability is essential for business survival and growth, capital and inventory investment, acquisitions, dividends and compensation for investment risk. Therefore, economic agents have an objective they are trying to optimise:

- Individual consumers seek to maximise utility
- Business firms maximise profits (or minimise costs)
- Not-for-profit entities maximise output.

Without optimising either utility, profit or output, there would be no incentive to invest and operate.

Second law of thermodynamics and entropy

The second law of thermodynamics is about the quality of energy. It states that, as energy is transferred or transformed, more and more of it is dispersed. The second law also states that there is a natural tendency for any isolated system to degenerate into a more disordered state. Any natural process in an isolated system progresses in the direction of increasing disorder, or entropy, of the system (Kondepudi, 2008).

To illustrate: when the sun shines on sand during the day, heat is transferred to the sand. At night, the heat is dispersed in the temperature of the beach. According to the first law of thermodynamics, energy cannot be created or destroyed, it can only be changed from one type to another. Therefore, all the sun's energy that reaches the beach during the day is captured by the sand and other surroundings. However, the status of this energy is not as useful as when it was embodied and concentrated in the sun (and is now more disorganised and dispersed). This tendency demonstrates the second law of thermodynamics for a system to move towards disorganisation and higher entropy.

Slack resources

Slack resources are the resources that an organisation may possess in excess of the minimum level it needs. A resource constraint, on the other hand, refers to an organisation with the minimum available resources it requires. Some commentators argue that a resource slack is positive, as it gives an organisation a level of protection from incidents that have a negative impact. Others believe that a resource slack could signal mismanagement or cause organisations to become complacent because there is diminished need to be resourceful or creative.

Transaction costs

Transaction cost theory was developed by Ronald Coase (1937) and Oliver Williamson (1975) to describe what individuals or organisations incur as part of a transaction. The theory postulates that hierarchical organisations may distribute resources more efficiently than an imperfect or limited bargaining system (like a market). There are three main types of transaction costs:

- Search and information costs – the costs of identifying a supplier or buyer
- Bargaining and decision costs – the costs of negotiating with a supplier or buyer
- Policing and enforcement costs – the costs of monitoring quality of received goods and services.

Transaction costs are important to economic agents because they are a key determinant of net returns. The way a business is organised can determine its control over transactions, and hence it costs. It is in the interests of management, at times, to internalise transactions to lower costs that may emanate from uncertainties about price and quality of external suppliers.

Velocity of money

In economics, the velocity of money refers to the speed at which the typical note or credit shifts around the economy. The same unit of money can be spent multiple times by different people (multiplier effect). Likewise, the speed at which economic agents spend money (and what portion of it they spend) tends to fluctuate.

Money velocity is a key input in calculating an economy's output and inflation. Money velocity should not be confused with the money supply of an economy. Supply refers to the total *amount* of money in circulation, whereas velocity is the *rate* of spending in the economy.

This means that an increased money supply may not necessarily equate to an increased economic output. The velocity of money may become a better indicator of the strength and vitality of an economy. This is because individuals and businesses tend to hoard money in times of economic uncertainty, rather than spend it (Gans, King, & Mankiw, 2014).

VUCA model

The VUCA model was introduced by the US Army and has since been adopted into business and leadership studies. It helps businesses to analyse and manage risk, through the four categories of volatility, uncertainty, complexity and ambiguity. These factors are used to assess the level of risk involved and determine an appropriate strategy for moving forward (Kinsinger & Walch, 2012).

- **Volatility** refers to situations that are unexpected, unpredictable or unstable. The unstable nature of the situation means it can change or vary violently, rapidly and disproportionally in unpredictable directions. A typical example of volatility is a natural disaster – the situation cannot be avoided, and it has significant effects.
- **Uncertainty** involves having some, but not all, of the information required to fully understand a situation or predict an outcome. This occurs because the prevailing state or conditions in future periods may not be discernible. Uncertainty may arise from not knowing how competitors will behave or what economic conditions might prevail in a future period. A situation may not be volatile, but may be uncertain.
- **Complexity** means that situations are complicated by the involvement of numerous interconnected and interdependent parts and variables. Complexity can be characterised by an absence of information or by an overwhelming volume (or surfeit) of information. Complexity often arises because the matter at hand is too intricate with respect to the observer's capacity to interpret and analyse. A situation may not be volatile or uncertain, but may be very complex.

- **Ambiguity** refers to a situation where the overall meaning, cause or effect are unknown, despite the available information. Such situations are often without precedent to guide decision-making. Ambiguity occurs when an observer does not fully know or understand the causal linkages within a context. A situation may be not volatile, uncertain or complex, but still be highly ambiguous.

The combination of the above factors creates a continuum relevant to deciding whether risk is manageable (non-systematic and diversifiable) or cannot be directly mitigated (systematic and non-diversifiable).

Weighted average cost of capital (WACC)

The weighted average cost of capital (WACC) is a financial measure that calculates a firm's aggregate cost of financing and acquiring assets with reference to the firm's debt and equity structure. WACC reflects the combined cost of debt and equity, with the proportional weighting of these in the total capital structure. It is calculated by the multiplication of the cost of equity and the portion of the equity, added to the cost of debt, multiplied by the proportion of debt. Once that WACC applicable to the optimal capital structure is achieved, additional debt may cause the WACC to rise, reflecting the added risk created by higher financial leverage. This measure is often employed as the discount rate in discount cash flow (DCF) analysis to create the present value of future cash flows. DCF is used for internal capital budgeting or business project valuation in mergers and acquisitions.

Part 2: Strategic tools used in developing a business plan

Blue ocean and red ocean

The concept of blue ocean and red ocean markets relates to whether market spaces are currently in use, with competing existing businesses. Blue ocean markets are untapped. They provide opportunities for new, innovative products and services, and opportunities for high growth. Businesses operating in blue ocean markets develop business strategies by creating new opportunities and responding to demand, rather than competing in existing industries. Red ocean markets are existing. Business operating in red ocean markets develop business strategies by focusing on their competition. They seek to win a bigger piece of a market that has set boundaries and can become oversaturated with less opportunity for profit and growth.

Blue ocean and red ocean markets both present risk. Blue ocean markets usually present greater opportunities for growth and profit, but there is a risk of overestimating demand.

In red ocean markets the risk is less acute, but businesses are entering a market where there are existing experienced competitors (Chan & Mauborgne, 2005).

Boston Consulting Group (BCG) Growth Share Matrix

The Boston Consulting Group created the Growth Share Matrix to assist organisations evaluate their products and services. It supports organisations to gain insights into what products best help them capitalise on market share growth opportunities. Businesses (or business units) are measured against their market growth rate and share of the market. Organisations can use the matrix to develop marketing strategies based on the ability of each product or service to generate profit. Figure 60 illustrates the Growth Share Matrix (Martin, 2018).

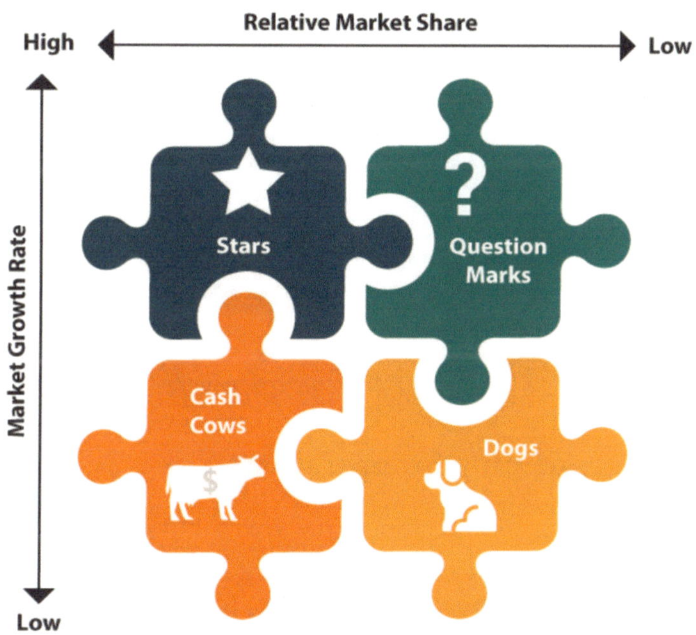

Figure 60: Boston Consulting Group Growth Share Matrix (Martin, 2018)

Five Forces

The Five Forces framework was created by Harvard Business Professor Michael Porter and has become one of the most useful and popular business strategy tools. It helps organisations to assess industry attractiveness, how trends will affect industry competition, which industries to compete in and how to position organisations for success. Porter (1996) identified five forces that make up the competitive environment, as illustrated in Figure 61.

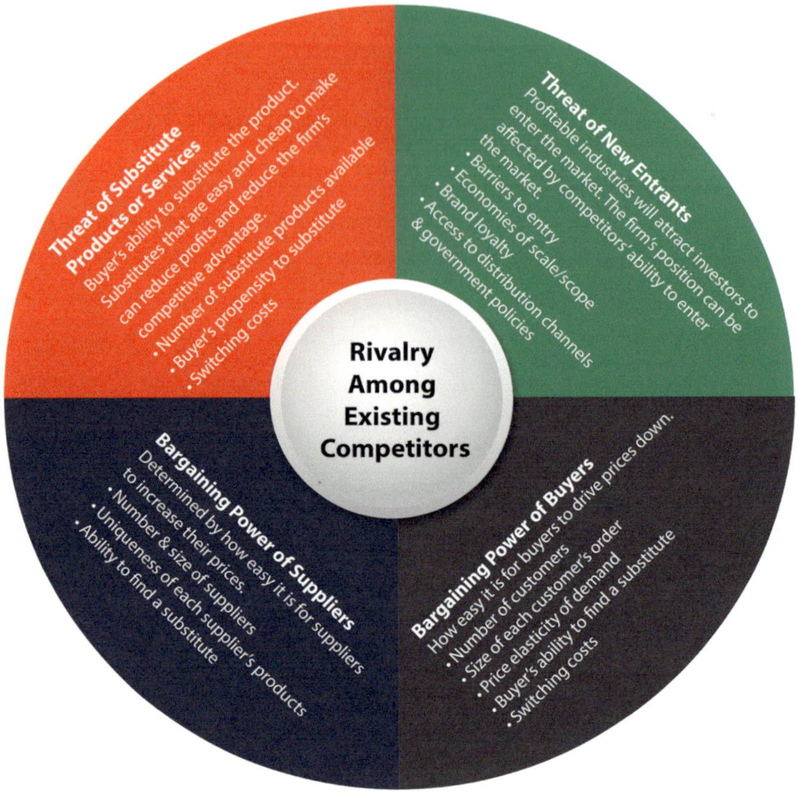

Figure 61: Porter's Five Forces, suitable for analysing market and industry structure

Five S (good housekeeping for operations)

Five S (good housekeeping for operations) involves the principle of waste elimination through workplace organisation, whilst maximising efficiency and profit. Five S comes from five Japanese words that roughly translate in English to sort, set in order, clean, standardise, and sustain. The Five S framework emphasises a specific mindset and tools to create efficiency and value. It also involves the practice of removing inefficiency by observing, analysing, collaborating and searching for waste. Five S provides the foundation for most quality management programs.

Kanban

Kanban is a workflow management method designed to help businesses visualise their work and maximise efficiency. It developed from a scheduling system used in Toyota's just-in-time production system, with production configured to consumer demand. Kanban methodology operates through a production board that provides real-time reporting. Work is visualised on the board (at its most simple level this may record work requested, in progress, and complete) and work in progress is limited to the extent possible. Explicit processes, procedures and policies are used to manage the workflow, and feedback loops are built into the production system (Kanbanize, 2020).

McKinsey Nine-Box framework

The Nine-Box framework was developed by McKinsey Consulting Group as an analytical tool for strategic business planning. The framework helps multi-business organisations to evaluate and prioritise investments among their businesses. The framework helps organisations decide which business units should receive more (or less) investment, what new products or business units are needed in the portfolio, and which products or business units should be diversified (McKinsey & Company, 2019; as illustrated in Figure 62).

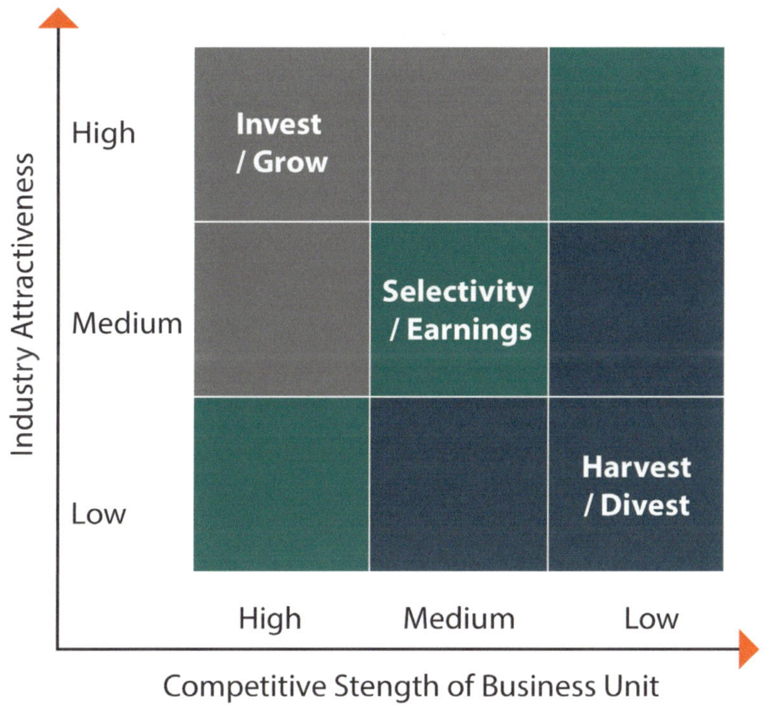

Figure 62: Nine-Box framework (McKinsey & Company, 2019)

PESTEL

PESTEL is an analytical tool used to support macroeconomic analysis. It considers external factors and helps to analyse their impact on the organisation or project (Aguilar, 1967). As illustrated in Figure 63, PESTEL helps organisations understand the big picture of their operating environment and may support them to minimise threats and take advantage of opportunities. This tool encourages organisations to think about the wider environment from both a short-term and long-term perspective.

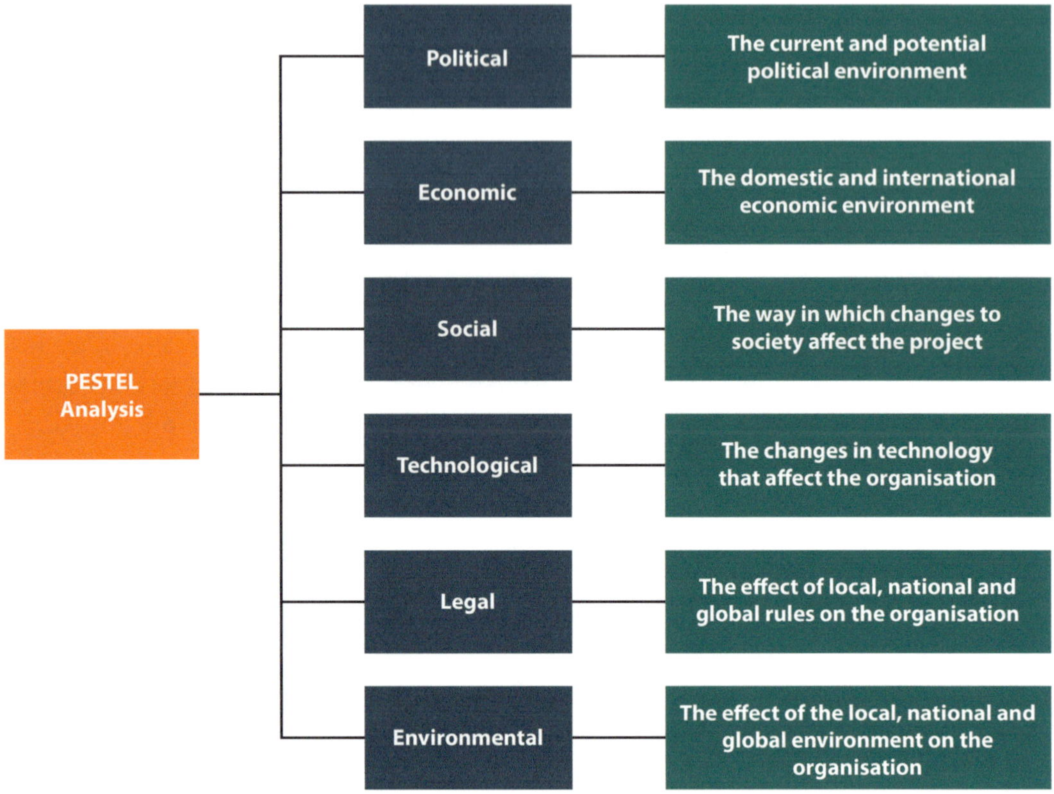

Figure 63: Elements of PESTEL analysis

SWOT

SWOT analysis, which was developed at Stanford Research Institute, is a technique for identifying an organisation's internal factors: strengths, weaknesses, opportunities and threats (as shown in Figure 64 below). SWOT analysis helps decision-makers address weakness and threats and to also capitalise on strengths and opportunities. SWOT analysis can identify key issues affecting an organisation, but it does not offer solutions.

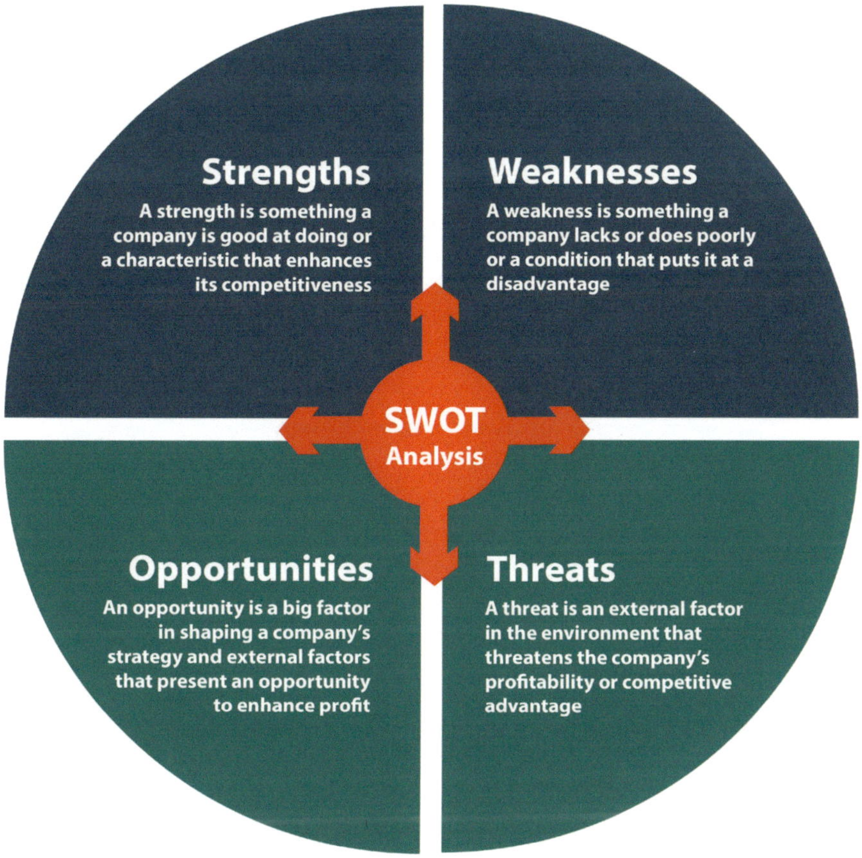

Figure 64: Main aspects of SWOT analysis

Total quality management (TQM)

Total quality management (TQM) is a management framework designed to build long-term success by having the organisation focus on improving quality and, thus, delivering customer satisfaction. The framework focuses on continuous improvement over the long term. TQM refers to customer requirements and postulates that improved quality is achieved through systematic analysis of workflows against external requirements. It is a continuous system.

Vision and mission

An organisation's vision is a summary of its ultimate goals: essentially, what it would like to achieve and what it would like to be known for in the future. A vision statement reflects an organisation's values and inspirations, and is intended to capture the heart and mind of each employee. It describes the future identity, is a source of inspiration and provides clear decision-making criteria (Hanson, Hitt, Ireland, & Hoskisson, 2017).

A mission is the organisation's business scope and fundamental purpose. A mission tends to be specific, indicating the industry the business intends to create, revolutionise or compete in, and who it will serve. A mission assists an organisation to move towards its vision, goals and objectives. It concentrates on the present by identifying the customer and critical processes, and informs the desired level of performance.

Taken together, the vision and mission help organisations to formulate business strategies. An organisation's vision tends to be longer term, whilst its mission can change in a medium-term response to economic, regulatory, environmental and market conditions (see Figure 65).

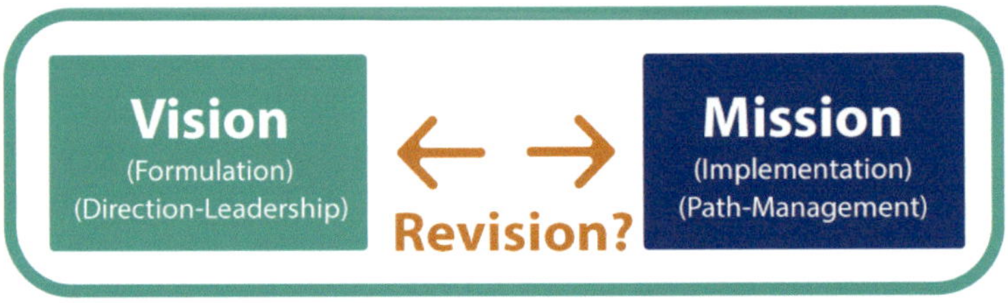

Figure 65: Review both vision and mission after the business plan has been compiled to ensure they are both pragmatic and credible

Part 3: Background theories of business strategy

Strategic management refers to the managerial process of forming a strategic vision, setting objectives, crafting a strategy, implementing and executing the strategy, and initiating corrective adjustments over time (Thomson & Strickland, 2001, p. 6). Key strategic management theories include:

- Profit-maximising theory (and competition-based theory) – based on the notion that the main objective of an organisation is to maximise profit. Competition-based theory suggests that organisations seek to develop sustainable competitive advantage over rivals in the marketplace
- Resource-based theory – a managerial framework used to analyse and determine the strategic resources that have the potential to enhance comparative advantage for the organisation (Barney, 1991)
- Survival-based theory – centres on the concept that organisations need to continuously adapt to their competitive environment in order to survive
- Market-based theories – centre on the industry and external market factors that determine profitability, with a focus on the strategies of cost leadership, differentiation and focus (Porter, 1980)

- Human resource-based theory – emphasises the importance of the human element in strategy development; highlights the motivation, politics and culture of organisations and the desire of individuals (Walker, 1978)
- Agency theory – used to explain and resolve issues in the relationship between principals (shareholders) and agents (managers); a central issue is the agency costs that stem from the 'divorce of ownership from control', where managers are responsible for money that is not their own (Bolton & Scharfstein, 1998; Jensen & Meckling, 1976)
- Contingency theory – used to explain that there is no best way to organise a company; the optimal strategy depends on prevailing internal and external factors at different times.

There are varied approaches to examining the feasibility and validity of the above theories:

- Process vs content approaches: The process approach involves formulating a business strategy through a series of activities, where the focus and scope deals with sequential identification, selection and implementation. The content approach, on the other hand, focuses on identifying parameters deployable by the organisation (e.g., product differentiation or niche market)
- Economic vs organisational approaches: The economic approach emphasises the need for organisations to develop their business strategy based on the microeconomic and macroeconomic conditions and the organisation's opportunities. This approach encourages a focus on the best way to position an organisation in terms of competition and the economic system. The organisational approach emphasises the organisational perspective and encourages a focus on improved internal components
- Internal vs external approaches: The internal approach suggests that organisations should develop strategies based on an analysis of their internal environment (resources, structure and culture). The external approach proposes that organisations should develop strategies based on an analysis of their external business environment (political, economic, social, cultural, technological, ecological, governmental and legal)[105]
- Prescriptive vs descriptive approaches: The prescriptive approach emphasises explicit, planned and logical processes. The process of formulating strategy is defined in advance and its specific components are decided before implementation. The prescriptive approach proposes the one optimal way to develop and implement organisational strategies for all types of organisations. The descriptive approach is concerned with the current reality and focuses on how organisational strategies are formulated and implemented in real organisations

105. The UTBS as presented in this book adopts and combines these two approaches.

- Competitive advantage approach: This focuses on the organisation's resources and distinctive capabilities as the basis for developing business strategy. Organisations can obtain their competitive advantage from resources (tangible and intangible) and capabilities (resource, skill, activity or capability) that are distinctive to those of competitors. This approach suggests that organisations should first identify their sources of competitive advantage before developing any business strategy.[106]

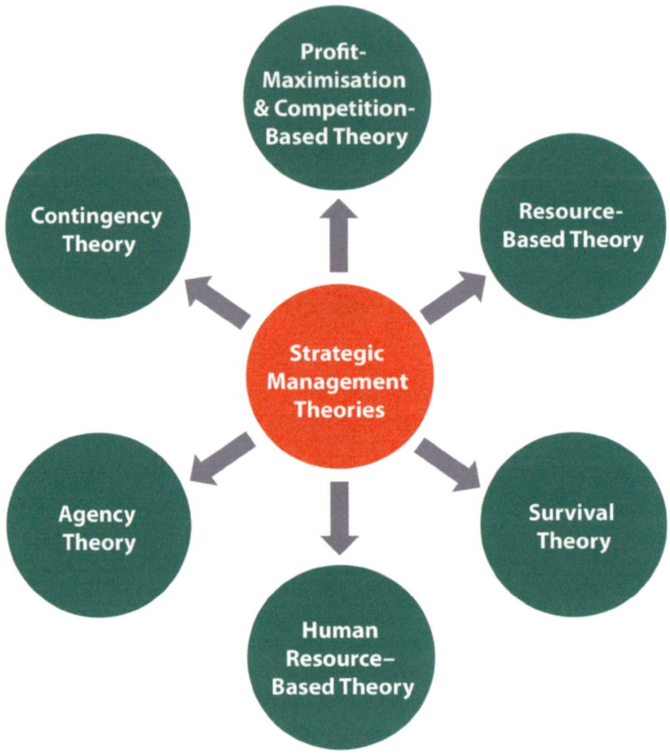

Figure 66: Some of the main schools of thought in strategic management theory

Competitive advantage

Competitive advantage is the basis for superior performance and can be obtained when an organisation develops or acquires a set of attributes (or executes actions) that allow it to outperform its competitors. A competitive advantage can increase profits whilst also enhancing the value for customers (Wang, 2014).

Competitive advantage can occur either because the organisation is able to deliver the same benefits as competitors, but at a lower average total cost, or because the organisation delivers benefits that exceed competitors' products. Porter (1987) notes that:

106. The UTBS as presented in this book also draws on this approach in conjunction with external environmental attributes.

> ... competitive advantage grows fundamentally out of the value a firm is able to create for its buyers that exceeds the firm's cost of creating it. Value is what buyers are willing to pay, and superior value stems from offering lower prices than competitors for equivalent benefits or providing unique benefits that more than offset a higher prices (p. 3).

Wang's (2014) research highlights two dominant theories of competitive advantage: market-based theory and resource-based theory. Alternative theories include the relational view of strategy, and transient advantage (see Figure 67).

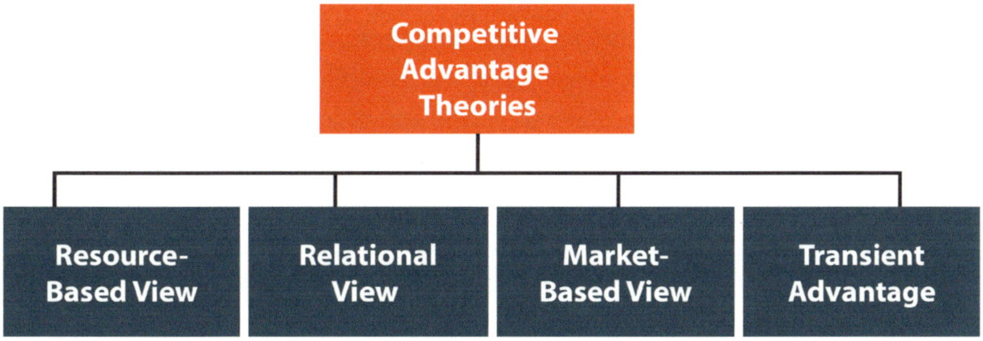

Figure 67: Some of the main theories of competitive advantage

Market-based view

Porter's (1987) market-based view is a widely used strategic approach to describe strategies for competitive advantage. It argues that the primary determinants of profitability or performance are industry and external market factors. To design an organisation's policies and strategy, the organisation must consider market trends and the nature of the industry's environment, then choose the adequate market combination for the product.

Michael Porter (1980) developed three generic business strategies for achieving above-average performance:

- Cost leadership – gaining competitive advantage by lowering prices to increase market share. A business can achieve this by lowering the costs of production, which will increase both sales and the business's profile
- Differentiation – gaining competitive advantage by crafting a product that is perceived as unique. The business may use marketing, high-quality product delivery, and research and development to create the perception of a unique product, allowing the business to charge an above-average price
- Focus – this has two variants: cost focus (the business seeks a cost advantage in selected target segments) and/or differentiation focus (the business seeks differentiation in other target segments).

Resource-based view

The resource-based view, developed by Penrose (1959), Wernerfelt (1984) and Barney (1991), focuses on how factors in the organisation's internal environment determine its competitive advantage. It also considers resources that organisations have developed to compete in the environment. The organisation's resources can be classified as physical, monetary and human (Ansoff, 1965). A firm's resources are a set of available factors owned or controlled by the organisation. These resources are converted into final products and services by using assets from other organisations and bonding mechanisms such as technology, information and incentive systems.

Capabilities refer to a firm's ability to deploy resources, usually in combinations, using organised processes. Capabilities also encompass the ability to take innovative action to create value for customers and achieve the goals and objectives of the firm. Capabilities are often information-based, tangible or intangible processes that are organisation-specific and developed over time (Amit & Schoemaker, 1993, p. 35). Business capabilities can be analysed in strategic planning processes; internal resources and core competencies derived from distinctive capabilities can provide the strategy platform that underlies an organisation's growth. Hooley and Broderick (1998) argue that the resource-based view ignores the nature of the market and focuses only on internal resources, which are important and should not be ignored, but are not sufficient. Amit and Shoemaker (1993) also argue that external market factors should not be ignored, because the organisation's internal and external conditions are linked.

Knowledge-based and transient view

The knowledge-based view argues that knowledge, know-how, intellectual assets and competencies are the main drivers of superior performance in the information era. Knowledge is the most important asset of any organisation. Grant (1991) explains that knowledge can be classified into two types: information and know-how. Tiwana (2012) highlights that competitors can copy technology, capital and product to gain market share, but it takes time to acquire knowledge. Knowledge, therefore, is more difficult to imitate.

Transient advantage theory argues that strategies should be formulated with the understanding that they will guide the organisation's behaviour for a prolonged period (McGrath, 2013). This means the dynamic business environment needs to be considered and strategies should be infrequently revised/reformulated.

Relational or network view

The relational view focuses on dyad/network routines and processes as an important unit of analysis for understanding competitive advantage (Dyer & Singh, 1998). The theory identifies four sources of competitive advantage: 1) relation-specific assets, 2) knowledge-sharing routines, 3) complementary resources and capabilities, and 4) effective governance. Wang (2014) defines a business structure as the arrangement of a formal or informal contract between different partners for buying, selling, collaboration or related business activity.

List of QR codes and links

Electronic versions of figures used in this book

https://www.sentinel9.com/utbs-diagrams/

Link to Planium Pro read-only version

https://www.planiumpro.com

Sentinel 9 Video: Part 1 – Conceptual Framework

https://www.youtube.com/watch?v=uYTN1kFF25E&list=PLOKcJXMjdgJDgGO7ZwWUHi29alQisS6ra&index=2&t=0s

Sentinel 9 Video: Part 2 – What is Strategy? Strategy vs Tactics

https://www.youtube.com/watch?v=N7DJy_AYLxM&list=PLOKcJXMjdgJDgGO7ZwWUHi29alQisS6ra&index=2

Sentinel 9 Video: Part 3 – Strategic Variables – Flow vs Stock

https://www.youtube.com/watch?v=2ghEBp95ATE&list=PLOKcJXMjdgJDgGO7ZwWUHi29alQisS6ra&index=3

Sentinel 9 Video: Part 4 – Strategic Games – Thinking Mode and Transaction Cost

https://www.youtube.com/watch?v=ti5q5kz7t-c&list=PLOKcJXMjdgJDgGO7ZwWUHi29alQisS6ra&index=4

Sentinel 9 Video: Part 5 – Strategic Axioms

https://www.youtube.com/watch?v=TaZhboieWjg&list=PLOKcJXMjdgJDgGO7ZwWUHi29alQisS6ra&index=5

Sentinel 9 Video: Part 6 – Definition of Risk – A Review

https://www.youtube.com/watch?v=zsthwgw62E0&list=PLOKcJXMjdgJDgGO7ZwWUHi29alQisS6ra&index=6

Sentinel 9 Video: Part 7 – What is Wealth?

https://www.youtube.com/watch?v=ZV56_NQcvuE&list=PLOKcJXMjdgJDgGO7ZwWUHi29alQisS6ra&index=7

Sentinel 9 Video: Part 8 – Business Strategy 1 – Underlying Concepts

https://www.youtube.com/watch?v=wGSFUv8HIW8&list=PLOKcJXMjdgJDgGO7ZwWUHi29alQisS6ra&index=8

Sentinel 9 Video: Part 9 – Business Strategy 2 – Applied Definitions

https://www.youtube.com/watch?v=zVXYoer_btY&list=PLOKcJXMjdgJDgGO7ZwWUHi29alQisS6ra&index=9

Sentinel 9 Video: Part 10 – Business Strategy 3 – Background Corporate Information

https://www.youtube.com/watch?v=0A9XpdjuA2Y&list=PLOKcJXMjdgJDgGO7ZwWUHi29alQisS6ra&index=10

Sentinel 9 Video: Part 11 – Business Strategy 4 – Formulation: External & Internal Analysis

https://www.youtube.com/watch?v=7T2Gjr40e0c&list=PLOKcJXMjdgJDgGO7ZwWUHi29alQisS6ra&index=11

Sentinel 9 Video: Part 12 – Business Strategy 5 – Implementation – Processes, Procedures, Communication

https://www.youtube.com/watch?v=BK3S4ucSXzo&list=PLOKcJXMjdgJDgGO7ZwWUHi29alQisS6ra&index=12

Sentinel 9 Video: Part 13 – Business Strategy 6 – Evaluation

https://www.youtube.com/watch?v=koHtdINfYUQ&list=PLOKcJXMjdgJDgGO7ZwWUHi29alQisS6ra&index=13

Sentinel 9 Video: Part 14 – Unified Theory of Business Strategy

https://www.youtube.com/watch?v=bS8yc7seyl8&list=PLOKcJXMjdgJDgGO7ZwWUHi29alQisS6ra&index=14

Sentinel 9 Video: Part 15 – Macroeconomics – System Reflection

https://www.youtube.com/watch?v=fPJqVvYDfj0&list=PLOKcJXMjdgJDgGO7ZwWUHi29alQisS6ra&index=15

Bibliography

Acedo, F.J., Barroso, C., & Galan, J.L. (2006). The resource-based theory: Dissemination and main trends. *Strategic Management Journal, 27*, 621–636.

Acs, Z.J. & Gerwolski, D.A. (1996). *Management and organization.* Upper Saddle River, NJ: Prentice Hall.

Aguilar, F.J. (1967). *Scanning the business environment.* New York: Macmillan.

Alchian, A. (1984). Specificity, specialization, and coalitions. *Zeitschrift Für Die Gesamte Staatswissenschaft / Journal of Institutional and Theoretical Economics, 140*(1), 34–49.

Amazon. (2019). Amazon Annual Reports, Retrieved from http://www.annualreports.com/Company/amazoncom-inc

Amit, R. (2014, November 18). *The latest innovation: Redesigning the business model* (transcribed conversation). Knowledge@Wharton. Retrieved from http://knowledge.wharton.upenn.edu/article/redesigning-business-model/

Amit, R. & Schoemaker, P.J. (1993). Strategic assets and organizational rent. *Strategic Management Journal, 14*(1), 33–46.

Anderson, E. (2019). Toyota's competitive advantage: Path dependency, dynamic, capabilities, and sources of inimitability—A contrastive study with Nissan. In R. Sanchez & A. Heene (Eds.) *Enhancing Competences for Competitive Advantage (Advances in Applied Business Strategy, Volume 12)* (pp. 87–120). Somerville, MA: Emerald Group Publishing.

Ankli, R. (1992). Michael Porter's competitive advantage and business history. *Business and Economic History, 21,* 228–236.

Ansari, A. & Batoul, M. (1997). World-class strategies for safety: A Boeing approach. *International Journal of Operations & Production Management, 17*, 389–398.

Ansoff, H.I. (1965). *Corporate strategy.* New York: McGraw Hill.

Aoki, K. & Lennerfors, T.T. (2013, September). The new, improved keiretsu. *Harvard Business Review.* Retrieved from https://hbr.org/2013/09/the-new-improved-keiretsu

ASIC. (2018). *Develop an investing plan.* Retrieved from https://www.moneysmart.gov.au/investing/invest-smarter/risk-and-return

Australian Bureau of Statistics. (2017). *Motor vehicle census, Australia* (Cat No. 9309.0). Retrieved from https://www.abs.gov.au/AUSSTATS/abs@.nsf/allprimarymainfeatures/AFE43252F544460ACA2582D60014CB0F?opendocument

Australian Bureau of Statistics. (2018). *Toyota the most popular choice for Australian drivers* (media release). Retrieved from https://www.abs.gov.au/ausstats/abs@.nsf/mediareleasesbytitle/D0EB682B27145F9CCA2584430019FAB7?OpenDocument

Australian Bureau Statistics. (2019). *Motor vehicle census, Australia* (Cat No. 9309.0) Retrieved from https://www.abs.gov.au/AUSSTATS/abs@.nsf/allprimarymainfeatures/06D0E28CD6E66B8ACA2568A900139408?opendocument

Australian Treasury. (2006). *Australian net private wealth.* Retrieved from https://treasury.gov.au/publication/economic-roundup-summer-2006/australian-net-private-wealth

Bain, J. (1968). *Industrial organization.* Hoboken, NJ: John Wiley & Sons.

Balmer, R.T. (2011). *Modern engineering thermodynamics.* Cambridge MA: Academic Press.

Barney, J.B. (1991). Firms resources and sustained competitive advantage. *Journal of Management, 17*(1), 99–120.

Barney, J.B. (2001). Is the resource-based "view" a useful perspective for strategic management research? Yes. *Academy of Management Review, 26*(1): 41–56.

Barney, J.B. (1995). Looking inside for competitive advantage. *Academy of Management Executive, 9*(4), 49–61.

Barron, E. (2013). *Game theory an introduction* (2nd ed.). Hoboken, NJ: John Wiley & Sons.

Bennet, N. & Lemoine, J. (2014, January–February). What VUCA Really Means for You. *Harvard Business Review.* Retrieved from https://hbr.org/2014/01/what-vuca-really-means-for-you

Berglof, E. & Perotti, E.C. (1994). The governance structure of the Japanese financial keiretsu. *Journal of Financial Economics, 36*(2), 259–284.

Berle, A. & Means, G.C. (1932). *The modern corporation and private property.* New York: Harcourt, Brace & World.

Berryman, R. (2014). *Amazon.com, Inc: A case study analysis.* School of Communication, Western Michigan University. Retrieved from https://www.academia.edu/8744694/Amazon.com_Inc._a_case_study_analysis

Bolton, P. & Scharfstein, D. (1998). Corporate finance, the theory of the firm, and organizations. *The Journal of Economic Perspectives, 12*(4), 95–114.

Campbell, T. (2014). *My big toe: A trilogy unifying philosophy, physics, and metaphysics: awakening, discovery, inner working.* Lightning Strike Books.

Cannivet, M. (2018, February). 3 Secrets of Amazon's Success. *Forbes.* Retrieved from https://www.forbes.com/sites/michaelcannivet/2018/02/02/3-secrets-of-amazons-success-anyone-can-emulate/#1e166bbc4826

Cantwell, J. & Santangelo, G.D. (2000). Capitalism, profits and innovation in the new techno-economic paradigm. *Journal of Evolutionary Economics, 10*(1/2), 131.

Carlyle, E. (2013, March). The year's biggest winner: Zara billionaire Amancio Ortega. *Forbes.* Retrieved from https://www.forbes.com/sites/erincarlyle/2013/03/04/the-years-biggest-winner-zara-billionaire-amancio-ortega/#1e7311d26fd9

Caruso, M. (2001). Stock prices and money velocity: A multi-country analysis. *Empirical Economics, 26*(4), 651–672.

Casson, M. (1990). *Enterprise and competitiveness: A systems view of international business.* Oxford: Clarendon.

Cavender, R, & Kincade, D.H. (2014). Management of a luxury brand: Dimensions and sub-variables from a case study of LVMH. *Journal of Fashion Marketing and Management, 18*(2), 231–248.

Caves, R.E. (1980). Industrial organization, corporate strategy and structure. *Journal of Economic Literature, 18*(1), 64–92.

Chan, W. & Mauborgne, R. (2005). Blue ocean strategy: From theory to practice. *California Management Review, 47*(3), 105–121.

Chandler, Jr., A.D. (1962). *Strategy and structure: Chapters in the history of the industrial enterprise.* Cambridge, MA: The MIT Press.

Chandler, Jr., A.D. (1990). *Scale and scope: The dynamics of industrial capitalism.* Cambridge, MA: Harvard University Press.

Chorafas, D. (2007). *Risk accounting and risk management for accountants.* Burlington, MA: Elsevier/CIMA Publishing.

Coase, R. (1937). The nature of the firm. *Economica, 4*(16), 356–405.

Cohan, P. (2018, February). 3 reasons Amazon is the world's best business. *Forbes.* Retrieved from https://www.forbes.com/sites/petercohan/2018/02/02/3-reasons-amazon-is-the-worlds-best-business/#48c24e736356

Collis, D.J. & Montgomery. C.A. (1998, May–June). Creating corporate advantage. *Harvard Business Review*, 71–83.

Conner, K.R. (1991). A historical comparison of resource-based theory and five schools of thought within industrial organization economics: Do we have a new theory of the firm? *Journal of Management, 17*(1), 121–154.

D'Aveni, R.A. (2004). Corporate spheres of influence. *MIT Sloan Management Review, 45*(4), 38–46.

Dadhe, A. (2014). *Strategic management.* Department of Management Sciences & Research, G.S College of Commerce & Economics, Nagpur, India.

Dallas, H., Michael A.H., Duane, I., & Robert E.H. (2013). *Strategic management: Competitiveness & globalisation* (6th ed.). South Melbourne: Cengage Learning Australia.

Denning, S. (2012, September). When will US firms become agile? Part 2: Internal agility at Zara. *Forbes.* Retrieved from https://www.forbes.com/sites/stevedenning/2012/09/20/when-will-us-firms-become-agile-part-2-internal-agility-at-zara/#17b2ea171117

Dhir, S. & Sushil. (2018). *Flexible strategies in VUCA markets.* Singapore: Springer Singapore.

Dierick, I. & Cool, K. (1989). Asset stock accumulation and sustainability of competitive advantage. *Management Science, 35*(12), 1504–1511.

Dixit, A., Nalebuff, B., & Sandler, T. (1992). Thinking strategically – the competitive edge in business, politics, and everyday life. *Journal of Economic Literature, 30*(2), 925.

Dompere, K.K. (2019). *A general theory of entropy: Fuzzy rational foundations of information-knowledge certainty.* Cham, Switzerland: Springer.

Dragone, D. (2007). *Intertemporal decision-making: Economic and cognitive perspectives.* Department of Economics, University of Bologna, Strada Maggiore. Retrieved from https://pdfs.semanticscholar.org/194f/ed54ad6e2c8dfade88f9e6e7edd414a2efeb.pdf

Dutta, D. (2002). *Third eyesight: Case study.* Reference article from Third Eyesight. Retrieved from https://thirdeyesight.in/articles/ImagesFashion_Zara_Part_I.pdf

Dyer, J. & Singh, H. (1998). The relational view: Cooperative strategy and sources of interorganizational competitive advantage. *The Academy of Management Review, 23*(4), 660–679.

Edwards, C.T. & Samimi, R. 1997. Japanese interfirm networks: Exploring the seminal sources of their success. *Journal of Management Studies, 34*(4), 489–510.

Ehrbar, A. (1998). EVA (Economic Value Added): The real key to creating wealth. *Ohio CPA Journal, 58*(4), 36–37.

Elsenhardt, K.M. (1989). Agency theory: An assessment and review. *Academy of Management Review, 14*(1), 57–74.

Farfan, B. (2019a). *Amazon's mission statement.* The Balance Small Business. Retrieved from https://www.thebalancesmb.com/amazon-mission-statement-4068548

Farfan, B. (2019b). *What is Apple's mission statement?* The Balance Small Business. Retrieved from https://www.thebalancesmb.com/apple-mission-statement-4068547

Ferdows, K., Lewis, M.A., & Machuca, J.A. (2005). *Zara's secret for fast fashion.* Harvard Business School Working Knowledge. Retrieved from https://www.researchgate.net/profile/Michael_Lewis38/publication/265035571_Zara's_Secret_for_Fast_Fashion/links/555b577408ae91e75e764e50/Zaras-Secret-for-Fast-Fashion.pdf

Ferrier, W.J. (2001). Navigating the competitive landscape: The drivers and consequences of competitive aggressiveness. *Academy of Management Journal, 44*(4), 858–877.

Feymean, R. (1965). *Seeking new laws: The character of physical law.* Cambridge, MA: The MIT Press.

Fisher, F. (1989). Games economists play: A noncooperative view. *RAND Journal of Economics, 20*(1), 113–124.

Folan, K. (2013, March). Will Zara be able to keep clothes cheap as labor costs rise? *Racked.* Retrieved from http://www.racked.com/2013/3/4/7684835/some-fastfashion-companies-will-survive-increased-labor-prices-but

Forbes. (2013, April). Toyota eyes big growth ahead in emerging markets. *Forbes.* Retrieved from http://www.forbes.com/sites/greatspeculations/2013/04/04/toyota-eyes-big-growth-ahead-in-emerging-markets/

Forbes. (2019) Billionaires, The richest people in the world. *Forbes.* Retrieved from https://www.forbes.com/billionaires/#621cba26251c

Frank, M.Z. & Shen, T. (2016). Investment and the weighted average cost of capital. *Journal of Financial Economics, 119*(2), 300–315.

Friedman, M. (1962). *Capitalism and freedom.* Chicago, IL: University of Chicago Press.

Gandhi, V. & Kumbharana, C. (2018). Comparative study of Amazon EC2 and Microsoft Azure cloud architecture. *International Journal of Advanced Networking Applications,* September, 117–123.

Gans, J., King, S., & Mankiw, N.G. (2014). *Principles of microeconomics.* South Melbourne: Cengage Learning Australia.

Gardner, R. (2003). *Games for business and economics* (2nd ed.). Hoboken, NJ: John Wiley & Sons.

Gawankar, S., Kamble, S., & Raut, R. (2015). Performance measurement using Balance Score Card and its applications: A review. *Journal of Supply Chain Management Systems, 4*(3), 6–21.

Gaynor, M., Harald, S., & Vogt, W. (2005). The volume-outcome effect, scale economies, and learning-by-doing. *American Economic Review, 95*(2), 243–247.

Geckil, I.K. & Anderson, P.L. (2016). *Applied game theory and strategic behavior*. Boca Raton, FL: CRC Press.

Ghemawat, P. & Nueno Iniesta, J.L. (2003). *Zara: Fast fashion* (multimedia case). Harvard Business School Case Study (Product 703416-HTM-ENG).

Graham, J.L. (1993). The knowledge link: how firms compete through strategic alliances (Review of the book by Joseph L Badaracco, Jr). *Journal of Marketing, 57*(4), 149–151.

Grant, M.R. (1991). The resource-based theory of competitive advantage: Implications for strategy formulation. *California Management Review, 33*(3), 114–135.

Grant, M.R. (2008). *Contemporary strategy analysis* (6th ed.). Oxford: Blackwell Publishing.

Grant, R.M. (2003). Strategic planning in a turbulent environment: Evidence from the oil majors. *Strategic Management Journal, 24*(6), 491–517.

Green, B. (1999). *The elegant universe.* New York: Vintage Books.

Grossman, S.J. & Hart, O.D. (1986) The costs and benefits of ownership: A theory of vertical integration. *The Journal of Political Economy, 94*(4), 691–719.

Hall, J. & Johnson. M.E. (2009, March). When should a process be art, not science? *Harvard Business Review, 87*(3). Retrieved from https://hbr.org/2009/03/when-should-a-process-be-art-not-science

Hamel, G. (2001). Revolution vs. evolution: You need both. *Harvard Business Review, 79*(5), 150–156.

Hanson, D., Hitt, M.A., Ireland, R.D., & Hoskisson, R.E. (2017). *Strategic management: Competitiveness & globalisation* (6th ed.). Boston, MA: Cengage Learning.

Harbott, A. (2011, March 3). *Analysing Zara's business model* (blog post). Retrieved from https://harbott.com/analysing-zaras-business-model-6ee755699a70

Hart, O. & Moore, J. (1990). Property rights and the nature of the firm. *Journal of Political Economy, 98*(6), 1119–1158.

Hashim, M.K. (2016). Approaches to formulating business strategy: A review. *Arabian Journal of Business and Management Review, 7*(1).

Hitt, M.A., Ireland, R.D., & Hoskisson, R.E. (1999). *Strategic management: Competitiveness and globalization: Concepts and cases.* Cincinnati, OH: South-Western College Publishing.

Hooley, G. & Broderick, A. (1998). Competitive positioning and the resource-based view of the firm. *Journal of Strategic Marketing, 6*(2), 97–115.

Hulland, J.S. & Kay, J. (1995). Foundations of corporate success: How business strategies add value. *Journal of Marketing, 59*(1), 109.

Inditex. (2020). *Who we are*. Retrieved from https://www.inditex.com/about-us/who-we-are

Ireland, R.D. & Webb, J.W. (2007). Strategic entrepreneurship: Creating competitive advantage through streams of innovation. *Business Horizons, 50*(1), 49–59.

Itami, H. (1987). *Mobilizing invisible assets.* Boston, MA: Harvard University Press.

Jensen, M. & Meckling, W. (1976). Theory of the firm: Managerial behaviour, agency costs and ownership structure. *Journal of Financial Economics, 3*(4), 305–360.

Juan, Y.C. & Ou-Yang, C. (2004). Systematic approach for the gap analysis of business processes. *International Journal of Production Research, 42*(7), 1325–1364.

Kahneman, D. (2013). *Thinking, fast and slow.* New York: Farrar, Straus and Giroux.

Kanbanize. (2020). *Kanban explained for beginners.* Retrieved from https://kanbanize.com/kanban-resources/getting-started/what-is-kanban

Kaplan, R.S. & Norton, D.P. (1996). *The balanced scorecard: Translating strategy into action.* Boston, MA: Harvard Business School Press.

Kaufman, S. (2015). *Unified reality theory: The evolution of existence into experience.* Milwaukee, WI: Destiny Toad Press.

Kay. J.A. (1993). *Foundations of corporate success: How business strategies add value.* Oxford: Oxford University Press.

Kay, J.A. (2003). *The truth about markets: Their genius, their limits, their follies.* London & New York: Allen Lane.

Kim, B. (2019). Competitive priorities and supply chain strategy in the fashion industry. *Qualitative Market Research: An International Journal, 16*(2), 214–242.

Kinsinger, P. & Walch, K. (2012). Living and leading in a VUCA world. *Thunderbird University,* 1–4.

Kippenberger, T. (2000). Remember the USP? (Unique selling proposition). *The Antidote, 5*(6), 6–8.

Kito, T., Brintrup. A., New. S., & Reed-Tsochas. F. (2014). *The structure of the Toyota supply network: An empirical analysis.* Said Business School Research Papers, University of Oxford.

Kolecki, J.C. (2002). *An introduction to tensors for students of physics and engineering.* Cleveland, OH: Glenn Research Centre & NASA. Retrieved from https://www.grc.nasa.gov/www/k-12/Numbers/Math/documents/Tensors_TM2002211716.pdf

Kondepudi, D. (2008). *Introduction to modern thermodynamics.* Hoboken, NJ: John Wiley & Sons.

Kotler, A. (2014). *Foundations of marketing.* Melbourne: Pearson Education Custom.

Kotter, J.P. (2007). Leading change: Why transformation efforts fail. *Harvard Business Review, 85*(1), 96–103.

Lam, J. (2017). *Implementing enterprise risk management: From methods to applications.* Hoboken, NJ: John Wiley & Sons.

Leavy, B. (2003). Assessing your strategic alternatives from both a market position and core competence perspective. *Strategy & Leadership, 31*(6), 29–35.

Leidecker, J.K. & Bruno, A.V. (1984). Identifying and using critical success factors. *Long Range Planning,* 17(1), 23–32.

Leonard-Barton, D. (1995). *Wellsprings of knowledge building and sustaining the sources of innovation.* Boston, MA: Harvard Business School.

Liang, F.S., Lee, L., & Sang, C.N. (2016, April). Risk management in a VUCA environment. *Institute of Singapore Chartered Accountants Journal.* Retrieved from https://isca.org.sg/media/778886/april-print-version.pdf

Lincoln, J., Gerlach, M., & Ahmadjian, C. (1996). Keiretsu networks and corporate performance in Japan. *American Sociological Review, 61*(1), 67–88.

Lindi, J. & Marques Da Silva, C. (2011). Value proposition as a catalyst for a customer focused innovation. *Management Decision, 49*(10), 1694–1708.

Lockett, A. & Thompson, S. (2001). *The resource-based view and economics.* Nottingham University Business School discussion paper, Nottingham University Business School.

Lopez, C. & Fan. Y. (2009). Internationalisation of the Spanish fashion brand Zara. *Journal of Fashion Marketing and Management, 13*(2), 279–296.

Malthouse, E.C. & Elsner. R (2006). Customisation with crossed-basis subsegmentation. *Journal of Database Marketing & Customer Strategy Management, 14*(1), 40–50.

Martin, M. (2018). *What is a BCG Matrix?* Business News Daily. Retrieved from https://www.businessnewsdaily.com/5693-bcg-matrix.html

Maschler, M., Solan, E., & Zamir, S. (2013). *Game theory.* Cambridge: Cambridge University Press.

McDonald, M. & Wilson, H. (2016). *Marketing plans: How to prepare them, how to profit from them* (8th ed.) Hoboken, NJ: John Wiley & Sons.

McGahan, A.M. & Porter, M.E. (2003). The emergence and sustainability of abnormal profits. *Strategic Organization, 1*(1), 79–108.

McGrath, R.G. (2013). Transient advantage. *Harvard Business Review, 91*(6), 62–70.

McGuire, J. & Dow, S. (2003). The persistence and implications of Japanese keiretsu organization. *Journal of International Business Studies, 34*(4), 374–388.

McGuire, J. & Dow. S. (2002). The Japanese keiretsu system: An empirical analysis. *Journal Business Research, 55*(1), 33–40.

McKinsey & Company. (2019). *GE-McKinsey Nine-Box Matrix.* Retrieved from https://www.mckinsey.com/business-functions/strategy-and-corporate-finance/our-insights/enduring-ideas-the-ge-and-mckinsey-nine-box-matrix

Mehri, D. (2012). Restructuring in the Toyota keiretsu during the Asian financial crash. *Journal of Organizational Ethnography, 1*(2), 138–157.

Mellen, C.M. & Evans, F.C. (2018). *Valuation for M&A: Building and measuring private company value* (3rd ed.). Hoboken, NJ: John Wiley & Sons.

Mintzberg, H., Ahlstrand, B., & Lampel, J. (1998). *Strategy safari: A guided tour through the wilds of strategic management.* New York: The Free Press.

Mintzberg, H., Quinn, J.B., Lampel, J., & Ghoshal, S. (2014). *The strategy process: Concepts, contexts, cases* (5th ed.). New York: Pearson Education.

Miyashita, K. & Russell, D. (1996). *Keiretsu: Inside the hidden Japanese conglomerates.* New York: McGraw-Hill.

Monahan, G. (2008). *Enterprise risk management: A methodology for achieving strategic objectives.* Hoboken, NJ: John Wiley & Sons.

Mukherji, J., Mukherji, A., & Hurtado, P.S. (2015). The impact of environmental uncertainty, strategic marketing activities, and strategic orientation on the financial performance of entrepreneurial firms. *Competition Forum, 13*(1), 4–57.

Nakajima, S. (1989). *TPM development program: Implementing total productive maintenance.* Cambridge, MA: Productivity Press.

Naoki, T. (1989). *The mechanism of vertical integration: A case study of the Japanese automobile manufacturing industry* (Doctoral dissertation). Washington State University, ProQuest Dissertations Publishing.

Neck, H.M., Neck, C.P., & Murray, E.L. (2017). *Entrepreneurship: The practice and mindset.* Thousand Oaks, CA: Sage.

Nelson, R. & Winter, S. (1982). *An evolutionary theory of economic change.* Cambridge: Belknap Press.

Nelson, R. & Winter, S. (2002). Evolutionary theorizing in economics. *The Journal of Economic Perspectives, 16*(2), 23–46.

Nelson, R. (1991). Why do firms differ, and how does it matter? *Strategic Management Journal, 12*(S2), 61–74.

Nelson, R. (2002). Bringing institutions into evolutionary growth theory. *Journal of Evolutionary Economics, 12*(1–2), 17–28.

Niles, N. (2010). A case study in strategic financial planning in health service organizations. *Journal of Business Case Studies, 6*(5), 23–29.

Nwachukwu, C., Chládková, H., & Fadeyi. O. (2018). Strategy formulation process and innovation performance nexus. *International Journal for Quality Research, 12*(1), 147–164.

Omalaja, M.A. & Eruola, O.A. (2011). Strategic management theory: Concept, analysis and critiques in relation to corporate competitive advantage from the resource-based philosophy. *Economic Analysis, 44*(1–2), 59–77.

Owen, G. (2013). *Game theory* (4th ed.). Bingley, UK: Emerald Group Publishing.

Park, H. (2004). *The grand unified theory of the firm and corporate strategy: Measures to build corporate competitiveness.* Korea Economic Research Institute (KERI) and Saginaw Valley State University. Retrieved from https://www.researchgate.net/publication/229051739_The_Grand_Unified_Theory_of_The_Firm_And_Corporate_Strategy_Measures_To_Build_Corporate_Competitiveness

Pearce, D. (1987). *Renegotiation-proof equilibria: Collective rationality and intertemporal cooperation.* Cowles Foundation Discussion Paper No. 855, Yale University.

Peirson, G. (2017). *Business finance* (12th ed.). North Ryde, NSW: McGraw-Hill Education.

Penrose, E.T. (1959). *The theory of growth of the firm.* Oxford, UK: Oxford University Press.

Piccoli, G. & Pigni, F. (2016). *Information systems for managers: with cases* (3rd ed.). Burlington, VT: Prospect Press.

Porter, M. (2002). Strategy and the internet. In *Harvard Business Review on Advances in Strategy* (pp. 1–50). Boston, MA: Harvard Business School Press.

Porter, M.E & Krame, M. (2006, December). Strategy and society: The link between competitive advantage and corporate social responsibility. *Harvard Business Review*, 78–92.

Porter, M.E. (1980). *Competitive strategy: Techniques for analysing industries and competitors.* New York: The Free Press.

Porter, M.E. (1987, May/June). From competitive advantage to corporate strategy, *Harvard Business Review*, 43–59.

Porter, M.E. (1990). *The competitive advantage of nations.* London: Macmillan.

Porter, M.E. (1991). Towards a dynamic theory of strategy. *Strategic Management Journal, 12*(Special Issue), 95–117.

Porter, M.E. (1994). *Toward a dynamic theory of strategy.* In R.P. Rumelt, D.E. Schendel, & D.J. Teece (Eds.) *Fundamental issues in strategy* (pp. 423–461). Boston: Harvard Business School Press.

Porter, M.E. (1996, November/December). What is strategy? *Harvard Business Review*, 43–59.

Porter, M.E. (1997). Competitive strategy. *Measuring Business Excellence, 1*(2), 12–17.

Powell, T.C. (2001). Competitive advantage: Logical and philosophical considerations. *Strategic Management Journal, 22*(9): 875–888.

Pressman, S. (2014). *Fifty major economists* (3rd ed.). New York: Routledge Taylor & Francis.

Reason, P. & Bradbury, H. (2001). Preface. In P. Reason & H. Bradbury (Eds.) *Handbook of action research: Participative inquiry and practice* (pp. xxiii–xxxi). London: Sage.

Reeves, M., Moose, S., & Venema, T. (2014). *BCG classics revisited: The growth share matrix.* Boston Consulting Group. Retrieved from https://www.bcg.com/publications/2014/growth-share-matrix-bcg-classics-revisited.aspx

Reve, T. (1990). The firm as a nexus of internal and external contracts. In M. Aoiki, B. Gstafsson, & O.E. Williamson, *The firm as a nexus of treaties* (pp. 133–161). London: Sage.

Ritala, P., Golnam. A., & Wegmann. A. (2014). Co-opetition-based business models: The case of Amazon.com. *Industrial Marketing Management, 43*(2), 236–249.

Robbins, S., Bergman, R., Stagg, I., & Coulter, M. (2015). *Management* (7th ed.). Melbourne: Pearson Australia.

Rogers, D. & Rempe, S. (2011). A first and second law for nonequilibrium thermodynamics: Maximum entropy derivation of the fluctuation-dissipation theorem and entropy production functionals. *Journal of Physics: Conference Series, 402.*

Roll, M. (2018). The secret of Zara's success: A culture of customer co-creation. *Martin Roll Business & Brand Leadership.* Retrieved from https://martinroll.com/resources/articles/strategy/the-secret-of-zaras-success-a-culture-of-customer-co-creation/

Ross, S.A., Westerfield, R.W., & Jordan, B.D. (2013). *Fundamentals of corporate finance* (10th ed.). New York: McGraw-Hill Irwin.

Rubin, P.H. (1990). *Managing business transactions.* New York: The Free Press.

Rumelt, R. (1974). *Strategy, structure and economic performance.* Boston: Harvard University Press.

Rumelt, R. (1984). Toward a strategic theory of the firm. In K. Lamb (Ed.) *Competitive strategic management* (pp. 556–570). Englewood Cliffs, NJ: Prentice Hall.

Rumelt, R., Schendel, D.E., & Teece, D.J. (1994). *Fundamental issues in strategy: A research agenda.* Boston, MA: Harvard Business School.

Rumlet, R. (1979). *Evaluation of strategy: Theory and models.* The University of California at Los Angeles. Retrieved from http://teaching.up.edu/bus580/bps/Rumelt,%20 evaluation%20of%20a%20business%20strategy.PDF

Ryan, F. (2016, January 14). The velocity of money. *American Thinker*. Retrieved from https://www.americanthinker.com/articles/2016/01/the_velocity_of_money. html#ixzz46rHni5A2

Salem, M., Solomon, J., Genaidy, A., & Minkarah, I. (2006). Lean construction: From theory to implementation. *Journal of Management in Engineering, 22*(4), 168–175.

Schiereck, D., Kiesel, F., & Kolaric, S. (2016). Brexit: (Not) another Lehman moment for banks? *Finance Research Letters, 19*, 291–297.

Schonberger, R.J. (1996). *World class manufacturing: The next decade.* New York: The Free Press.

Sergio, J. (2011). *Strategic management: The theory and practices of strategy in (business) organizations.* Kgs. Lyngby, Denmark: DTU.

Shapiro, C. (1985). Patent licensing and R&D rivalry. *American Economic Review, 75*(2), 25–30.

Shapiro, C. (1989). The theory of business strategy. *Rand Journal of Economics, 20*(1), 125–137

Shimokawa. K. (1985). Japan's Keiretsu system: The case of the automobility industry. *Japanese Economic Studies, 13*(4), 3–31.

Simon, H.H. (1961). *Administrative behavior.* New York: McMillan.

Simpson, B.P. (2010). Two theories of monopoly and competition: Implications and applications. *Journal of Applied Business Economics, 11*(2), 2.

Sirmon, D.G. & Hitt, M.A. (2003). Managing resources: Linking unique resources, management and wealth creation in family firms. *Entrepreneurship Theory and Practice, 27*(4), 339–358.

Soliman, F. & Edmond, J. (2015). The impact of balance score card implementation on supply chain firms. In F. Soliman (Ed.) *Business transformation and sustainability through cloud system implementation* (pp. 240–257). London: IGI Global.

Southern California Injury Prevention Research Centre (SCIPRC). (2008). *A guide to strategy evaluation: Evaluating your city's approach to community safety and youth violence prevention.* UCLA School of Public Health. Retrieved from http://www. ph.ucla.edu/sciprc/pdf/Evaluation_Guidebook_July08.pdf

Spence, M. (1973). Job market signalling. *Quarterly Journal of Economics, 87*(3), 355–374.

Spence, M. (1979). Investment strategy and growth in a new market. *The Bell Journal of Economics, 10*(1), 1–9.

Spulber, D.F. (1984). Economic analysis and strategic management. *Journal of Economics and Management Strategy, 26*(3), 87–110.

Spulber, D.F. (1993). Economic analysis and management strategy: Survey. *Journal of Economics and Management Strategy, 1*(3), 535–574.

Spulber, D.F. (1994). Economic analysis and management strategy. *Journal of Economics and Management Strategy, 3*(2), 335–406.

Statista. (2020). Annual net revenue of Amazon from 2004 to 2019. Retrieved from https://www.statista.com/statistics/266282/annual-net-revenue-of-amazoncom/

Stewart, I. (1997). *Does God play dice? The new mathematics of chaos* (2nd ed.). New York: Penguin.

Storbacka, K., Strandvik, T., & Grönroos, C. (1994). Managing customer relationships for profit: The dynamics of relationship quality. *International Journal of Service Industry Management, 5*(5), 21–38.

Stowell, S.J. & Mead, S.S. (2016). *The art of strategic leadership: how leaders at all levels prepare themselves, their teams, and organizations for the future.* Hoboken, NJ: John Wiley & Sons.

Takeishi, A & Noro, Y. (2017). *Keiretsu divergence in the Japanese automotive industry: Why have some, but not all, gone?* CEAFJP Discussion Paper Series 17–04. Retrieved from http://ffj.ehess.fr/upload/Discussion/CEAFJPDP-17-04.pdf

Teece, D., Rumelt, R., Dosi, G., & Winter, S. (1994). Understanding corporate coherence: Theory and evidence. *Journal of Economic Behavior and Organization, 23*(1), 1–30.

Thomson, A. & Strickland, A. (2001). *Strategic Management.* New York: McGraw Hill Irwin.

Tilles, S. (1963, July). How to evaluate corporate strategy. *Harvard Business Review.* Retrieved from https://hbr.org/1963/07/how-to-evaluate-corporate-strategy

Tiwana, A. (2012). Novelty-knowledge alignment: A theory of design convergence in systems development. *Journal of Management Information Systems, 29*(1), 15–52.

ToughNickel (2018, December 12). *Zara's business operations and strategy: How and why they work.* Retrieved from https://toughnickel.com/industries/Business-Operations-of-Clothing-Retailer-Zara

Toyoda, E. (1985). *Toyota: Fifty years in motion.* Tokyo: Kodansha International (Harper and Row).

Toyota Motor Corporation. (2018a). *Annual Report (as filed with the US Securities and Exchange Commission).* Retrieved from http://www.toyota-global.com/pages/contents/investors/ir_library/sec/pdf/20-F_201803_final.pdf

Toyota. (2018b). *Investor update: FY2 2018 financial results.* Retrieved from https://www.toyota.com.au/finance/-/media/tfa/toyotafinance/investor-information/investor-presentations-pdfs/tfal-investor-relations-presentation_fy-ending-31-march-2018-final.pdf

Toyota. (2019). *Toyota global: Safety and health.* Retrieved from http://www.toyota-global.com/company/history_of_toyota/75years/data/automotive_business/production/safety/index.html

Tradegecko. (2018, June 25). *Zara supply chain analysis – the secret behind Zara's retail success.* Retrieved from https://www.tradegecko.com/blog/zara-supply-chain-its-secret-to-retail-success

Turban, E., Volonino, L., Wood, G.R., and Gesser, G.H. (2015). *Information technology for management: Digital strategies for insight, action, and sustainable performance* (10th ed.). Hoboken, NJ: John Wiley & Sons.

Turocy, T.L. & von Stengel, B. (2001). *Game theory.* CDAM Research Report LSE-CDAM-2001-09. Retrieved from http://www.cdam.lse.ac.uk/Reports/Files/cdam-2001-09.pdf

United States Army War College. (2012). *Developing strategic thinking leaders in the U.S. Army.* Retrieved from file:///H:/Subject14%20Strategic%20Business%20Planning/ArticlesFolder/VUCA%202012.pdf

Varian, H. (1989). *What use is economic theory.* University of California. Retrieved from file:///H:/Subject14%20Strategic%20Business%20Planning/ArticlesFolder/Varian%201989%20What%20use%20is%20Economic%20Theory..pdf

von Neumann, J., & Morgenstern, O. (1944). *Theory of games and economic behavior.* Princeton, NJ: Princeton University Press.

Walker, J.F. (1978). Linking human resource planning and strategic planning. *Human Resource Planning, 1,* 1–18.

Wang, H. (2014). Theories for competitive advantage. In H. Hasan (Ed.) *Being practical with theory: A window into business research* (pp. 33–43). Wollongong, Australia: Lulu.

Wehrl, A. (1978). General properties of entropy. *Reviews of Modern Physics, 50*(2), 221–260.

Weinberg, S. (1992). *Dreams of a final theory.* New York: Pantheon Books.

Wen, Y. (2014, September 1). *What does money velocity tell us about low inflation in the U.S.?* Federal Reserve Bank of St Louis. Retrieved from https://www.stlouisfed.org/on-the-economy/2014/september/what-does-money-velocity-tell-us-about-low-inflation-in-the-us

Wernerfelt, B. (1984). A resource-based view of the firm. *Strategic Management Journal, 5*(2), 171–180.

Westwood, J. (2013). *How to write a marketing plan* (4th ed.). London: Kogan Page Limited.

Wheelen, T.L. & Hunger, J.D. (1993). *Strategic management and business policy* (9th ed.). Upper Saddle River, NJ: Person/Prentice Hall.

Willems, K., Janssens, W., Swinnen, G., Brengman, M., Streukens, S., & Vancauteren, M. (2012). From Armani to Zara: Impression formation based on fashion store patronage. *Journal of Business Research, 65*(10), 1487–1494.

Williamson, O.E. (1975). *Markets and hierarchies: Analysis and antitrust implications.* New York: The Free Press.

Williamson, O.E. (1985). *The economic institution of capitalism.* New York: The Free Press.

Williamson, O.E. (1996). *The mechanism of governance.* New York: Oxford University Press.

Williamson, OE. (1991). Strategizing, economizing, and economic organization, *Strategic Management Journal, 12*(S2), 75–94.

Womack, J., Jones, D., & Roos, D. (2007). *The machine that changed the world: The story of lean production—Toyota's secret weapon in the global car wars that is now revolutionizing world industry.* New York: Simon & Shuster.

World Bank. (2018). *The changing wealth of nations.* Retrieved from https://www.worldbank.org/en/news/infographic/2018/01/30/the-changing-wealth-of-nations

Wright, P. (1987). A refinement of Porter's strategies. *Strategic Management Journal, 8*(1), 93–101.

Wright, P.M., Dunford, B.B., & Snell, S.A. (2001). Human resources and the resource based view of the firm. *Journal of Management, 27*(6), 701–721.

Yakovleva, Y. (2017). *Effective business planning. Case Study: Company X.* Unpublished bachelor thesis, Lahti University of Applied Sciences, Finland.

Yang, C.C. & Yant, K.J. (2013). An integrated model of the Toyota production system with total quality management and people factors. *Human Factors and Ergonomics in Manufacturing & Service Industries, 23*(5), 450–461.

Yun, S.K. (1984). SU (8) Theory of Multigenerational Grand Unification. *Physical Review D, 29*(7), 1494–1503.

About the author

Dr Rod Samimi
B.Eng (Hons), M.Comm (Hons), PhD

Rod Samimi has more than 30 years' experience in direct business management, commercial advisory work and academic research in the engineering, construction and professional services sectors. He currently works in investment banking with direct private business involvement in industrial technology, educational services and software applications.

Rod's corporate experience includes seven years in the oil industry, 10 years in manufacturing and construction, and over 10 years in business consulting and research. He has been involved in various business operations, including mature steady-state, distressed restructuring, growth and expansion, and start-ups.

Rod has also been involved in international mergers and acquisitions across Australia, Asia, Europe and the Middle East. He has a wide range of experience raising equity and debt capital in international markets. He participates on the boards of a number of private entities, with direct operational involvement.

Unified Theory of Business Strategy is the culmination of more than 10 years' postdoctoral research, both independently and within large institutions. Rod brings to the book an innovative blend of academic training and direct practitioner experience, across both physical industries and professional services.

Made in the USA
Monee, IL
12 September 2026

62979082R00126